THE COMPLETE IDIOT'S GUIDE TO

Microsoft® PowerPoint® 97

by Nat Gertler

A Division of Macmillan Publishing
201 W. 103rd Street, Indianapolis, IN 46290

This book is for my father Eugene and his wife Poco, who are planning to soon set out on the open road and see what America has to offer. I hope this adventure brings them vast pleasure and cool knick-knacks!—Nat Gertler

International Standard Book Number: 0-7897-0933-3
Library of Congress Catalog Card Number: 96-71448

98 97 96   8 7 6 5 4 3 2 1

Interpretation of the printing code: the rightmost number of the first series of numbers is the year of the book's printing; the rightmost number of the second series of numbers is the number of the book's printing. For example, a printing code of 96-1 shows that the first printing of the book occurred in 1996.

Screen reproductions in this book were created by means of the program Collage Complete from Inner Media, Inc., Hollis, NH.

Printed in the United States of America

Publisher
Roland Elgey

Editorial Services Director
Elizabeth Keaffaber

Publishing Director
Lynn E. Zingraf

Acquisitions Editor
Martha O'Sullivan

Managing Editor
Michael Cunningham

Product Development Specialist
John Gosney

Production Editor
Mark Enochs

Director of Marketing
Lynn E. Zingraf

Cover Designers
Dan Armstrong
Barbara Kordesh

Designer
Barbara Kordesh

Illustrations
Judd Winick

Technical Specialist
Nadeem Muhammed

Indexer
Eric Brinkman

Production Team
Kim Cofer
Diana Groth
Maureen Hanrahan
Linda Knose
Chris Morris
Lori Price
Daniela Raderstorf

*Special thanks to Faithe Wempen for ensuring the
technical accuracy of this book.*

We'd Like to Hear from You!

As part of our continuing effort to produce books of the highest possible quality, Que would like to hear your comments. To stay competitive, we *really* want you, as a computer book reader and user, to let us know what you like or dislike most about this book or other Que products.

You can mail comments, ideas, or suggestions for improving future editions to the address below, or send us a fax at (317) 581-4663. For the online inclined, Macmillan Computer Publishing has a forum on CompuServe (type **GO QUEBOOKS** at any prompt) through which our staff and authors are available for questions and comments. The address of our Internet site is **http://www.mcp.com** (World Wide Web).

In addition to exploring our forum, please feel free to contact me personally to discuss your opinions of this book: on CompuServe, I'm at 10436,2300, and on the Internet, I'm **jgosney@que.mcp.com**.

Thanks in advance—your comments will help us to continue publishing the best books available on computer topics in today's market.

John Gosney
Product Development Specialist
Que Corporation
201 W. 103rd Street
Indianapolis, Indiana 46290
USA

Although we cannot provide general technical support, we're happy to help you resolve problems you encounter related to our books, disks, or other products. If you need such assistance, please contact our Tech Support department at (800) 545-5914 ext. 3833.

To order other Que or Macmillan Computer Publishing books or products, please call our Customer Service department at (800) 835-3202 ext. 666.

Contents at a Glance

Contents

A Installing PowerPoint 259

B Windows 95 and Windows NT Primer 261

Speak Like a Geek: The Complete Archive 273

Index 283

Introduction

Welcome to *The Complete Idiot's Guide to Microsoft PowerPoint 97*, your user-friendly, low-calorie guide to using PowerPoint. PowerPoint is a tool that lets you put together slide shows, interactive displays on your computer, and other sorts of presentations. This book will get you using it quickly, easily, and effectively. Once you get the hang of PowerPoint, you'll find it so easy to put together a clear and exciting presentation that everyone at work will ask you to make their presentations for them! Soon, you'll become Executive Vice President In Charge Of Presentations. You'll glory in the success and riches! But then you go too far! You'll try to take over the company, and lose the power struggle. You'll find yourself without a job, and all that money you made you'll have lost on a bad investment in grapefruit futures. You've got nothing but the clothes on your back and the knowledge of how to make a good presentation, but that's all you need. You come up with a great idea for a new company, create a convincing presentation to show to the Wall Street bigwigs, and next thing you know you're back on top, more successful than ever! And it will all be thanks to *The Complete Idiot's Guide to Microsoft PowerPoint 97*.

You're welcome.

This Book Is Full of Good Stuff

There's a lot of good stuff in this book. Early in the book are the basics of using PowerPoint, so you can start putting presentations together quickly. Later in the book you get to see more of PowerPoint's special features so that you can make fancier presentations, and ones that look exactly like you want them to. All through it is advice on making creative decisions to let your presentation have impact. There's so much good stuff in here that it's amazing we didn't throw in a pound of chocolate!

Browsing Through the Book

If you're as lazy as I am (and that's saying something!) you probably don't want to spend a lot of time reading about things you're never going to use—and odds are that with all the features of PowerPoint, you'll never use them all. This book is broken up into chapters. There's a few chapters you have to read to get the hang of PowerPoint, but most chapters you can skip reading until you decide you need to know about that specific topic. Each chapter starts with a list of the things you'd learn by reading that chapter, so you can decide whether to skip it. Think of it as a buffet of knowledge, and you can always come back for seconds!

Part 1: A Running Start

The chapters are grouped into parts. The first part is designed to get you going with PowerPoint. There's a chapter that lets you know what PowerPoint is, what it does, and what it's good for. Right after that, we get you up and running, putting together a simple presentation, including information about how to save presentations on your hard disk and get them back later, and how to display them on your computer screen. Then there's a chapter on how to get help when you have a PowerPoint question, which will come in handy no matter what you're doing. All in all, Part 1 is a must-read, and should be the first thing you read.

Part 2: Building Your Presentation

There's a lot of things you can put into a presentation, such as text, charts and graphs, lists, logos, pictures, and chocolate (which is good for bribing customers during sales presentations). I can't help you with chocolate, but the rest of these elements are each covered in chapters in Part 2. The first chapter, which tells you how to arrange the basic units of a presentation, is a must-read, and odds are you'll be using text and have to read that one as well. For the rest, just take a look at the first paragraph, see what the section's about, and skip over it if you don't need it. You can always come back to them later, if you need to.

Part 3: Fancy, Flashy, Fabulous Features

Part 3 is full of chapters on things like flying text, interactivity, moving pictures, sound, and other whiz-bang effects that'll make your presentation as fancy as a Stephen Spielberg movie (or at least a Buzby Berkeley musical). Depending on what sort of presentation you're giving, though, you may not be able to use these things. After all, there's no way to put a movie onto an overhead projector sheet, and if you figure out a way to get sound onto a piece of paper, you'll be earning so many millions that you'll be able to hire someone to make presentations for you. (I am certainly willing to accept such a job at a huge salary!) If you're going to be showing your presentations on a computer display, on a Web page, or on video tape, you should look at this part and see what each chapter has to offer. If you're just doing overheads, standard slides, or printing your presentation out, skip this part and use the time you save to sneak out to the movies. (Just tell your boss you're doing research on traditional mass-market presentation media!)

Part 4: Sharing the Presentation with Others

Designing your presentation is only half the battle. Once you've done that, you have to know how to show it to other people. This might mean knowing how to print it out, how to get it onto slides, how to turn it into a Web page, or how to engrave it in chocolate.

Each of these (except the chocolate one, alas) and more are covered in Part 4. You only have to read up on the methods you're going to use. If you're not going to use PowerPoint to create Web pages, for example, there's no need to read the chapter on how to do so... even though I slaved for hours on end over a hot keyboard creating that chapter for you, checking each fact and carefully turning each phrase several times to make sure it was just right! Aw, go on, skip it!

Part 5: Getting the Most Out of PowerPoint

This last part is a bit of a weird one, since it has less to do with *how* to use PowerPoint and everything to do with *why* you're using PowerPoint. While there is a chapter on using information from Microsoft Word and Excel with PowerPoint, the other chapters are about what makes for a good presentation. A presentation that looks good but doesn't make a lot of sense is like a date who looks good but doesn't make a lot of sense; it may be fun for the thrill of it, but it's not going to do you a lot of good in the long run. There's a chapter on what you should put in your presentation, and one on how to speak to people as part of your presentation.

The Rest of the Book

There's a table of contents in the front and an index in the back, both of which are handy if you need them but I doubt you'll just be sitting down and reading them. Toward the back is an appendix about how to install PowerPoint, if you're not lucky enough to have someone install it for you. If you're fairly new to windows, or aren't fully comfortable with the terminology, the second appendix tells you about how to use Windows and what the various parts of it are called.

Further back is a section called *Speak Like a Geek*, which is a glossary full of techno-terms you might run into and what they mean to regular people. That's a handy reference if you need it. And before Part 1 there's an introduction, and it's too late to decide if you want to read that, because you're already most of the way through it!

The Language of the Book

There's a few standard tricks that are used in this book to make things clear. For example, if I tell you to hit a key, click on a button, or select a command, the command name, button name, or key will be printed **like this**. If I want you to hold down the Shift, Alt, or Ctrl keys and press another key, it will look like: press **Shift+G** to get a capital G.

If I tell you to type something, the phrase that you type will look like this. When I'm giving you a definition to a word, we'll put the new word in *italics* (slanty letters).

If you look around this page, you'll see a number of *sidebars*, gray separate sections that are not part of the normal reading. The ones on this page explain about the sidebars you'll run into later in the book.

Check This Out! sidebars

Sidebars with this picture are used to tell you about special features and other little bits of information that it might be handy to know. This is where you'll find shortcuts for doing hard tasks, and other ways of saving time.

Techno Talk sidebars

This picture means that the sidebar is letting you know some technical details about how something works. You don't need to know this stuff to use PowerPoint. If you understand the technical side of computing, it may be interesting, and if you don't understand technical, this is a good place to learn. Don't let this symbol scare you away!

New in PowerPoint 97

This picture is used to let you know when there's a new useful feature that was not in older versions of PowerPoint.

Ack! Nowledgements!

I'd like to thank the gang at Que for dragging me into yet another of these books. Particular thanks go to Martha O'Sullivan, who has helped me with most of my books. Points to John Gosney for his editorial work on this book. I'd also like to thank the editors of my comic book and prose fiction projects for all their understanding during the hectic days spent getting this book done. And a big thanks goes to my sidekick, Anita, who just made homemade ice cream.

I'll Trade These Marks for Other Marks!

The names *PowerPoint*, *Office*, *Word*, and *Excel* are trademarks of Microsoft Corporation. For that matter, the name *Microsoft* is a trademark of Microsoft Corporation. Perhaps someday we will all be trademarks of Microsoft Corporation! Any other trademarks mentioned are owned by their respective owners.

Part 1
A Running Start

You've got this absolutely great computer on your desk, with all the latest bells and whistles (which is a stupid expression, considering just how old bells and whistles are). You're all ready to play Revenge of the Space Bunnies II in all of its multimedia splendor, but someone wants you to do something useful (yawn) with the machine and get it to put out a presentation!

This part will get you going. You'll learn the most important things about PowerPoint and about using Windows 95, and then zoom! you're making a simple presentation. Once that's got your confidence up, we'll tell you about what to do when things go wrong!

Chapter 1

What the Heck Is PowerPoint Anyway?

PowerPoint sounds like the name of the superpower belonging to the villainous Human Finger. "Do not dare stop my nefarious scheme, Lady Power, or I shall be forced to PowerPoint your helpless boyfriend right into oblivion!" But if I could teach you that, I wouldn't. You might use it for your own nefarious schemes, and besides, I'd rather spend the time using it for my own nefarious schemes. ("Give me all your chocolate donuts, or I shall be forced to PowerPoint your jelly ones into an unsightly mess!")

PowerPoint is a software tool that lets you create presentations. That opens up the question of "what is a presentation?"—a question that is so important that it needs to be put in great big letters:

What Is a Presentation?

When someone is standing up in front of a group of people, using slides and overhead projectors to display various reasons why you should invest in his new fast-food franchise Lotsa Lard, *that's* a presentation.

When you're watching the local access cable TV channel, and they're showing an endless loop of fancy screens listing when last month's bake sales and fund drives were, *that's* a presentation.

When you're in a motel, and there's a computer screen displaying a list of local attractions, and you just have to touch on the name of the local amusement park and it shows you a short film clip about how great and wonderful the rides are, and then tells you that the park is open only in months with a W in the name, *that's* a presentation.

When you're on the World Wide Web, and you find a Web site that is nothing more than a bunch of pages telling you how wonderful that Web site is, *that's* a presentation.

When the moon hits your eye like a big pizza pie, *that's* not a presentation. It's painful, that's what it is.

What Is the Point in PowerPoint?

If you think about an overhead projector presentation, you might not see that much point to PowerPoint. Sure, it can put text onto the sheet, but so can a word processor. And PowerPoint can put a picture on the sheet, but so can a modern word processor. And PowerPoint can help create charts and graphs, but some of that stuff isn't too hard to cut and paste from a spreadsheet into your word processor. And PowerPoint can create nicely designed consistent backgrounds for your overheads, which, well, your word processor can't.

And PowerPoint also has built-in capabilities for creating *speaker's notes*, cheat sheets that let you see the slide along with some notes of what you want to say to the audience. And it will also print out handouts, with all the overheads reproduced, several to a page, that the people you are talking to can refer to later, after they realize that they spent the whole presentation trying to fish the pen cap out of their pants pocket without standing up.

MultiMedia in PowerPoint Is ReallyGood and ReallyEffective

If you're showing a presentation using something that can show motion (such as on the computer, or on video tape), then you get to use a whole passel of pleasing PowerPoint properties:

➤ Your text can move, slide, and scroll.

➤ You can have fancy transitions where one display fades away while another appears.

➤ You can put digitized film clips into your presentation. You can add sound, either just little highlights of sound or a complete narration built in.

➤ Your presentation can even start and stop an audio CD in your CD-ROM player. That way, if you have a boring part in your presentation, you can suddenly start playing the National Anthem, and everyone will have to stand at respectful attention while your presentation continues!

Interactivity: What We Used to Call "Doing Stuff"

If the person seeing the presentation is seeing it on a computer screen, your PowerPoint presentation can be interactive. Basically, this means that the user clicks something (or, if you have a touch screen, touches a point on the screen), and something happens. For example, you can have a screen where you click one place to learn more about the brand new luxury time-share condominiums in scenic Siberia, or click another place to learn *much* more about the condominiums.

If you're letting people see your presentation via the World Wide Web, then you can have things to click that take the viewers out of this presentation and show them things on other Web sites.

Fresh Webbing

Using PowerPoint to create Web pages is a new feature in PowerPoint 97 (although you could do it with an add-in program before). This was added because so much is suddenly happening on the Web. If your main goal is to design a Web site, PowerPoint isn't the best tool for that (things like Microsoft FrontPage are better), but the features are great for letting you take a presentation created for something else and also use it on the Web.

PowerPoint Does the Work

PowerPoint can't do all your work for you—Only you know the information that is going to be in your presentation. What it can do is take care of many of the little things that go into making the presentation nice, and let you worry about the big things. PowerPoint has templates waiting for you, which are already structured like good presentations, and all you have to do is fill in the information. If you're doing a sales presentation, for example, you can use a template designed for sales presentations, broken into sections where you talk about the strengths of your product, how it meets customer needs, where it beats the competition, and so on. Once you put in the information ("Diggity Donuts have the biggest hole in the industry, for easy holding," "Diggity Donuts fit precisely into the customer's stomach," whatever), you'll have a complete presentation, with nice backgrounds and transitions already selected for you.

But you aren't stuck with doing things the way PowerPoint wants. You can start your presentation from scratch, or you can use a template and then change around whatever you want. You're in control. PowerPoint is a smart tool, but it is still your tool (as opposed to that artificial intelligence-powered lawn mower that got too smart and is now ruling a small nation).

Don't Let the Power Make You Forget the Point

If you saw an ad for Brougham's Amazing, Wonderful, Ultra-Fine, Classy, Improved, A-1 Recycled Gallstones, would you buy them? Not even if they were half off? Of course not. All the fancy packaging in the world can't save a bad concept. PowerPoint gives you many great tools you can use to fine-tune your presentation, but it makes it easy to spend all your time fine-tuning the look of things (making it dangerously easy to overlook the actual information you're presenting!)

Your goal should be to communicate information, and all of PowerPoint's tricks are just tools to that end. If you spend a lot of time adding all the latest bells and whistles (not that bells and whistles are new, but it's easier than saying "all the latest multimedia doohickeys and interactive thingamaboobles") rather than figuring out what has to be in your presentation and how to make it clear, your presentation will be bad. Spend more time on the information than you do on the details of the presentation.

But the Nifty Stuff Is Still Useful

If your presentation is so poor it doesn't communicate the information, then your good concept will get lost. Your words and concepts should hold attention on their own, but wise use of design and multimedia can effectively carry the information. Staying totally wrapped in your content and not paying any attention to how to present it will leave you with a long, boring presentation few will choose to pay attention to. Try to achieve a balance between the substance of your presentation and the gift wrap you put it in.

Chapter 2

A Quick and Easy Presentation

In This Chapter

➤ Start PowerPoint

➤ Build a simple presentation that doesn't do anything you want to do, but works!

➤ Save your presentation, and get it back later

Experts will tell you that the proper way to start any new activity is to study what you are to do carefully, read up on all the materials, and proceed in tiny steps as you learn. This is why experts so rarely seem to be having any fun.

Fun is had by people who make the cake without the recipe, by people who hop onto their tricycle before learning the proper hand signal for a left turn, by people who don't study the fine and historic art of crafting fiction and instead just make something up! Let's throw caution to the wind and jump in with both feet! (And if you think it's easy to jump feet first into the wind, you haven't tried it!)

In this chapter, I'll show you how to quickly make a simple presentation. It won't be a presentation that you'd ever actually want to show, and it sure won't show you every feature of PowerPoint. It will, however, give you a basic sense of what PowerPoint does and how it does it, and that will come in handy when we start talking about the steps of the presentation that you *do* want.

Jump-Starting PowerPoint

A computer program is different from a car. (Surprise!) After all, a car is still useful even when it isn't running; you can just sit in the front seat and listen to the radio (although that will run down the car's batteries, and later you'll have trouble getting a spark), or you can sit in the back seat and smooch (which will start you sparking all by itself). But until you start the computer program running, it's just a bunch of information on your hard disk.

To start PowerPoint, click the **Start** button. On the **Start** menu that appears, click **Program**. Another menu appears to the right of the **Start** menu. If there's an entry on the menu marked **Microsoft PowerPoint**, that's the one you want to click. If there isn't, click the entry marked either **Office** or **Microsoft Office** (it will have a little picture of a folder next to it), and another menu appears. That menu will have the **Microsoft PowerPoint** command, which you can now click and start the program!

Ordering the Menu

The Program menu lists all of the *folders* (which lead to another level of menus) first, in alphabetical order, followed by a list of commands, in alphabetical order. Finding the one you're looking for should be easy, if you have the alphabet memorized!

To Know the PowerPoint Window Is to Love the PowerPoint Window

You can tell that PowerPoint has started when its window appears. It's full of good stuff!

The top of the window has the same information as any main program window: a title bar and a menu bar. Below that are several rows of buttons, arranged in logically grouped sections called *toolbars*, with more toolbar space at the bottom of the screen. Keep working with windows, and soon you'll have seen more bars than a worker on Hershey's assembly line! (Of course, they also get a lot of kisses...)

You'll see a small window with a funny-looking animated character (called the *Assistant*). If he's asking you what you want to do, click on **Start Using PowerPoint** to get him out of the way for the moment. If he's not asking you anything, ignore him for now—you'll learn more about him in Chapter 3, "Help Is on the Way"—but if he makes a funny face at you, feel free to make one right back!

Smoothly Buttoned Up

The toolbar buttons in PowerPoint 97 (and other parts of Microsoft Office 97) look different from those on any older products, including Windows 95. Instead of each button being raised, they look smooth against each other, without even a line dividing one button in a group from the next. However, when you pass the pointer over a button, it sticks out, so you can see where its edges are. When you push the button in by clicking on it, it still looks stuck in.

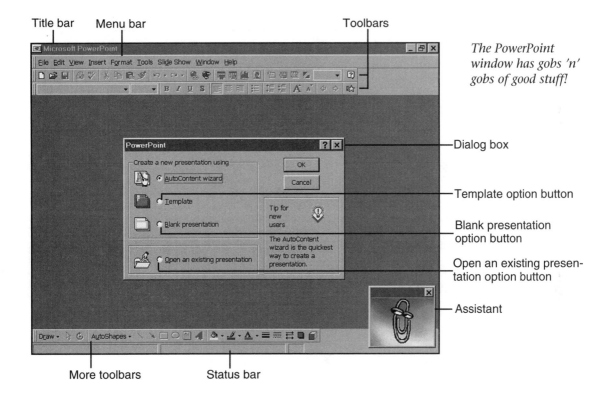

The PowerPoint window has gobs 'n' gobs of good stuff!

Wake Up the Wizard!

When the screen appears, it has a dialog box in the center of it. PowerPoint knows that you want to be working on a presentation, but it doesn't know what presentation. The dialog box offers the choice of not one, not two, but three (not four, not five!) ways of starting a new presentation, as well as the option of continuing work on a presentation that you've already started.

When this dialog box comes up, the **AutoContent Wizard** method of creating a new presentation is at the top of the list. *Wizard* is Microsoft's term for a procedure that takes care of a lot of little bits of work for you. *AutoContent Wizard* is an automatic system that will put together the basics of a presentation for you, so you only have to put in the original material you want to present—it already has good designs and formats for a wide range of types of presentations. Letting the computer do the work is a wonderfully lazy way of getting something done. Click the **AutoContent Wizard** option button; then click the **OK** button to get the wizard working for you!

Working with the Wizard

Once you start the wizard, a window marked **AutoContent Wizard** appears. In the left part of the screen is a list of six steps that you'll have to go through in order to get the wizard to do its job. The first step is simply **Start**, and you accomplish that step by clicking the **Next** button at the bottom of the window.

Step Back, Jack!

If you make a mistake on any of the wizard steps and realize it while working on another step, simply press the **Back** button. It will take you back to the previous step.

The AutoContent Wizard holds your hand through the few steps it takes to put together a basic presentation. Here, we see the list of presentation types available.

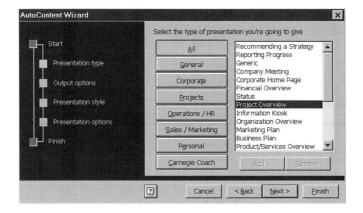

Presentation Type-Casting

In the next step, you have to pick a type of presentation to design. At the right side of the window is a list of types of presentations that you can make. Depending on the way that PowerPoint was installed, you may see a lot of different types of presentations that you may want to do someday (and others that you may never want to do, and can't even imagine anyone wanting to do them). Click the one marked **Project Overview** to select that type of presentation, and it becomes *highlighted* (appear in a different color, so you can tell it from the rest of the list). Then, click the **Next** button to move to the next step.

Skipping Up the Steps

The next two steps want you to pick how the project will be presented. The computer will already have guessed what you want, and its guesses are right, so you don't have to correct it. Click the **Next** button twice to move through these steps. Zoom!

Making Your Presentation Feel Entitled

It's time to pick a title for your presentation, something that reflects what the presentation is about. Now, you may have some great ideas for presentations, but I've got one I've been aching to do, and you can help me with it!

When Que contracted me to write this book, they bought a lot of rights. They got U.S. rights, translation rights, book on tape rights, but they got something even more valuable: the theme park rights! That's right, if Que and their corporate partners want to, they can now make *The Complete Idiot's Guide to PowerPoint: The Ride!* Thrill to the attack of the giant buttons! Look out for the flying text! You're in for the presentation of your life!

So what I want you to type into the **Presentation title** field is **Complete Idiot's Guide to PowerPoint: The Ride**. Put your name into the **Your name** field (if you can't remember it, type **Pocahontas Gertler**, although that's probably not your name. If it were, could you forget it?). Delete everything in the the **Additional information** field.

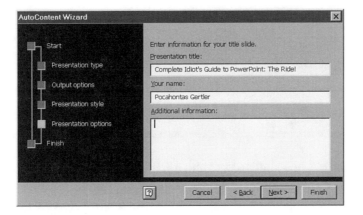

With this form filled out, you're ready to click on Finish and let the Wizard do the work.

With all that information entered, click that **Next** button to move on to the final step. The final step is clicking the **Finish** button, which you can do with aplomb. (If you're all out of plombs, do it with a prune.)

The Outline Is the In Thing!

PowerPoint puts together the presentation for you. A PowerPoint presentation is made up of individual segments, called *slides*, even though they may end up being slides in a slide-show, computer screens in an on-screen display, sheets of paper in a hand-out, overheads in a projected show, or Web pages. I suppose *slidesorscreensorsheetsoroverheadsorwebpages* was just too big a thing to call them! (And calling them *Morty* was just too informal.)

Outline view shows you how PowerPoint puts the presentation together. That means that it shows you a numbered list of slides. For each slide, you see the contents of that slide, including the main discussion point and the *bulleted* (dotted) list of other discussion points underneath it. (There are other views you can use, which I'll discuss in Chapter 4, "Sliding Slides into Place."

Miniature version of your first slide

The outline mode display puts your slides in line, oddly enough.

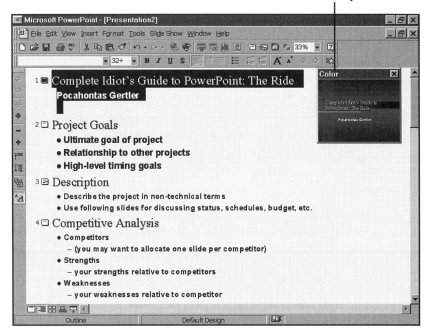

Notice that except for the first slide listed (which has the title), the contents of the slides don't say a thing about the thrilling adventure that is *Complete Idiot's Guide to PowerPoint: The Ride*. The wizard isn't *that* smart. It doesn't understand what your title is about. (That doesn't meant that the wizard is stupid, of course, just illiterate. Just because a wizard can cast a spell doesn't mean that it *can* spell!) What the wizard has put in is some guideline text, which includes concepts and guidelines for the types of thing that should be contained on each slide.

There's also a window over the outline display, which shows you what one slide from the presentation looks like. It should look nice and pretty and colorful, but it may be a little small to read. Don't worry, this is just a miniature version! You won't have to restrict your audience to leprechauns and other small creatures.

Replacing Words with More Words

At this point, your presentation is totally generic, except for the title. You'll have to change it before you can really feel it's yours. If you were working on a real presentation to show others, you'd probably replace most of the text. However, in the interest of being efficient (or, if you're like me, lazy), just change it a little bit—just one line of text. Specifically, go to slide 2 (Project Goals) and change the first point (**Ultimate goal of project**).

To do this, first you have to tell the computer what you're going to change. This is called *selecting*. Slide your pointer over to the line you're going to change. The pointer, at this point, will be turn into a large capital **I**. Slide that to the left of the first letter of what you're going to select, push down the left mouse button, and drag it to the end of the phrase. As you do this, the words will magically, mystically (well, electronically) change color to show you which words you have selected. Instead of being black letters on a white background, the letters turn white and the background turns black.

Selection Correction Directions

If you somehow end up selecting the wrong thing, don't worry! Click any unselected text to clear the selection. Then try selecting the what you meant to select in the first place!

Type **Finally, a ride as fun as crafting a presentation**! When you start to type the words, the phrase you had selected disappears, and what you type appears in its place. Now you have a custom presentation designed to sell the world on the greatest amusement ride ever conceived! It's now time to see this presentation in action.

Presenting: Your Presentation!

Now that you have everything in place, it's time to put on a show. Pull down the **View** menu and select the **Slide Show** command. The screen goes blank, and the computer spends a little time thinking little computer thoughts ("I think, therefore, I am—a chipmunk!")

Then the title slide appears. There, in big letters, is the name of the ride we've all been waiting for! Sit and stare at it, with its big white letters and lovely colored background. You can stare for a long time, because it's not going anywhere. It's just staying there, staring back.

The title slide for this title's ride.

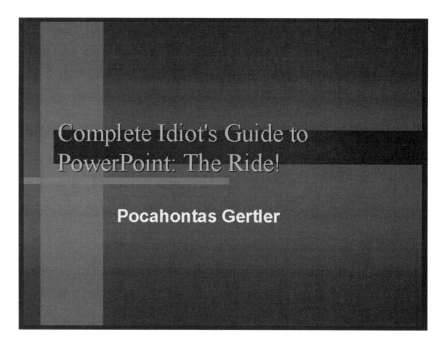

Sliding Through the Slides

There is, of course, a way to move on to the next slide. I asked my techno-geek friend how to do this, and she said "Initially, one is best served by configuring one's port (or, if one is alternately dextrous, starboard) index digit into extended position. Place said limb attachment onto the elongated horizontal entry device that is designated for the insertion of representation-free characters. Depress said rectangular solid and then release it, with a reasonable degree of rapidity."

But those of us who aren't so geeky can just *press the spacebar.*

The new slide replaces the title slide with the next slide all at once. (This is just one way to get rid of the old slide and bring on the new one. The effects used when switching slides in computerized slide shows are called *transitions.* You'll learn more about these and other special effects in Chapter 15, "Tricky Transitions and Terrific Timing.")

If you keep pressing the spacebar, you will move through the eleven slides that make up the presentation. After the last slide, the slide display goes away, and you will return to the PowerPoint window with the outline in it. The quick and easy presentation is complete, and you can feel proud of your accomplishment.

And the good news is that making a slide show that tells what you want it to tell, instead of just a bunch of preprogrammed slides, isn't much harder than that. Oh, you can make it hard, if you're one of those people who like to organize and fine-tune every little thing ("Oh, it's all wrong! The red in that background is far too scarlet! I need a burgundy!"). But you're closer than you probably realize to making presentations that get the job done.

Hallelujah, the point we added is presented!

Save the Show

Now that you've made your first show, you have to learn to *save* it, to store it on your hard disk. If you don't, then when you leave the program, the computer totally forgets about your show. In this case, that might not be so bad; like *My Mother, The Car* proved, some shows are worth forgetting. But to do everything right, you should save it.

Click the **Save** button. A dialog box appears, with the *cursor* (the blinking line you see while typing text that shows you where the text will go) already in the **File name** field. Type a name for the presentation (**PowerPoint Ride** should do fine); then press **Enter**. Powerpoint stores all the information about the presentation in a file called *PowerPoint Ride.ppt* (with *ppt* standing for PowerPoint.) I'll show you later how to get that file back, if you ever want to see that presentation again.

Leaving PowerPoint, and Returning to the Real World

Now that you're done with creating your presentation, it's time to leave the program. Simply click the **Close** button (the **X** button on the title bar) and the program *closes*. The program is still on your computer's hard disk, so you can run it again any time you want. It just isn't running now. And hey, it's earned the rest!

Presentation Regeneration Information

When you want to get the presentation back and look at it again (or even work on it further), here's what you do: Start PowerPoint. When it shows you the opening dialog box, click the **Open an existing presentation** option button; then click **OK**. Another dialog box with a list of presentations appears (the ones with .ppt as their extension). Click the name of the presentation you want to bring back, click **OK**, and the presentation will be loaded again!

Loading Without Leaving

If you're done working with one presentation and want to work with another, you don't have to leave PowerPoint. Just save the work you've done on the first presentation, then click the **Close Window** button on the menu bar (not the one above it on the title bar!)

 Next, click the **Open** button. It will show you the list of presentations and allow you to select another one to load!

The Least You Need to Know

➤ You start PowerPoint by clicking the **Start** button, pointing to **Program**, and then selecting **Microsoft PowerPoint** from the sub-menu that appears.

➤ The AutoContent Wizard can help you create a presentation quickly and easily.

➤ To change text, first *select* the text you're getting rid of (drag the mouse across it); then type the text that you're adding.

➤ To start the presentation display on your computer, open the **View** menu and select the **Slide Show** command.

➤ Press the **spacebar** to move from one slide to the next.

Chapter 3

Help Is on the Way

In This Chapter

➤ Avoid panicking

➤ Get answers to PowerPoint questions

While you're working on your presentation, you are likely to have many questions, ones like "How do I make a black background?" or "What does this button do?" or "Isn't it lunch time yet?" If you're lucky, you have a nearby handy-dandy expert who can answer all of your questions for you (if you are *really* lucky, you'll find a billion dollars, and you can hire a crew of people to make your presentations for you, as well as to bring cold sodas and warm pizza, but that's a little much to hope for).

Unfortunately, we don't all have a handy-dandy expert, and even experts get time off. Besides, if you bother your expert with every little question, he's likely to become annoyed, and annoyed experts can do some *really* nasty things to your computer.

The Author's Favorite Reference

You already have an easy-to-use, technologically simple source for answers right there by you. Just look around. Is it next to the book? No, check the other side. Maybe it's under the book? Wait, now I remember—it *is* the book! Yes, *The Complete Idiot's Guide to*

Microsoft PowerPoint 97 is more than just a handy bug-squasher, it's very good at answering questions, because of the following advantages:

➤ It has a nice, big Table of Contents.

➤ It's broken into chapters by subject.

➤ There's a detailed index in the back.

➤ You can look up answers even when you're away from your computer.

➤ I make money on each copy sold.

However, there are answers that you won't find here. PowerPoint has many little features and options not in here. Also, there are some things that you can get a quicker answer with on the computer. Plus, you may not always have the book with you when you're using PowerPoint, particularly if you borrowed this copy from a friend or a library. (If you did borrow, there's at least one very good reason you should go out and buy a copy: I make money on every copy sold. Forgive me repeating the point, but it is one that is near and dear to my heart.)

Your On-Screen, On-the-Spot Office Assistant

When you're using PowerPoint, you probably see a small square window with an animated character in it that doesn't seem to have anything to do with PowerPoint. (If you don't, click this button and it will appear. Your button may or may not have the light bulb on it.)

This animated fellow is your *Office Assistant*. He's always got an eye on what you're doing and can answer your questions at any time. Sometimes, he's just sitting still; sometimes, he's bopping back and forth in animated motion, but sometimes he's offering advice—and he's always ready to answer questions.

Office Assistant Offers Assistance

Sometimes, the Office Assistant realizes you might not know the best way to do something, or are doing it awkwardly. When this happens, a light bulb appears, the light bulb being the recognized international symbol for an idea. (However, it's a yellow light bulb, which means it's a bug light.)

When you see that light bulb, click the **Office Assistant**. A comic-strip-style word balloon with advice in it appears. In addition to written advice, the balloon may also hold some buttons you can click to let the Assistant help you get the job done. The Office Assistant will only volunteer this particular piece of advice once, so pay attention!

When the light is on, click Office Assistant for all kinds of useful information.

(If someone else has been using this copy of PowerPoint, you can make sure that the Office Assistant doesn't skip the tips that it's already shown the other person. Right-click the Assistant, select **Options** from the shortcut menu, click the **Reset My Tips** button then the **OK** button. The Assistant will suddenly have amnesia, forgetting that it ever told anyone anything!)

Your Office Assistant Is Better Than a Wizard
Earlier versions of PowerPoint had a feature called *Answer Wizard* that did a lot of the same things, but the Office Assistant can actually help you with the process it suggests!

Ask Your Assistant

The Assistant is pretty good at answering "How do I...?"-type questions. If you have a question like that, click the Assistant and a word balloon appears. The Assistant's smart enough that the balloon may already have a list of topics it *thinks* you might want to know about. If you're interested in something that's on the list, simply click the topic, and a window of information pops up, often with a more detailed list of topics to pick from.

The Office Assistant really wants to help, but it needs to know what you need help with. It gives you a whole list of possible topics, and if you want something else, you can just type it in.

Whether or not the Assistant provides a list, it will provide a space for asking a specific question. Just start typing, and your question will appear in that space. Press **Enter**, and the Assistant will try to answer your question.

And this is when you learn that the Assistant isn't very smart.

Cartoons are never very smart. Even Mister Peabody, genius inventor of the Wayback machine, never went back in time and invested in Microsoft in the early days. The Assistant will not come up with a specific answer to your questions. Instead, it will produce a list of topics that it thinks can answer your question. You get to click one of the topics and hope it has the right information.

You see, the Assistant isn't smart enough to understand the question. Instead, it looks for certain key words that tell it what topic is being talked about. If you ask **How do I add a button to the toolbar?**, it will give you a list of topics, one of which is the right one (Add a button to the toolbar). However, if you asked **How do I button my shirt?** or even **Button, button, who's got the button?**, you'd get exactly the same list of topics. The Assistant just recognizes the word *button* and pulls up its list of button-related topics.

Changing Your Assistant

Depending on how your copy of PowerPoint was installed, you may have a choice of different Office Assistants. They all offer the same advice; the only difference is how they look. Some look more goofy and fun, and some look more businesslike—just like your real-life coworkers!

Techno Talk

Short on Assistants? Each Assistant installed on your system takes up a lot of disk space. That's why some of the Assistants that you see here may not be installed.

To change yours (your Office Assistant, not your real-life coworkers), right-click your Assistant to get a shortcut menu. From that menu, select the **Choose Assistant** command. A dialog box appears, with a tab named **Gallery** displayed. There are two buttons marked **Back** and **Next** that let you flip through all of the Assistants on your system. Once you find the one you want, click the **OK** button to use it. (If the Assistant tells you that it needs the Microsoft Office CD, get that CD, put it in your CD-ROM drive, and click **OK**.)

What's This Button?

PowerPoint has many on-screen buttons, each of which displays a little picture that tells you exactly what the button does...or would, if you could read the mind of the graphic designers. For example, there is one button that has a picture of the Earth, with arrows pointing in two directions on it. Does this control the direction in which the Earth spins? No, it just adds a toolbar full of World Wide Web control buttons on it to the display. This is a curious design for a button, because the world does not rotate around the Web... unless you're a spider!

These are the different Office Assistants that you can use. They may look different, but they all give the same advice!

However, most of you aren't spiders. (At least, I hope not! Not that I would mind taking money from a spider. I'm not prejudiced. Heck, some of my best friends have eight legs. Okay, four of my best friends have eight legs between them.) For you, each button has a name that explains, basically, what it does. To see the name of a currently usable button, just point to it. After a second, the name of the button appears in a yellow box. This is called a *ScreenTip*. For example, point to the little Earth-with-arrows button and you will see the button's name, *Web Toolbar*, and that gives you more information than the picture of the Earth did.

What Is "What's This?"

If you pull down the **Help** menu, you'll find a command simply known as **What's This?** Sounds mysterious, eh? If you select this command, the pointer changes into an arrow with a question mark. If that's all it did, it might be mysterious, but it wouldn't be useful.

If you use that pointer to click a button or select a command from a menu, the button or command takes effect. Instead, a box pops open with a short explanation of the thing you clicked. Try clicking the button with the little picture of the Earth, and you will get this explanation: **Web Toolbar: Displays or hides the Web toolbar.**

Contents and Index: A Whole Lot of Help

The Office Assistant and the What's This pointer are handy for simple and short questions. If you need more information than this, and you want to flip through it and bounce easily from topic to topic as you try to learn something, go straight to the Help Topics. This is a complete reference work ready for you to use. And lucky for you, it's a reference work about PowerPoint! (At first, Microsoft was going to put *The Beginner's Guide to the Care and Feeding of Broccoli* into the system before they came up with this brainstorm.)

To access this reference work, pull down the **Help** menu and select the **Contents and Index** command. A Help dialog box opens, giving you access to this hidden warehouse of information.

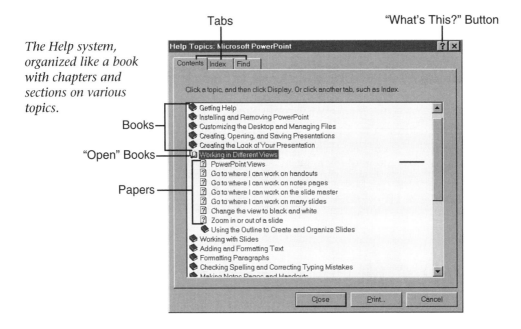

The Help system, organized like a book with chapters and sections on various topics.

Contents: They're Not Just for Breakfast Anymore!

The information in the Help system is organized like a book, but you aren't going to want to read it straight through. There are two main ways to find what you want: look in the table of contents or look through the index. (There's a third way that searches through the whole book for a word that you pick. That sounds like a great idea, but it ends up being about as practical as trying to figure out how your car engine works by sitting under the hood while someone else drives.)

To hit the Table of Contents, click on the **Contents** tab in the Help dialog box. A list of topics appears, each with a little book next to it. That book means that this is a big topic, and its broken up into sections. Double-click on the book, and the list expands to show all the sections in that book. Some of the sections will have a piece of paper next to them, and some will have a book next to them. Double-clicking on the books expands the list further. Double-clicking on the paper displays that help entry on the screen.

For example, if you want to know about how to add another button to one of PowerPoint's toolbars, you'd open up the **Customizing PowerPoint** book. In there, you'll find a **Customizing Toolbars and Menus** book. In there is a paper marked **Add a button to a toolbar**. Double-click that, and you'll get a display with the information that you want.

If you want to close a book that you have open, double-click it again. The list of sections of that book will disappear quicker than a bowl of mice at a python party.

Thumbing Through the Index

To look something up using the index, click the **Index** tab in the Help dialog box. This tab has two areas: a text entry field and an alphabetic list of help topics, many with subtopics. If you have a good grasp of the traditional order of the alphabet, you can use the scroll bar to go through the list and find the topic that you want.

If you want to find the topic faster, you can type the first word of what you're looking for into the text box. As you type, the part of the list starting with that word will appear in the list section.

Once you find the topic you are looking for (or if you find a topic that you aren't looking for but it sounds fascinating anyway!), double-click it. You might go right to the Help information you wanted, or you might be taken to a shorter list of related topics, which you can select one topic from.

Using What You Get

When the Help information appears, it may just be something that you read, and when you finish, you click either the **Close (X)** button or the **Help Topics** button (if you want to get back to the dialog box to look something else up).

However, some Help information has more than that. Some have a list of steps that you can leave open while you work on doing what it says. Others have *hyperlinks*, places to click on to get more information.

Help Printing Help To print out a Help topic, right-click it and select the **Print Topic** command from the shortcut menu. A Print dialog box appears. Click **OK**!

You can recognize these hyperlinks because they have a gray button or a green underline. The pointer turns into a pointing finger when you pass over them (someone obviously never told your computer that it wasn't polite to point).

Click a hyperlink and you might see a small, quick explanation of what you clicked appear in a box. Or the whole Help window might move to another page of information about what you clicked. If it moves on to another page, you can get back to the page you were on by clicking the **Back** button. (And here you were hoping the Back button would cause the computer to scratch your back for you! Boy, when computers can do that, they'll *really* be user-friendly!)

The Help display has lots of things you can click for more help.

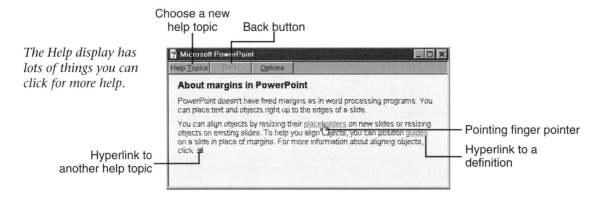

Choose a new help topic

Back button

Pointing finger pointer

Hyperlink to a definition

Hyperlink to another help topic

The World Wide Web Is a Huge Helpful Haven

The Help system is full of information that people need. Well, actually, it's full of information that the folks at Microsoft *thought* that people were going to need when they were making up the Help system. That's close, but it's not quite the same thing.

Check This Out...

Improving a Point It's a good idea to check out the Online Support Web site from time to time, even if you don't have a question. Microsoft often offers additional files to add features to their products, available for free just by downloading them from the Web site!

After all, no matter how much effort you put into expecting how someone is going to use something, they will still surprise you. I remember one toy that our parents bought for us. It was a soft doll of a little old lady, one of those where you pull the string and it talks. It was a perfect gift for rambunctious kids: soft, nondangerous, engaging, respectful, and most of all, nonviolent. So what did we do with it? We used it as a hand grenade! Pull the string, count to three, and throw it into another kid's room! If the doll finished saying its phrase before being cleared out of the room, we considered the grenade to have "gone off," and the people in the room to have been "blown up."

Computer users are a lot like that. The people who design the programs spend a lot of time figuring out how you are going to use the program, and then you turn around and try to do something with it they never thought of. This can create two types of questions that can't be answered in the Help files: "How do I do such-n-such?" and "When I do such-n-such, why does the program stop working?"

Because new questions pop up, Microsoft has a Web site devoted to answering them. If you have your system set up to access the World Wide Web, you can get to it by pulling down the **Help** menu and selecting the **Microsoft on the Web** command. A second menu appears, where you will select **Online Support**. When you pick this, PowerPoint loads your Web browser and gets it to display the Web site. (You may have to enter your Internet password information.)

PowerPoint 9-1-1

Sometimes, the answer just can't be found. You've checked the book, asked the Office Assistant, gone through the Help Index, checked the Web site, asked the expert down the hall, asked the guy who was stealing a donut from the expert down the hall, and what you need to know just doesn't seem to be out there. What to do?

It's time to call up Microsoft! If anyone knows, they should! Microsoft has a whole flotilla of people just sitting by the phone, waiting for you to call. (Well, not just you. But I'm sure they'd love to hear from you as well!) Microsoft's technical support staff are friendly, quick, and know lots and lots of answers.

But that's why you should use them last. Oh, the problem is not that they know the answers, but that everyone knows that they know the answers, so everyone calls them. Sometimes, you can get through to them very quickly, but other times, it takes quite a while, because everyone is trying to ask them things at once. You may spend a lot of time on hold, waiting to get through.

To get information on how to call them, pull down the **Help** menu and select the **About Microsoft PowerPoint** command. A window opens up, giving you certain information about your copy of PowerPoint (the revision number and things like that). On the bottom of the window is a **Tech Support** button. Press that, and you'll see a list of Help topics on how to contact Microsoft's helpful helpers! (Leave the About Microsoft PowerPoint window open, though, because the technical support people will need some of that information to help you out.)

The Least You Need to Know

➤ Clicking the **Office Assistant** icon causes the animated Office Assistant character to appear.

➤ When the Office Assistant has a light bulb with him, click it to get some suggestions about what you are doing.

➤ If you need help figuring out how to do something, click the Office Assistant and type in your question.

➤ The **Help, What's This?** command turns your pointer into an arrow and a question mark. Click the arrow or question mark on anything to find out what it is.

➤ The **Help, Contents and Index** command brings up a complete Help guide with a Table of Contents and an Index.

➤ When using the Table of Contents, double-click a book to see more information on that topic. Double-click a paper to see Help information on that topic.

➤ The **Help, Microsoft on the Web, Online Support** command will bring up a Web page of Help information if you're properly connected.

➤ To find out how to reach Tech Support, use the **Help, About Microsoft PowerPoint** command and click the **Tech Support** button.

Part 2
Building Your Presentation

A presentation is like a salad. You can put a lot of things into it, and make it fancy, or you could put a few things into it, and keep it simple. And some people will look at you weirdly if you give it to them without dressing.

In this part, you'll learn about putting the basics into your presentation salad—the lettuce, the croutons, those little cherry tomatoes that go squish in your mouth. We'll get to the fancy stuff, the endives and anchovies, later.

Chapter 4

Sliding Slides into Place

In This Chapter

➤ Create new slides

➤ Get rid of old slides

➤ Slip a slide from one place into another

➤ View your slides several different ways (front, back, and slideways!)

A *slide* is a single part of a presentation. If you're dealing with a printed presentation, it's a single page. If you have an on-screen presentation, it's a single screen display. And if you're using a slide projector, a slide is a slide!

A *slide show* is a group of slides, organized in a specific order or with a specific choice of paths from one slide to the next. A *presentation* is one or more slide shows, stored together, which may also contain notes on the slide shows. A whole bunch of presentations, organized together with a break for lunch, is a *long, boring symposium*, but those are, thankfully, outside what this book covers.

Looking Slideways

PowerPoint provides a number of different ways for you to look at slides. Each is good for some things and not so good for others, so it's a good idea to get used to them all. Popping from one way of looking at things to another is easy; you can change your view quicker than a politician changes an opinion. At the lower left part of the PowerPoint screen is a set of buttons, each of which gives you a different view to your slides.

Slide View? Aren't They All Slide Views?

Clicking this **Slide View** button puts you into *Slide View*, where you can see the slides on-screen one at a time. Each slide appears about half the size it would be in an on-screen slide show. You can move from viewing one slide to another by using the scroll bar at right to move up or down through your slide show.

In Slide View, you get a good look at one slide at a time.

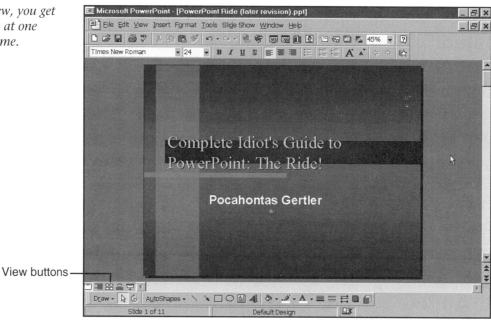

View buttons—

The Slide View is good for changing the contents of a slide. It's really the only view that lets you add or change charts, pictures, movies, logos, and sound to an existing slide. Other views let you change text, but not the other contents of a slide.

Slide View has its weaknesses, though. It only lets you see one slide at a time, which means that it isn't very good for finding a slide, adding new slides, getting rid of old slides, or changing the order of slides. And because it does show you as much of the detail as it can, it can be slow if you're using complicated slides, particularly if you're using a slow computer. (Isn't it funny that you don't remember *buying* a slow computer? You remember buying a lightning-fast state-of-the-art machine! Yet over the years it has somehow been replaced with a slow computer....)

Viewing the Outline Isn't Out of Line

When you made the quick presentation in Chapter 2, "A Quick and Easy Presentation," you used the *Outline View* to change text. You can see this at any time simply by clicking the **Outline View** button.

You'll use Outline View often because it shows a lot at once and you can do a lot with it. For each slide, it shows you a little icon of a slide followed by the text of the slide. This is great for getting the sense of the entire presentation at once, since you can see the text from a number of slides at the same time and in easy-to-read form. You can also make quick text changes, delete slides, and move slides around (Outline View isn't any good for adding pictures, sounds, charts, animation, or exotic Caribbean spices, though).

Use Slide Sorter for the Slides' Order!

The *Slide Sorter View* is great for rearranging your slides. Click this button and you'll see small versions of your slides, several of them on-screen at a time. The slides are arranged in rows, with the first slides going from left to right on the first row, then the next slides on the second row, and so on. You can use the scroll bars to see slides further on in the show.

Slide Sorter View is great for rearranging slides, and for finding a specific slide in the set. You can't change what's on any of the slides here, but you can rearrange the slides to your heart's content (if rearranging slides makes your heart content).

Check This Out...

Automatic Transition

In Slide Sorter View, if you see a little slide icon underneath one of the slides, try clicking it. Right there on the mini version of the slide, you'll see how the transition takes place from the previous slide to this one! This only appears if a transition has been chosen. (You'll learn more about transitions in Chapter 15, "Tricky Transitions and Terrific Timing.")

In Slide Sorter View, you can see many slides at once—and quickly shuffle them.

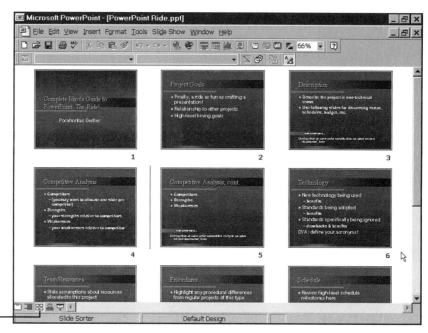

Transition indicator

Note the Notes Page View

PowerPoint can print out a cheat-sheet, so you can have a listing of notes about each slide to refer to while making your presentation. The Notes Page View is designed just to allow you to work on these notes, displaying one slide and a place to edit the notes for each page.

To learn more about making the notes for the Notes page, check out Chapter 20, "Reaching a Crowd: Slides, Overheads, Projection Screens, and Network Presentations." (No, don't check it out *now!* Wait until you learn about creating slides before you try adding notes to them!)

The Notes Page View is very good for adding notes, but not much good for anything else. Some consider being good for just one thing *specializing*; others consider it *being lazy*.

Slide Show: The Show-Off View

Clicking this button starts showing your slide show. There are also commands for starting the slide show on the View menu and the Slide Show menu, but this button has one important difference: it starts the slide show with whatever slide you are currently working on. If, for example, you are in Notes Page View and are looking at the third slide in your show, clicking this button shows the slide show starting at the third slide. To move to the next slide, hit the **spacebar**.

This is the clearest display of how your final presentation will look, since it's basically your final presentation. However, it's no good for changing things. Trying to change things while the slide show is going would be like trying to change your spark plugs while driving.

Show-Stopping To stop the slide show, right-click; then select **End Show** from the shortcut menu.

Selecting Slides

Before you start changing, moving, or otherwise mutilating slides, you have to tell PowerPoint which slide you're working with. The different views have different way of doing this, just to keep you on your toes:

➤ In the Slide View and the Note Pages View, you don't have to select slides. Since each only displays one slide at a time, PowerPoint figures that the slide displayed is the one you want to work with. And it's right!

➤ In the Outline View, click the little slide icon to the left of the slide text. The text of the slide you've selected will reverse colors.

➤ In the Slide Sorter View, just click the picture of the slide you want to select. You can't get it any easier than that! (Well, you could hire an entire staff of slide-selecting personnel, but you probably have better uses for your money. If you don't, could you send me some?)

Selecting More than One Slide

If you want to select more than one slide at a time (if you want to move or delete a whole group of slides, for example), and you're in Slide Sorter View, hold down the **Shift** key while selecting. You can keep selecting as many as you want (but leave some room for dessert). In Outline View, select a group of them by clicking the first one then holding down **Shift** and clicking the last one. In either view, to select them all, hit **Ctrl+A**.

Adding a Slide

You can add a new slide in any view except the Slide Show. To add a new slide, first select the slide you want the new slide to follow. Click the **New Slide** button and a dialog box appears.

A dialog box appears with a display of different layouts for your slide. Some of these layouts contain places for charts, pictures, or movies. Pick a layout that looks the way you want your slide to appear. If it isn't exact, you can rearrange things later. Select the layout; then click **OK**.

A New Slide to Start With If you want to add a new slide as the very first one in your slide show, you have to add it somewhere else, and then move it into the first position. (You'll see how to move it later in this chapter.)

The New Slide dialog box shows small pictures of the different slide layouts you can add. Selecting a picture brings up a description of the slide on the right of the dialog box.

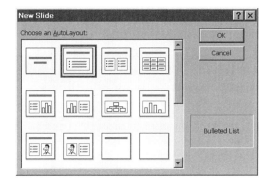

Don't worry now about adding the text or other contents of the slide; I'll show you how to do that in the next chapter.

Slide Deleting

To delete a slide, go into the Slide Sorter View, select the slide, and press **Delete**. Boom! It's gone, never to be seen again!

Didn't Mean to Delete it?

If you delete a slide that you didn't mean to delete, just click on the **Undo** button! It's good for undoing all sorts of mistakes! You can even click repeatedly on it to undo the last few steps, one at a time.

Sliding a Slide Around

Sometimes, you want to rearrange your slide show, to get things in a more logical order. Other times, you want to rearrange other people's slide show, just so they get really confused when they're doing their presentations. Let's face it: you're mean!

To do this, go into Slide Sorter View, because sorting your slides is sort of what this view is all about. Select the slide (or slides) that you want to move; then drag them. The slides don't actually move as you drag them, but you will see a vertical line moving in-between slides, following the pointer as well as it can. Get that line in front of the slide that you want to move these slides in front of, and then release the mouse button. The slides will be rearranged just as you want them to be!

Sliding into Second: Duplicating Your Slide

To make a copy of a slide, select the slide; then pull down the **Edit** menu and select **Duplicate**. The second copy appears immediately after the first.

Why would you want to do this? Sometimes, you just want to have a slide appear more than once in your slide show. For example, you might want to end your show with a copy of the title slide, so that people are left with a reminder of what this presentation was all about.

Sometimes, however, you may want to just create nifty effects. For example, let's say you have a computer-based presentation with a slide that says **Complete Idiot's Guide To PowerPoint: The Ride is the world's fastest**. Make two copies of that, so now you have three identical slides in a row. Replace the word **fastest** with **biggest** on the second slide, and with **best** on the third. Now when you step through the slide show, it will look like it's one slide, with just the last word changing. Keen, eh?

Sliding into First, then Stealing Second

If you want to steal a copy of a slide from another presentation and put it into yours, you can do it! (Make sure you get permission from whoever made the slide.) You can reuse all the slides you want. You can even put on a "greatest hits" retrospective of your favorite slides.

To do this, first select the slide that you want the new slide(s) to appear after. Then pull down the **Insert** menu and select the **Slides from Files** command. The Slide Finder dialog box appears. Click the **Browse** button. A list of your presentation files will appear. Select the one that has the slide(s), then click on the **Open** button.

Now, the name of the presentation you selected appears in the File text box on the Slide Finder dialog box. Click the **Display** button, and the first three slides in the presentation appear in the lower half of the display. You can scroll through the presentation with the scroll bar beneath the slides. Select the slides that you want by clicking on them. (You can select more than one, and you don't even have to hold down the **Shift** key.) Then click the **Insert** button, and the slide (or slides) will be added to your presentation!

The Slide Finder dialog box lets you see the slides in the presentation that you're copying from. If you want to copy them all, click on the Insert All button.

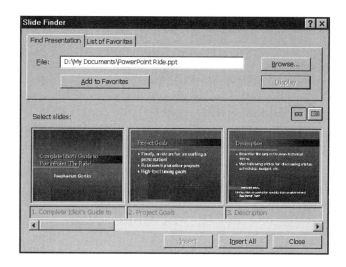

The Least You Need to Know

➤ There are five different slide viewing modes.

Click for **Slide View**. The slide you are viewing is automatically considered selected.

Click for **Outline View**. To select a slide in this mode, click the small slide icon before the text.

Click for **Slide Sorter View**; then click a slide to select that slide.

Click for **Note Pages View**. The slide you are viewing is automatically considered selected.

To view the Slide Show starting from the currently selected slide, click the **Slide Show View** button. You cannot select slides in this view.

➤ To add a slide, select the slide you want to appear before it; then click **Insert New Slide** button.

➤ To delete a slide, select the slide and press **Delete**.

➤ To move a slide, use Slide Sorter view. Select the slide, and drag the it until a vertical line appears before the slide you want to put this slide ahead of.

➤ To copy a slide, select the slide; then select **Edit, Duplicate**.

Chapter 5

The World of Words

In This Chapter

➤ Put words on your slides

➤ Make words bigger and smaller

➤ Makes words bold and italic

➤ Create lists, so you'll no longer be listless!

➤ Correct misspelled words (and mess up correct ones, if you want!)

Words are very important. Sometimes, they're very, very important. If you're getting paid by the word, they can be very, very, very, very, very, very, very important. (That's 75 cents worth right there!)

It's possible to create a presentation without any written text. Most of the time, you'll not only be using text, you'll be using lots and lots of it.

Brave New Words for Brave New Slides

If you've just created a new slide, the best view to add words in is the Slide View. In that view, you'll see that your new slide has the phrase Click here to add text wherever text is going to be on the slide. That phrase is so full of depth and meaning, which boils down to this: to add text, click there!

But you have to do more than just click there! That was too easy! After you click there, you have to type the text. As you type, what you type appears on the screen. If you make a mistake, hit the **Backspace** key to get rid of it, and keep typing. (If you decide not to add any text at all, hit the **Esc** key and escape out of it!)

Some text areas are specifically designed for lists. If you start typing in one of those, a *bullet* (a dot) will appear before what you type. Every time you hit the Enter key, a new line will start with another bullet.

Reworking Your Words (or Rewording Your Work)

Sometimes, you want to change words on one of your slides. Perhaps you've discovered better words, or maybe you've just discovered that you're allergic to the word "agenda." Whatever the reason, changing what you've typed is easy.

First, *select* the text you're going to change. (Remember, this is done by pointing to the start of the first word you want to change, holding down the mouse button, and dragging to the end of the last word you want to change.) The selected words will show up in a different color. Start typing the new text, and the old text, feeling unwanted, will leave immediately.

Select Tricks

To quickly select a word, double-click on it. To select a whole paragraph, triple-click. And if you click a hundred times on the word, you get... a tired clicking finger!

Word-dos: Styling Your Text

Remember way back, in your great-grandmother's day, they had a device called a *typewriter*. This method of putting words on paper created letters that all looked alike. A typed shopping list looked the same as a contract, which looked the same as a love letter. Really important words like "one-third off" looked the same as unimportant words like "heretofore." This was a great way to be understood, but an absolutely horrible way to look hip, fashionable, and obscure.

Luckily, PowerPoint has a full set of tools to make your words look fancy. Now you can make your words so heavily designed that they're as hard to read as one of those modern magazine ads! You can even create the sort of teeny tiny text that they use to tell you that use of this product may lead to spontaneous human combustion.

Leapin' Letters: Bold, Italic, Underline, and Shadow

You can quickly add some basic effects to your text. Select the text you wish to emphasize, and then click:

B To get **bold** text (or press **Ctrl+B**)

I To get *italic* text (or press **Ctrl+I**)

U To <u>underline</u> text (or press **Ctrl+U**)

S To give the text a small shadow, as if it were hovering over the page.

(If you don't see these buttons on the screen, right-click the buttons you do see, and select **Formatting** from the menu that appears. This will make the Formatting toolbar appear.)

You can combine these effects by clicking more than one button. If you want to get rid of the effect, just select the text and click the button again. The button will pop out, and the text will be back to normal.

Check This Out...

Font-astic Formatting

Use the **Format, Font** command to get a dialog box which will let you choose to make text *embossed* (raised), *subscript* (smaller and below the rest of the text), or *superscript* (smaller and above the rest of the text).

Colorful Language

There's little that can make your text stand out more than color. Red is a particularly good one; that's why we have terms like *red letter days*, *red ink*, and *The Scarlet Letter*. PowerPoint automatically uses a color that shows up well against the background, but you can change that color at any time.

A To change the color of text, first select it. Then head down to the bottom of the screen and click on the small drop-down arrow to the right of the Font Color button. A small menu pops up, which has

Check This Out...

Invisible Text A neat trick is to turn shadows on, then make your text the same color as the background. The text will seem to disappear, with only the shadows visible, but that's enough to be clearly readable. Try it!

a bunch of little colored squares on it. Just click on the square of the color you want. If you want to change more text to that color, you can select that text and click on the Color button. (If you don't see the toolbar at the bottom, right-click on any toolbar you do see, and select **Drawing** from the menu that appears. The button will now be seen.)

Don't actually use all the different style options on the same slide. If you mix more than 3 on a slide, it becomes as hard to read as a bowl of alphabet soup!

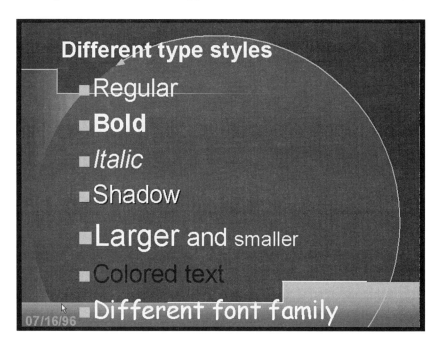

Sizing Up (and Down) Your Words

Some concepts call for huge words, like "I love you!" or "Free donuts!" Others call for a mite more delicacy, like "I only love you because you give me free donuts." By changing the *font size* (the size of the letters), you can create a sense of importance and make sure that the most important thing is seen first. Keep clicking on the **Increase Font Size** and **Decrease Font Size** buttons until the selected text is as big or as small as you want it.

The Font Size field shows you how big your letters are (measured in *points*, 72nds of an inch). You can fine-tune the size by changing the number there.

Font   Drop-down arrow   Increase Font Size

Arial   28   B I U S

Font size   Decrease Font Size

The Formatting toolbar has lots of buttons to control the look of your text.

It's Too Small

Remember that when you're working in Slide View, you're seeing the slide half-sized. Text that is too small to read at that size might be fine when displayed on the computer screen, and large text may look humongous. You probably shouldn't be putting so much on a slide that you need to type very small—unless you're using PowerPoint to create one of those car lease ads with all the legal details about how you can pay thousands of dollars every month for 10 years and still not own the darn thing!

Just Put One Font in Front of Another

There are a lot of different *fonts* (type designs), ranging from the boring to the unreadable. Somewhere in between, there are some you should actually think about using. Click on the drop-down button next to the font field, and you'll see a list of fonts on your system. Select a font from the list, and the selected text will now appear in that font.

If you aren't familiar with the fonts you have, you should spend some time getting friendly with them. When you have some time to spare, select a sentence and see what it looks like with each font on your system. Some will look better than others. Some of the fancier ones may only have capital letters, and will replace all of the lowercase letters with squares. Remember which ones look good, so you can get them back when you need them. The ugly ones you can use for when you put your competitor's name on the slide!

Founts of Fonts
There are plenty of fonts available for download from the Internet. You can also get CD-ROMs with hundreds or even thousands of fonts on them. Many of these are considered *display fonts*, which are too fancy to write letters with but can be good for titles.

41

Speling Is Emportent

All the pretty letters in the world won't do you any good if they don't form words. Misspelled words are hard to understand, and they make you look both stupid and sloppy. And some day, your old grade school English teacher may be watching your presentations, and it would be horrible to have her drag you back into third grade spelling class at this point!

PowerPoint has a *spell checker*, a program feature that will go over all the words on your slides and make sure that they are all indeed words, showing that you didn't make a major typo and that your cat didn't trundle across the keyboard while you weren't looking. (I was once filling out my Township Pet Registration form when my cat jumped on the typewriter, bringing the cat, typewriter, and my last bottle of white-out smashing to the floor at once. Poor little fejo;lwwq/'vv!)

You don't even have to tell PowerPoint to check your work. As you type, PowerPoint is constantly looking over your shoulder, just waiting for you to make a mistake so it can point out the mistake and laugh at you. Okay, it doesn't laugh out loud, but you know that somewhere, deep inside, it's laughing. When you type something that it thinks is a mistake, it will underline the word with a wavy line.

Fixing the Misteak

If you recognize your mistake, you can simply fix it, and the wavy line will go away. If you don't know what the right spelling is, or if you think you do have the right spelling, right-click on the word and a menu will appear.

At the top of the menu is a list of words that it thinks you might have meant. If the right word is there, just select it from the menu. PowerPoint will take away your wrong word and slide in the right one, and no one will be any wiser! If PowerPoint doesn't recommend the right word, try replacing it with another guess at the right spelling. Even if you don't get it right, you might get close enough for PowerPoint to make the right suggestion.

Right-clicking on a typo brings up a list of suggested fixes.

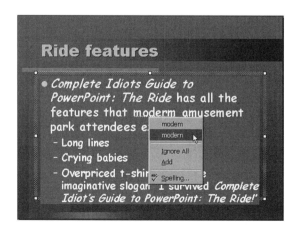

My Spelling is Ryght, Dadgummit!

PowerPoint is a know-it-all. It thinks that just because it doesn't recognize a word, it must be misspelled. Sometimes it's right, and sometimes it's wrong. There are a lot of things that PowerPoint doesn't know, including a lot of names. If PowerPoint incorrectly corrects you, feel free to laugh at it.

If PowerPoint calls something a typo, and it isn't, there are three things you can do:

➤ Ignore the wavy line. (Don't worry, the wavy line won't show up in the finished slide show!) The problem is that if you ignore the wavy line when it isn't a misspelling, it's hard to notice it when there really is one.

➤ Right-click on the word and select **Ignore All** from the menu. This lets PowerPoint know not to count that same word as a mistake again in this presentation. (It will still count it as a mistake if you use it in another presentation.)

➤ Right-click on the word and select **Add**. This tells PowerPoint to add the word to its dictionary, so next time it will not count it as a mistake.

> **Check This Out...**
>
> **One Dictionary for the Whole Office** All of the Microsoft Office products use the same dictionary file to check spelling. If you add a word to the dictionary in PowerPoint, then Word (for example) will also recognize it!

Missed Mistakes

There are mistakes that you can make that PowerPoint has no way of noticing. That's because many typos accidentally turn one word into another. If you put, say, "Compete Idiom's Glide" on a slide, PowerPoint will not complain a bit, because everything in it is a word. PowerPoint is not smart enough to recognize that none of them are the right words. Congratulations! You are smart enough to out-smart the error-catching technology!

These mistakes are best battled with the power of the human brain. Read over your presentation or, better yet, get someone else to read it over. Murphy's Law says that any mistake you don't catch will be seen by every member of your audience!

Alignment Assignment

Usually, we see text where each new line starts right below the previous line, but each line's end is in a slightly different place, depending on the length of the words on the line. This is the easiest thing for most people to read. But dagnabbit, we've put a lot of work into designing this presentation, so maybe it should be just as much work to read it!

There are three different choices for how your lines of text will line up. While your working on a block of text, you can click on:

To get *left alignment* (the text lines up the usual way).

 To get *center alignment* (each line of text is centered across the text area, giving it a balanced look). This is good for titles.

 To get *right alignment* (the ends of the lines are stacked neatly, but the beginnings of the lines don't line up). This creates a new-wave look for short lists, but isn't very useful.

Spreading the Lines

If you have a slide that doesn't have much on it, and you don't want it to look so empty, you could add more material to it—but that would be work! It's a lot easier just to make your existing text fill up more space. Making the lettering bigger is one way of doing this, but another way is to increase the space between lines. Click on this **Increase Paragraph Spacing** button, and the lines start to spread apart. The more times you click, the further apart they go!

If you want to fit more onto your slide, you can squish the lines together. Clicking this **Decrease Paragraph Spacing** button decreases the space between lines. Don't get *too* enthusiastic with this, though! Within a few clicks of the button, you'll have the lines squished so close that they are overlapping.

Lust for Lists!

Lists are very popular in presentations. There's nothing like saying that your product will make the customer:

➤ Rich

➤ Healthy

➤ Irresistible to members of the appropriate sex

Many of the slide layouts that PowerPoint's AutoLayout feature offers have list areas. You can recognize them in the layout pictures in the New Slide dialog box because they show lines of text that start with a *bullet* (a dot).

Entering text into a list works just like regular text, except that every time you hit **Enter**, a line is skipped and a bullet is put in front of the line. The Increase and Decrease Paragraph Spacing buttons work differently as well, changing just the size of the space between items on the list, rather than the space between each line of text.

Demotion of De List

Individual items on your list may have their own lists that go with them. When the previous list tells your customer that your product will make them healthy, you may want to list the individual health benefits (a healthy glow, washboard abs, and the end to cavities). This sub-list should be indented further than the normal list.

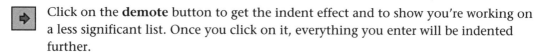 Click on the **demote** button to get the indent effect and to show you're working on a less significant list. Once you click on it, everything you enter will be indented further.

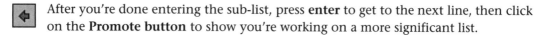 After you're done entering the sub-list, press **enter** to get to the next line, then click on the **Promote button** to show you're working on a more significant list.

Bite the Bullet

Lists don't have to have bullets. To remove bullets from a list, select the list, then click on this button. The bullets will disappear. Click the button again, and they reappear.

If you want to use a different-looking bullet, you can do that too! Select the whole list, then pull down the **Format** menu and select the **Bullet** command. The Bullet dialog box displaying a whole bunch of bullets will appear, and you can click on the one you want. If you don't see any you want, there's a Bullets From drop-down list that lets you select a different font to take the bullet from. There's also a Color drop-down button that lets you pick the color of the bullet, and a Size field where you can enter the caliber... er, *size* of the bullet! Once you've selected your bullet, click on the **OK** button to use it!

Color ——

Pick another list of bullets ——

Size ——

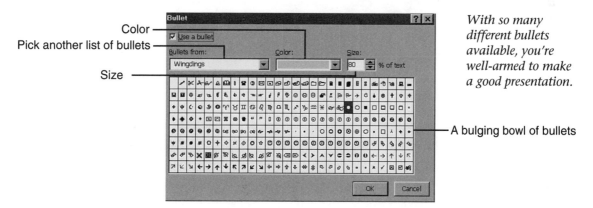

With so many different bullets available, you're well-armed to make a good presentation.

—— A bulging bowl of bullets

45

The Least You Need to Know

➤ To start putting text on a new slide, click where it says Click here to add text.

➤ To change text on an existing slide, select the text that you want to change and then type over it.

➤ If you don't see the Formatting toolbar, right click on any other toolbar and select **Formatting** from the menu that appears.

➤ The following Formatting toolbar buttons allow you to format and manipulate text:

B Bold: Makes text bold

I Italics: Italicizes text

U Underline: Underlines text

S Shadow: Casts a shadow

A Increase Font Size: Makes text bigger

A Decrease Font Size: Makes text smaller

Left Alignment: Aligns text to the left

Center Alignment: Aligns text to the center

Right Alignment: Aligns text to the right

➤ The drop-down arrow at the right end of the font field opens a drop-down list from which you can select a completely different type style.

➤ If you type a word that PowerPoint doesn't know, a wavy line will appear under it. Right-click on the word to see a menu that will let you pick the correct word, or to teach PowerPoint this word.

➤ When entering a list, each time you hit Enter you start a new item on the list. Each item starts with a bullet, unless you click on this **Bullets** button to stop the bullets.

Chapter 6

Layout: Not Just Something You Do in the Sun

In This Chapter

➤ Arrange boxes of text and other slide contents

➤ Change each box's size

➤ Overlap boxes

➤ Add boxes, remove boxes, and even group boxes!

Learning how to lay out your slides is very important. Extremely important. The fate of civilization may depend on it.

Well, okay, it's not *that* important. Heck, with all of the nice built-in slide designs that PowerPoint provides, you may not need to know it at all. But still, knowing this could help you make your presentation look that much better—and isn't that more important than civilization?

Boxes in Slides? I Thought Slides Went in Boxes!

The design of a slide is broken down into areas called *boxes*. Each box holds one *object*, one piece of your slide. For example, if you have, a slide with a title, a list, and a chart, you'll have three boxes: one for the tile, one for the list, and one for the chart. You could have a slide with no boxes, but that would be a blank slide.

Each box is a rectangular shape, even if it's holding something that isn't rectangular, such as a circular picture or New Jersey. (Not that you can actually put New Jersey itself onto a slide, but if you could, it would be in a rectangular box.) On the slide designs that PowerPoint starts you off with, none of the boxes overlap, but you can overlap them if you want.

Selecting and Moving Boxes

To select a box, go into Slide View and click on the box's contents. When you do this, eight little white squares will appear around the edges of the box, one at each corner and one at the center of each edge. These white squares are *sizing handles*, which you'll use if you want to change the size of the box. On some boxes, an edge line appears around the box as well.

The line and white boxes around the list show that it's selected. Don't confuse that with the dotted line around the space for a chart.

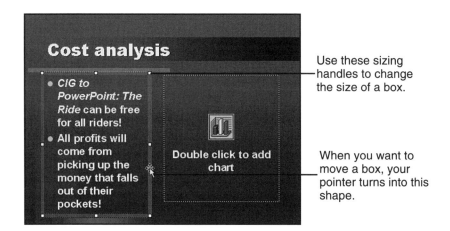

Use these sizing handles to change the size of a box.

When you want to move a box, your pointer turns into this shape.

Moving boxes is easy. Just point to an edge of the box, and your pointer should turn into an arrow with arrowheads pointing in all four directions (useful, I suppose, to very clumsy hunters). Push down the mouse button and drag the rectangle wherever you want it to go! You can even drag it off the edge of the slide, but if you do, it won't be in your slide show! (Although you can make some nifty effects by dragging it just over the edge of the slide, so *part* of it shows up in the show.)

Sliding It from Slide to Slide

To move a box from one slide to another slide, a different method comes into play. Just follow these easy steps:

1. First, select the box you want to move (if you're doing a text box, re-select it by grabbing the edge, so PowerPoint doesn't think you're trying to select just some of the text).

2. Then, click on the **Cut** button, which will *cut* the box off of the slide.

3. Finally, go to the slide that you want to put the box on, and click the **Paste** button, which will *paste* it onto the page. Then you can move the box into place.

Clipboard Concerns

When you use the cut button, it takes whatever you cut and stores it into a place in memory called the *clipboard*. When you paste, whatever's on the clipboard gets copied onto the page. You can use cut without paste to just eliminate a box. You can also keep pasting the same thing several places, as it isn't removed from the clipboard when you paste it.

Resizing Boxes, for When Size Matters

Sometimes, you find you want a bigger box, such as when you have more text than will fit in the box you have. Sometimes you want smaller box. Let's face it, you're just never satisfied!

If you want to make a box that is wider or narrower, grab one of the sizing handles on the middle of the sides of the box. Use the handle to drag the size to where you want it.

To make the box taller or shorter, grab the handle on the middle of the top or bottom of the box and use it drag that edge where you want it.

To shrink or grow the whole box, but still keep the same basic shape, hold down the **Shift** key and drag one of the corner handles. PowerPoint will make sure that the ratio between the width and height remain the same.

To make the box crunchier, coat it with a thin layer of chocolate then sprinkle on Rice Krispies-compatible breakfast cereal!

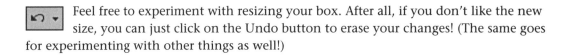 Feel free to experiment with resizing your box. After all, if you don't like the new size, you can just click on the Undo button to erase your changes! (The same goes for experimenting with other things as well!)

Time to Play Spin the Box!

Just because a box has to be a rectangle does not mean that it has to be a straight up-and-down. You can tilt the box, or rotate it, to put your title at a jaunty angle, or just to tilt a chart a little bit to get on the nerves of precise people (you know, the sort who wander around your house, straightening your paintings).

Check This Out...

Precisely Tilting

If you hold down the Shift key while rotating the box, it will rotate in precise 15 degree steps, so that there's only 24 different positions you can rotate it to. This is handy if you want to rotate several things the same amount.

To do this, first select the box that you want to take for a spin. Click on the **Free Rotate** button on the lower edge of your screen. The sizing handles on the box will disappear, and you will start to see green dots before your eyes. Don't worry, these dots are *rotation handles*. Grab one of those handles and drag it around. An outline will show how the box rotates, turning around the box's center, which stays still. Once you've got the outline where you want it, release the button, and the box will tilt into position. The contents of the box become tilted as well, so you get tilted words, tilted pictures, tilted New Jersey, whatever.

After you've tilted it, click on the **Free Rotate** button again to return to a normal pointer.

The Box Is a Pushover

If you want to quickly push the box over on its side, click on the **Draw** button. A menu will pop up. Select **Rotate or Flip**, and a sub-menu will appear. From that menu, select either **Rotate Right** or **Rotate Left**, and the object will be rotated 90 degrees. To turn it upside-down, just do this twice. And if you do it four times in a row, the box will be back where it started and you will have successfully wasted 20 seconds!

Boxes on Top of Boxes

You can create some interesting effects by *overlapping*. No, overlapping doesn't mean licking the cone after all the ice cream is gone—it means putting one box on top of another box. By doing this, you can put text on top of pictures, text on top of other text, pictures on top of each other, or even New Jersey on top of Idaho (if you could get them into boxes).

Getting a box on top of another box is no problem: just move it over. The real question is how you choose which box goes on top and which goes on the bottom.

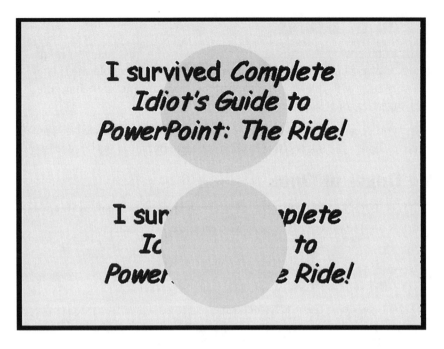

The order in which things are piled makes a big difference. These two piles have the same objects overlapping, but in the bottom one, the circle is on top, hiding the text.

Boxes Going Up and Down (Aren't Those Called Elevators?)

To change where a box is in a stack, first select it. Then right-click on it, and a shortcut menu will appear. Select **Order** from this menu, and you'll see a sub-menu with four commands on it.

If you only have two boxes in your pile (now that's not much of a pile, is it?) then you'll select **Send to Back** (which takes the selected box and puts it at the bottom of the pile) or **Bring to Front** (which makes it the top of the pile).

If you've got a real serious pile, there are a couple of other commands that come in handy. Selecting **Bring Forward** will move the selected box up the stack by one, so if you have the third box in the pile selected, it will bring it up so it's the second. **Send Backward** does just the opposite, lowering the item in the pile by one.

Check This Out...

Search for the Missing Box

To work with a box, you have to be able to select it. Usually, this is easy, but if you have a small box buried under larger boxes, there may be no visible part to click on. The trick is to dig down through the pile. Select whatever's on top, and send it to the bottom. Keep doing that until you've dug down through the pile and found the missing box!

Groups: Boxes Full o' Boxes

Sometimes, you'll want to take several boxes and treat them as one, just like you might want to squish a bunch of marshmallows together and treat them as one big mega-marshmallow. This is very handy if you've got a mixture of text and pictures that you want to copy or move together, or if you're making mega-s'mores.

In order to do this, first you're going to have to select several boxes, to show what you want to pull into a group. That's a trick worthy of its own little headline, so here it is:

Selecting Multiple Boxes at Once

First, select one of the boxes. Then, while holding down the **Shift** key, click on the other boxes. The sizing handles on each box will appear, showing that it is selected.

Quickly Select a Bunch

If all of the boxes you want to select are close together, and there aren't any other boxes mixed in with them, you can select them all in one smooth motion. Point to a spot up and to the left of the boxes, hold down the mouse button, and drag to below and to the right of the boxes.

Bringing the Group Together

Once you've got all the boxes selected, it's time to make a group out of them. Click on the **Draw** button, and select the **Group** command from the menu that appears.

Kazowie! Suddenly, all of these boxes are one big box! Instead of having a bunch of different handles, they've got one set of handles. Everything that you can do to individual boxes, you can now do to this one big box.

Bringing Loners into the Group

Any box that PowerPoint's AutoLayout feature built into the slide won't want to join in the group. If you have one of these selected, you won't be able to use the group command. However, you can fool PowerPoint into forgetting that a box was put there by AutoLayout. To do this, click the **Draw** button, select **Change Autoshape**, then pick **Block Arrows** from the submenu. A display of arrow shapes will appear. Click on any one of them. (The box your working with may look strange at this point—don't worry, we'll have it back to normal in a moment.)

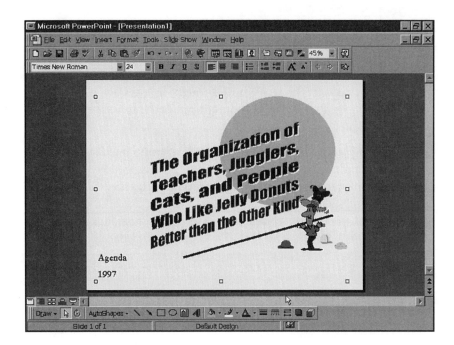

If we can put words, pictures, shapes, lines, and logos into a single box, then why can't we have world peace?

Next, click **Draw** and select **Change Autoshape** again, but this time select **Basic Shapes** and click on the rectangle in the upper left corner. The box should now look the way that it originally did, but PowerPoint has now forgotten it's a special box. If you select the pieces for your group again, you'll be able to group them just fine! (And don't worry that you don't know what that Autoshape feature is yet. I'll be teaching you about it in Chapter 8, "Lines and Shapes: Good Things in Variable-Size Boxes.")

Driving the Group Apart

There's always a way to drive any group apart. You could become the Yoko Ono of the PowerPoint box set with this ability! Select the group, click on the **Draw** button, and select **Ungroup**.

Unkazowie! All of the boxes in the group are their own selves again, each with their own handles. If you want to do something with just one of these boxes, click off the side of the slide (to clear the selection), then select that box.

Reunion Tour '97: Bringing the Group Back Together

Giving the Group a New Member If you already have a group, and you want to add another box to it, you don't have to break up the group. Just select both the group and the new box and then select **Draw**, **Group**.

Theoretically, you should never put your group together until you're absolutely sure every piece of the group is perfect. In the real world, though, if you wait until everything is perfect to do something, you'll never get anything done!

If you do discover that part of the group needs to be changed, resized, or moved, you'll have to take the group apart using the Ungroup command described earlier. Once you've made the change, though, you don't have to go to all the trouble of selecting everything. Just click on the **Draw** button and pick the **Regroup** command, and all the boxes from the group will rejoin!

The Least You Need to Know

➤ The items on a slide are called *objects*. Each object has its own *box*.

➤ To select a box, click on it. To select several boxes at once, hold down the **Shift** key and click on them each in turn.

➤ To move a box, click on its edge and drag it.

➤ To change the size of the box, click on one of the *sizing handles* (white squares) and drag it into position.

 ➤ Selecting a box, then clicking the **Cut** button will cut the box from the slide, storing a copy of it on the clipboard.

 ➤ You can paste a copy of the last thing you cut onto any slide by going to that slide and clicking the **Paste** button.

 ➤ To rotate a box, click on the **Free Rotate** button, then drag one of the green dots at the corner of the box.

➤ *Grouping* turns a bunch of boxes into a single box. To do this, select the boxes, the click on the **Draw** button and select the **Group** command. The **Ungroup** command on the same menu breaks a group back into separate boxes.

Chapter 7

WordArt: Your Logo-Making Low-Calorie Friend

In This Chapter

➤ Create colorful fancy logos and titles

➤ Stretch and shape your words

➤ Give even shallow phrases visual depth

➤ Fire half of your art department

A good logo or an impressive-looking title can really set the stage for a good, impressive presentation. PowerPoint's WordArt feature makes such impressive logos a snap. It's an excellent tool for when you're trying to pass off your teeny little company as a huge conglomerate.

Instant Logo

You can throw together a logo in a few seconds, which is particularly good if you already told the boss it would take all week.

To get started, go into Slide View and get the slide where you want your logo to appear. Click on the **WordArt** button on the Drawing toolbar, and a grid of thirty different logos appear. They all say the words *WordArt*, but they all look different. There are curvy WordArts, shiny WordArts, rainbow-colored WordArts, more different WordArts than you'd ever thought you'd see or, frankly, than you'd ever want to!

WordArt Is EveryWhere

The WordArt function is not only available in PowerPoint, but also in other Microsoft programs such as Word and Excel. The things you learn in this chapter will serve with those programs as well, and the designs you make in any one of these programs can be used with the others.

The WordArt dialog box offers you 30 different designs to work with.

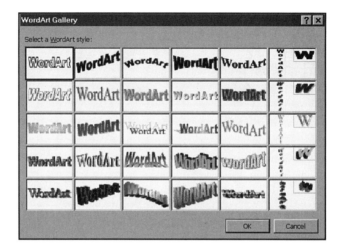

Immediately, you think "this is a great tool to use if you're creating a logo for a company called WordArt, but otherwise…" But never fear; you can change the text to anything you like. Double-click on the style of logo that you want, and a dialog box pops up asking for the text that you want to use. The text field says Your Text Here, and if you really want your logo to say this, just go ahead and click the **OK** button now.

Of course, if your company doesn't happen to be named *Your Text Here* (and why not? It's a name no one else seems to be using!), you can type the company name, the title, or whatever words you want to be a work of art. If you want your logo to have multiple lines of text, just press Enter between lines. (The text box has automatic word wrap if you type long lines, but the new lines it starts only appear in the text box, not in the finished logo.)

Click on the **OK** button, and your WordArt logo masterpiece will appear! And wow, it is impressive looking, isn't it? And it would be even better if it were another color? Or a little wider? Or the letters were spaced a bit farther apart?

WordArt Adjustments

Moving and resizing your WordArt are done just as with any other object. When you change the size of the box, the logo will automatically redraw to reflect the new size. But the logo doesn't necessarily fit inside the box; the box is the size that the WordArt would be if it was flat, but since a lot of WordArt is angled and three-dimensional, the logo may extend beyond the edges of the box.

Sizing handles　　Shaping Diamond

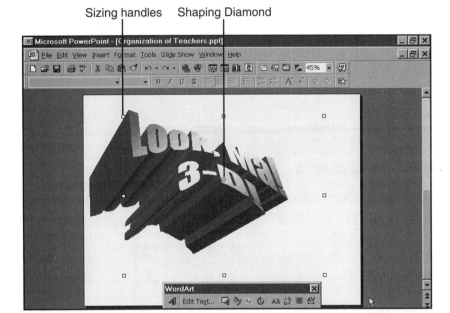

The WordArt often extends beyond the edges of the box.

In addition to the white squares around the edges of the art, you should also see one or two yellow diamonds. Dragging these diamonds around changes the shape of your logo. Exactly what it changes depends on the type of design that you chose. If you experiment with a diamond, you should quickly see what it does (or, if you don't, you can remain ignorant, which is supposed to be blissful).

An Old Angle on a New Diamond

If you've used previous versions of WordArt, you haven't seen this diamond before. However, the things that the diamond changes are the same as used to be changed by the angles and sliders set by the Special Effects button.

Buttons for the Indecisive

When you select the WordArt object, a WordArt *toolbar* (group of buttons) appears on the screen. Two of these buttons are for redoing things you've already done. These buttons are only useful if you don't do everything perfect the first time. Just in case there are any imperfect people out there, I'll tell you a bit about them.

If you click on the **WordArt Gallery** button, the gallery of 30 different designs reappears. Double-click on any design to change your words to that design. If you look at all the designs and decide that you were right in the first place (and had merely underestimated your perfectness), click on the **Cancel** button.

The **Edit Text** button brings up the Edit WordArt Text dialog box again. Of course, you can use this to change the words in your logo, but that's not all. Now that we're not rushing through it on an attempt to break the World Logo-Making Speed Record, we can check out some of the other features that this dialog box has to offer.

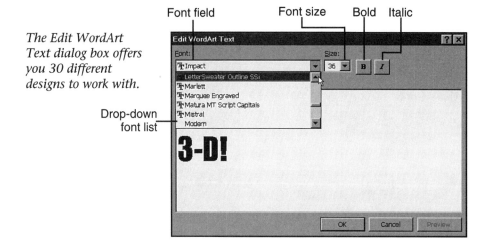

The Edit WordArt Text dialog box offers you 30 different designs to work with.

There are a pair of buttons that can make your text bold or italic. The italic is a little tricky, since italic normally makes your words slanty, but some logo designs will straighten them back up. Italic versions of letters are a little more ornate than the plain version in some fonts, such as Times New Roman, so it may be worth trying the change to see what effect it has.

The real powerhouse here is the Font drop-down list. Open it, and you'll see a list of fonts that you can use for your logo. Some of the fonts you're used to seeing may not be on this list, since only outline fonts are listed. Select a font, and your text will now appear in the font in the Text field. Click on the **OK** button, and that font will be twisted, stretched, and colored to make your logo.

TrueFacts About TrueType

When a letter is shown on the screen or printed out, what you see is a pattern of dots that make up the letter. Some fonts are stored on disk in files that have dot patterns for all the letters in each of a number of sizes. With TrueType fonts and other outline fonts, one precise mathematical description of the outline of each letter is stored. When Windows wants to display test using an outline font, it stretches the outline to the size it wants, then figures out what dots it takes to fill the outline. The outline is very easy for the computer to resize, stretch, warp, and work with in other ways that would be hard to do with a dot pattern. This is why WordArt uses only outline fonts.

If you have a very fancy logo style, with lots of curves or 3-D or other tricks, you're probably best off using a fairly simple font. A fancy font can be hard to read after you do all that stuff to it.

WordAerobics: Getting Your Logo in Shape

The WordArt Shape button lets you change the shape of the face of your logo. You may not be able to get your logo ship-shape, but you can make it wave-shape, bridge-shape, or any of dozens of other shapes. Click on this button, and a visual menu will appear, with pictures of all the different shapes. Click on the shape you want, and your logo will be stretched into that shape.

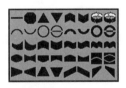

Choose your WordArt shape from these forty fine forms.

Free Rotate: Spinning at No Cost

The **Free Rotate** button on the WordArt toolbar is the same as the one on the drawing toolbar. However, it has a bit of a different effect in WordArt than you might expect. Dragging one of the green dots doesn't rotate the whole image of the logo. Instead, it rotates the basic design of the face of the logo. If you take a look at the next picture, you'll see the difference this makes. The lower version of the logo is just a rotated version of the top one. Notice that the lower version has the 3-D perspective effect still pointed toward the top, instead of pointed toward the bottom as you might expect after turning it upside-down. Notice also that the color fade still goes from top to bottom, even though what had been the bottom is now the top. Finally, notice that an upside-down logo is a really dumb idea, unless you're planning to give your presentation in Australia.

59

Turning the logo upside-down doesn't just give you the same picture, upside-down. (But if you put both logos on the ride, people watching it could still read it while the ride is doing a loop-de-loop!)

Fit to Print

There's an old Egyptian saying about how a person sizes their letters. Unfortunately, I don't know any old Egyptians, so I don't know what this saying is, but I'm sure it's pithy and wise.

Here are a few buttons on the toolbar that let you adjust how the letters fit in the shape:

The WordArt Same Letter Heights button stretches all of the smaller letters on a line (such as lowercase letters) to be the same height as the biggest letter. This looks pretty cool if you're designing a logo for a 1960s rock band (although if they don't have a logo by now, it may be too late!), but it looks kind of silly for most things. In addition, it stretches things like periods, commas, and apostrophes until they become unreadable.

Closing Space

Stretching all the letters to be the same height as the biggest does have one side-effect that can be useful. If you have a logo with more than one line of text, this will decrease the space between lines. If you have a multi-line logo in all capital letters with no punctuation, try this button and see how it looks!

The WordArt Vertical Text button switches the logo between having the letters run horizontally and having them stacked vertically. Horizontally is usually better. If you need a tall logo, it's usually better to make a wide logo and rotate it. That's what most publishers do for the titles that go on the spines of books. (Of course, if you take a look at the spine of this book, you'll realize that I couldn't make up my mind *which* direction the words should go in, so you have to wiggle the book to read it!)

In a multi-line logo, one line is always going to be shorter than the others, and won't make it all the way across the space provided. If you don't want that uneven look, the WordArt Alignment button lets you set how to deal with that problem. It brings up a menu listing six ways of dealing with this. The first three options move the shorter lines to the left, the middle, or the right of logo, respectively. The **Word Justify** option expands the size of spaces between words on the short line, pushing the first and last words to the edges. (This doesn't go any good if you only have one word on the line.) The **Letter Justify** option increases the size of the spaces between letters on the short line, stretching the line to fit the space. The last option is usually the best one: **Stretch Justify**, which stretches out the letters themselves to fit the space.

Finally, the WordArt Character Spacing button lets you adjust how much space is between letters. When you click on this button, a menu appears, listing five levels of closeness. Choosing **Very Loose** creates a very open, formal look. On the other end of the scale, **Very Tight** closes up the space so much that letters may actually overlap, creating a very energetic effect. It's a lot easier getting your letters tight now than before WordArt was invented; back then, it took a fifth of Scotch to get them really tight.

Color Commentary: Filling in the Letters

So far, we've mostly worried about the shape of your logo, but there is more to a logo than just shape. After all, would rainbows be as impressive if they were all gray, instead of the colors of the lovely trout from which they get their name?

To fill your letters with your choice of colors, click on the down arrow to the right end of the Fill Color button on the Drawing Toolbar. A menu will pop up that has about 8 to 16 little colored boxes. Click on one of those boxes, and your letters will become that color.

But hey, what's all this 16 color stuff? The *cheap* box of crayons always had 16 colors. You should demand more to choose from! And you'll get it, too, because on that menu is also a selection marked **More Fill Colors**. Select that, and a Colors dialog box appears with two tabs. The first tab shows hundreds of colored hexagons that you can select from. Double-click on the one you want, and that color will fill your text.

You can pick from all the colors of the spectrum. Well, all the colors of the hexagon.

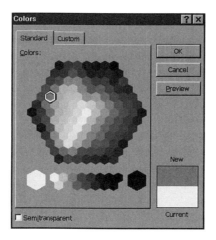

If you don't see just the right color there, try the **Custom** tab, which has thousands of different shades spread out across a rainbow-like grid. The color you click on will appear in a band at the right, in a range of brightnesses from very dark to very bright. Click on that band at the brightness level you want, then click on the **OK** button. Between the color setting and the brightness setting, you actually have over 16 *million* colors available. Now *that's* a lot of crayons!

Frilly Fills for Fabulous Fun

Having 16 million colors at your fingers is dissatisfying when you can only use one at a time. If you click on the down arrow to the right of the Fill Color button and select the **Fill Effects** command, you'll find where the really powerful stuff lurks! The Fill Effects dialog box appears, listing four tabs that contain even more stupefying fill options:

➤ **Gradient** lets you include fades from one color to another color. To use this, first click on the **Two colors** radio button. To the right, two drop-down menus will appear, marked Color 1 and Color 2. Open Color 1 and select a color from those displayed. (If you don't like any shown, you can select **More Colors**, which will bring up the same Color dialog box described in the last section.) Repeat this with Color 2.

Fancier Fades for Fade Fanciers!

Click **Preset** for access to the Preset Colors drop-down list of predesigned color combinations, including some like Gold and Chrome designed to look like metal. Silence may be golden, but if you want your words to be golden, this is the route to go. (Selecting the direction of the fade and the variation are done the same way as before.)

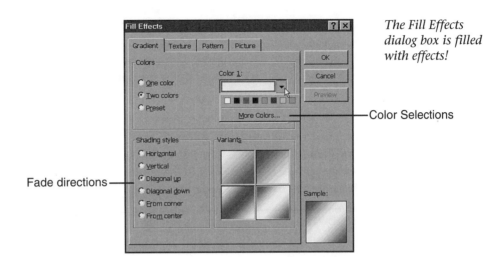

The Fill Effects dialog box is filled with effects!

Color Selections

Fade directions

The lower left of the dialog box has a list of directions in which the fade can take place. You can pick a horizontal fade, which will give you a sunset-like effect, or a fade from the center, which creates sort of a glow. Fades from the corner are "in" right now; that's what you call a fade fad! When you select a fade, you will see two or four variations of that sort of fade in the squares at the right. Click on the variation you want, then click on the **OK** button, and you'll see that fade in your work!

➤ **Textures** is the next tab on the list. Clicking on it lets you give your logo the trustworthy look of solid marble, the powerful look of the mighty oak, or the wimpy look of a crumpled shopping bag. An assortment of textures is displayed. Click on any one of these, and your text will take on that appearance.

Putting the Yours into Textyours

The Textures tab has an **Other Texture** button that lets you add your own textures. Textures are just images that repeat well (for example, if you put one right next to another or one on top of another, you don't see where one ends and another begins; it looks like a continuous picture). Use any art program to create such an image. (You can also borrow them from sets of Web backgrounds.) Clicking on the Other Texture button brings up a Select Texture file navigator that lets you select the file with the image. Select the image and click on the **OK** button, and that image will be added to the group of textures you can choose from.

➤ The **Pattern** tab lets you fill your logo with a two-color pattern, such as stripes or checkerboards. At the bottom of the tab are two color selection drop-down lists, one for **Foreground** and one for **Background**. Use these two lists to select two different colors. You'll see an array of patterns using those colors above the menus. Double-click on the pattern that you want, and it will fill the letters.

➤ The **Picture** tab lets you fill your logo with any picture you want. Just think: your logo could have a picture of you in it! You've always been a person (or alternate life form) of your word, and now you'll be a person *in* your word! To do this, you'll need to already have the picture stored in digital form (as a JPEG file, for example) on your hard disk. Then just follow these steps:

1. On the Picture tab, click on the **Select Picture** button. A Select Picture file navigator will appear. Click on the drop-down button at the end of the Look In field to get a list of disks on your system.

2. Select the disk that has the file. A list of folders on that disk appears below that. Double-click on the folder that has the picture file.

3. When that folder opens up, a list of files will be displayed. Double-click on the name of the picture file. The file navigator goes away, and your picture appears on the tab.

4. Click on the **OK** button, and the picture you selected will be stretched and shaped to fill your logo!

When you fill a logo with a picture, remember how large the logo will appear in the actual presentation. Small pictures look bad when blown up.

Outlinear Thinking

You can put an outline around all the letters of your logo. This is particularly neat when you have a fancy logo against a fancy background, so that there's a clean edge between them.

To pick a color for your outline, click on the down arrow at the right of the Line Color button on the Drawing toolbar. A color selection menu will appear, letting you pick from several colors or select **More Line Colors** to get the Color dialog box. When you select a color, PowerPoint uses all its brain power in figuring out that if you want an outline color, you must want an outline, and the outline appears! (To get rid of the outline, open the **Line Color** menu and pick **No Line**.)

To set the thickness of the line, click on this button. A menu showing different thicknesses of lines appears. Pick the one you want. (You can pick the one you don't want, if you want, but I don't know why you'd want to.)

You can even turn the line into a dotted line by clicking this button, but dotted lines usually look ugly as outlines for WordArt lettering. Then again, sometimes ugly is hip! (Or so I've kept trying to convince my dates...)

Who Knows What Shadows Lurk in the WordArts of Men?

Shadows are cool. That's because the sun is blocked from them.

To build such coolness into your logo, click on this button. A menu of green boxes with gray boxes under them appears. Some of the shadows make it look like the logo is hovering just over the page, casting a shadow on it. Others make it look like the logo is standing vertical, casting a shadow on the ground. Click on the shadow design you like, and that type of shadow appears on your logo. If you want to get rid of the shadow, click on **No Shadow** on that menu. (Of course, the only thing that doesn't cast a shadow is a vampire. Do you really want a vampire logo?)

To fine-tune the shadow, click on the **Shadow Settings** button on that menu. A new toolbar appears. This has four buttons with pictures of green boxes with arrows, one with an arrow in each direction. These are used to move the shadow, as if you were moving the light. (It's much easier to move the sun on a computer than in real life!) The button at the right end lets you select the color of the shadow, and works like all the other color-selection menus. It also has an added option called **Semitransparent Shadow**. Click on that, and your shadow looks like a shadow in a well-lit room, one which only darkens things a bit, rather than blocking things out altogether!

3-D or Not 3-D, That Is the Question

The 3-D features of WordArt let you do two things: *extrude* your logo, so it looks like it has physical depth as well as width and height, and to *rotate* your logo. Of course, you can already rotate your logo in the same plane as the slide (the same sort of direction that the hands move on a grandfather clock); 3-D also lets you rotate it against the vertical axis (like when you turn a clock around to fix it) or against the horizontal axis (like when you push a grandfather clock forward, so that it smashes to the floor).

3-D 4-U

 To quickly shove your logo into 3-D, click on the 3-D button on the Drawing toolbar, which is the master button for all 3-D operations. A menu will pop up, showing a square turned into 3-D with various rotations and extrusions. Click on the way that you want your logo to be 3-D-ized, and PowerPoint will leap to work. (If you have a lot of text in your logo, it may take a few seconds for the logo to draw. Remember, Rome wasn't made 3-D in a day!)

Check This Out...

2-Don'ts of 3-D

There are two things that don't work when you're 3-Ding your logo: shadows and outlines. Both will disappear when you turn your logo into 3-D.

Rotation Creation Station

If you click on the 3-D button and select **3-D Settings** from the menu, a new toolbar will appear on your screen. This toolbar has all the tools you need for fine-tuning your logo's 3-D aspects. On it there are four buttons with pictures of arrows wrapping around poles. Click on any one of these buttons to rotate the logo a little bit in the same direction as the arrow.

Rotate the logo   Extrusion and lighting controls

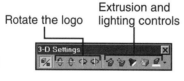

The 3-D Settings toolbar is filled with effects!

Extrusion and Intrusion

The five buttons on the right of the 3-D settings toolbar control the extrusion. Clicking on the Depth button brings up a menu of different lengths for the extrusion. You can pick various sizes from zero to infinity! Yes, your words can go on forever!

The Direction button brings up a menu that lets you pick the direction of the extrusion. It can go straight back, or head off in any of eight directions. This menu also has two commands called *Perspective* and *Parallel*. These affect how the farther-away parts of the 3-D object look. If you choose **Parallel**, the far away parts look the same size as the close parts. If you choose **Perspective**, things get smaller as they get farther away. Usually, Perspective is better. (Why, all things look better once you put them in perspective.)

PowerPoint pretends that there is a lamp shining on the extrusion, creating light and dark areas. To move the lamp isn't hard; after all, it's light work! Just click the Lighting button and you'll be able to pick from eight lamp directions. There are also three choices for the brightness of the light.

Clicking the Surface button brings up a menu with four choices of what your extrusion is made of. All this really affects is how shiny it is. **Matte** is not very shiny, **Plastic** is somewhat, and **Metal** is quite shiny. The fourth choice is **Wire Frame**, which shows just the edges of your entire logo.

Why a Wire?

Very few logos look good in Wire Frame mode. However, a logo in this mode gets displayed very quickly, because the computer has less to figure out. If you have a slow computer, you may want to use this mode while you work on getting the rotation just right, then switch to one of the solid modes.

The final button, 3-D Color, is the color of the extrusion. Clicking on the arrow at the right of this button gives you the normal color selection options. It will not, however, let you select any gradients, patterns, or textures; extrusions have to be solid colors.

Logo A-Go-Go

Watch out! Now that you know how to do it, you'll be tempted to write all your letters in 3-D metallic perspective lettering with marble fronts!

The Least You Need to Know

➤ Click on the **WordArt** button to start making a logo. Then double-click on a style, then enter your text.

➤ You can select your font on the text entry dialog box.

➤ The WordArt Alignment button on the WordArt toolbar lets you select how WordArt deals with a short line of text in a multi-line logo.

➤ Clicking the down arrow to the right of the Fill Color button lets you select a color to fill the logo with, or to choose fancy Fill Effects.

➤ Fill Effects include *gradients* (fading from one color to another), *patterns* (simple two-color patterns), *textures* (full color representations of stone, wood, and other material), and *picture* (filling in the logo with any picture you provide).

➤ The down arrow to the right of the Line Color button lets you select a colored outline for your logo. The Line Style button lets you select the line thickness.

➤ To pick a style of shadow for your logo to cast, click on the Shadow button.

➤ The 3-D button lets you turn your logo into a 3-D object. It will bring up a menu of basic 3-D rotations and extrusions.

➤ Selecting **3-D Settings** from the 3-D menu brings up the 3-D toolbar. This has buttons to control rotation and the color, material, length and angle of the extrusion.

Chapter 8

Lines and Shapes: Good Things in Variable-Size Boxes

Remember how I told you that you could pick and choose which chapters to read? (What? You didn't read the introduction? *Nobody* ever reads the introduction!) Whether you saw that or not, when I told you that, I lied. If you're going to read this chapter, you should read the previous chapter first.

Why? Because much of the way that the AutoShape feature works is the same as how the WordArt feature works. Much of the stuff that I put in the last chapter also applies here, and I didn't want to waste your time by telling it to you twice. (Okay, I didn't want to waste *my* time by typing it twice!)

The Simple Shapes

Things that are simple you use all the time. You use a kitchen knife several times a day, whether it's for chopping chicken, opening the plastic packet of hot dogs, or affixing a "you ate all my Krunchy Puffs!" note to your roommate's headboard. On the other hand, the Amazing Electro-Deluxe Avocado Peeler With 37 Attachments sits gathering dust on the pantry shelves, a stark reminder of Aunt Edna's bad taste in presents.

With shapes, it's the same thing. The simple ones (rectangles, ovals, lines, and arrows) you'll probably use all the time, so they each have their own handy-dandy button on the bottom row of buttons.

Lines and Arrows and Bars, Oh My!

Straight lines are very useful, and not just to set up punch lines. PowerPoint lets you quickly draw more lines than you can shake a stick at. (Although shaking a stick at lines seems like quite a waste of time to me.)

 In order to draw a line, click on the **Line** button. Point to where the line starts, then drag the mouse to where the line ends, and your line will appear.

 Arrows are just lines with pointy ends. Hunters may not realize that, but PowerPoint does. Draw a line with an arrow just like a line without one: click the **Arrow** button and then drag on the slide.

 After you've drawn a line (with or without an arrow), you can decide whether it's a line or an arrow by clicking on the **Arrow Style** button. A menu of different arrow styles appear. You can pick an arrow with a number of different types of pointy ends. You can pick an arrow with both ends pointy. (Hunters hate arrows like that, because you always prick your finger while shooting them.) You can even pick an arrow with no ends, in which case it turns back into a line.

 To change the thickness of the line, click on the **Line Style** button and pick a thickness.

 To make a dotted line (or a dotted arrow), click on the **Dash Style** button and pick a dotting style.

 Finally, you can set the line's color by clicking on the down arrow next to the Line Color button.

Jumpy Line?

If the end of your line seems to jump as you draw it, you have the *Grid* feature turned on. This feature treats the slide like a piece of graph paper, keeping all your points and corners at the intersections of lines. You can turn this off by clicking on the **Draw** button and selecting **Snap**, **To Grid**, or you can override it by holding down the **Alt** button while you draw shapes.

Un-Awful Ovals and Cor-Rect-Angles

The Rectangle and Oval buttons let you draw rectangles and ovals, respectively. Click on one of them, point to where you want one corner of the rectangle to be, then drag to the opposite corner. If you're drawing an oval, it will be an oval that goes to the edges of the rectangular area you dragged.

A square is just a rectangle designed by someone who couldn't make up his mind which side should be longer. A circle is just an oval that forgot to stretch. Drawing a square or a circle is the same as drawing a rectangle or oval, only you hold down the **Shift** key while you do it. PowerPoint will make sure that it's equal on all sides.

Sometimes you may need a rectangle or an oval with its center at some precise point. Now, if you're very good at drawing these objects the normal way, you can center them yourself. But if you aren't a self-centered person, try drawing them by pointing where you want the center to be, then hold down the **Ctrl** key as you drag the mouse to an outer corner.

Colors and Lines and Fills and Shadows and All the Fancy Gook

Now that you've got your shape in place, you want it to have the right color and the right outline and maybe you even want shadows or 3-D effects. The way that you do all of that stuff is exactly the same way that you did it with WordArt! That's right, just back up a few pages, the instructions are all there. I'll wait here while you go back and reread them.

(Tumm-tadiddle, toodley-tum, tummy-doodly-doot!) You're back? Good! Now on to:

Fancy Shapes: They Aren't Just for Marshmallows Anymore!

Circles and squares are fine for everyday use, but you have company coming, and you need something fancier! You need squiggles and arrows and happy faces! Is PowerPoint equipped? You betcha! Just click on that **AutoShapes** button, and you'll get a menu of types of shapes. Each type has its own submenu, showing you all the shapes it has to offer! Let's head down the list one by one.

Here are all the different shapes you can use, grouped by type. One hundred fifty-one shapes at your fingertips!

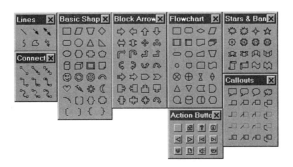

Lines

The top row of the Lines submenu shows you straight lines, but heck, we already know how to do those. But under those, we get curvy lines of various sorts, and those are a lot more exciting. The first of these makes smooth curves: just click on where you want some key points of the line to be, and PowerPoint will shape the curve to match. The other two let you draw any line you want—at least, any line you can manage with your mouse, which is not the world's easiest-to-use drawing tool. Just select one of them, then hold down the left mouse button as you draw.

Check This Out...

Line Altering

If you create your own line, and you want to make adjustments to it, click on the line then click on **Draw** and select **Edit Points**. The key points on your line will show up as black squares. On a straight line, there are only two: one at each end. But you can click anywhere on the line and drag to create a new key point and move it where you want it. Using this method, you can turn a simple straight line into a zig-zag of any proportions you like.

If you want to make your own object shape, use any of those non-straight line choices, and end your line at the same place that you started. PowerPoint will assume that you're making a shape, and will let you fill it in.

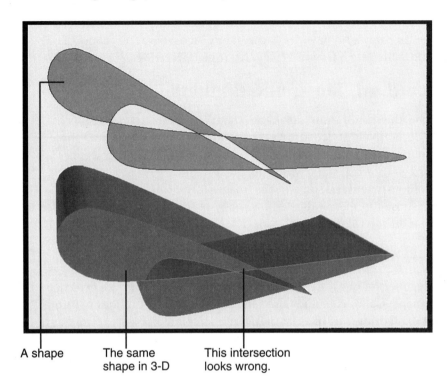

If you cross lines while creating a shape, PowerPoint considers some areas to be outside your shape, as seen at the top. The intersections don't look right when you make the shape 3-D.

A shape   The same   This intersection
               shape in 3-D   looks wrong.

Connectors

Charts are very important in an organization. Without an organizational chart, the only way to tell who is boss is to see who doesn't get yelled at when they're late. Many charts need connecting lines to show how things are related. The Connectors submenu has a variety of these. Some of these are basic straight lines, others are angled or curved lines. You use them all just like straight lines: point to the starting point, and drag to the end point. Unlike a regular line, connectors "snap" to existing objects on your slide, so the connectors neatly tie one object to another. You can even make a dotted line or change arrowheads by using the appropriate buttons.

Many connectors will show yellow diamonds in the middle when they are selected. Dragging this yellow diamond will change the path that the connector takes, which is very handy when you're trying to route it around other objects on a diagram.

Basic Shapes

This is a collection of various shapes. A couple of them have built-in shading for a 3-D effect without using the 3-D features. If you choose one of those, remember that they look best without any outline. Most of these have yellow diamond controls that let you change them in interesting ways. My favorite is the happy face where the yellow diamond lets you turn the smile into a frown. What a feeling of power!

Block Arrows, Flowchart, Stars, and Banners

These three menus have the sort of standard shapes that their name describes. Block arrows are big, thick, decoratively styled arrows. The Flowchart submenu has all the special figures you'll need for computer and process diagrams. Stars and Banners has scrolls, banners, and stars—not real stars, which are great flaming gas bags, but nice precise little foil-medallion-type stars. Some of the images of stars on the menu have numbers inside them; those numbers indicate how many points the star will have. The number will not appear on the shape itself.

Callouts

Callouts are special members of our little AutoShape family, because they are designed to hold text within the shape. Callouts include not only simple boxes with lines pointing from them (useful for explaining part of a picture), but also comic-book-style word and thought balloons (useful for showing that part of your picture is thinking).

Three types of callouts: a word balloon, a callout with a visible box, and a callout without a visible box.

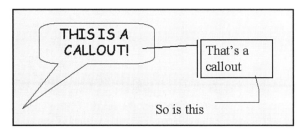

After you draw your callout, you can start typing, and it will appear in the text area. Callouts are like other text boxes; you can resize them, justify the text, use different fonts, and so on.

Keep Callouts Flat

As with any other shape, you can use the 3-D features on the callouts. However, the 3-D will not affect the text in the callout. If you're just extruding the callout, that's not a problem, but if you rotate the callout, the text won't rotate with it. If you want rotatable text, you will need to use WordArt.

Action Buttons

Action Buttons are designed specifically to be used with interactive presentation features, which is something that doesn't show up in this book until Chapter 13, "Click Here for Interactivity." I explain this stuff in there, where it will make more sense.

Getting Your Text Into Shape, Literally

You can put text into any of these shapes, except for lines (which don't have any space for text). To do this, click first on the **Text Box** button, then on the shape. The rectangle around the shape turns into a text box, and you can start typing.

The big difference between this and a normal text box is that the text starts in the middle of the box, rather than at the top. This way, it's more likely to end up in the shape, rather than on its edge. If you add more lines, PowerPoint keeps the text centered in the rectangle.

Changing Shape: I Never Metamorph I Didn't Like

If you change your mind about the shape you want, you can change it without having to redo all the outlines, colors, and text that you chose. Just click on the **Draw** button and select **Change AutoShape** from the menu. There you'll see a menu of all the shapes (except for Lines and Connectors—this process doesn't let you work with Lines and Connectors at all) and will be able to pick the one that you want.

Remember, you can also rotate and flip the shapes, just like any other box. All the commands are in the **Draw** menu.

The Least You Need to Know

➤ Drawing a shape involves just selecting a shape from the toolbar or AutoShape menu, then dragging the mouse from one corner of where you want the shape to another.

➤ If you hold down the **Ctrl** button while drawing the shape, the place where you started dragging will be considered the center of the shape, rather than the corner.

➤ If you hold down the **Shift** key while drawing an oval, it will be a perfect circle.

➤ If you hold down the **Shift** key while drawing a rectangle, it will be a perfect square.

➤ Many shapes show yellow diamonds when you select them. These can be dragged to fine-tune the shape in different ways.

➤ The colors, fill effects, outline, shadows, and 3-D effects work the same on shapes as they do on WordArt.

➤ Callouts are shapes with pointers and text areas. After you create a callout, you are expected to enter the text.

 ➤ You can put text on any shape by clicking on the **Text Box** button, then on the shape.

 ➤ If you draw a line or an arrow, clicking on the **Arrow Style** button will give you a menu where you can select which ends have arrowheads and what type of arrowheads they have.

Chapter 9

Putting Pictures in Their Places

In This Chapter

➤ Put pictures on your slides

➤ Trim the pictures down to size

➤ Cast a shadow for your picture (no, I don't mean "In this movie, Alec Baldwin will play The Shadow.")

➤ Fill the shapes with words

They say that a picture is worth a thousand words, but have you ever tried to trade one in? Where do you take that old photo of Mara Friedman eating cake at your cousin's bar mitzvah to get, say, a thousand choice adverbs? Once again, *they* don't seem to know what they are talking about.

A picture *is* worth paying attention to. By putting the right picture in your presentation, you'll not only get that attention, you will make good use of the attention you get.

Where Do Pictures Come from?

In order to put a picture on your slides, you're going to need to have a picture, and it will have to be stored on a file that your computer can read. By *picture*, we don't necessarily mean a photograph. It could be a drawing, a logo, a ray-traced rendering; any flat visual item is considered a picture. (Computer people often refer to these as *images* and editorial people call them *graphics*, but we'll be genuine human people and call them pictures.)

Get Pre-Made Pictures

There are lots of pictures already out there in computer format. Many folks sell CD-ROMs full of photos and drawings that are specifically meant for people like you (and even people shorter than you) to use as part of their own computer creations. In addition, the Internet is full of pictures that you can download to your PC and use. (Just because you *can* download and use it doesn't mean that you're *allowed* to. If the creator has put the picture in the *public domain*, that means that he has waived copyright on it and it is free to use. Otherwise, you have to get permission.)

PowerPoint even comes with a library of drawings called Clip Art that you can use in your presentation. Clip Art works a little differently than other pictures. I'll explain how to use the Clip Art pictures later in this chapter.

PC: Picture Creator

There are plenty of programs out there that let you create your own pictures. There's even a basic one that you got for free with Windows, called Paint. (You'll find it in your **Programs**, **Accessories** menu if you click the **Start** button.) Some of these programs let you paint a new picture using the mouse. Others let you create imaginary objects or areas in the computer's mind, then let you pick a point to photograph the object from (these are *3-D rendering* or *ray-tracing programs*).

If you use one of these programs, you have to make sure that it can save files in a graphic format that PowerPoint can use. There are hundreds of different formats out there, but the good news is that almost everything these days stores in a format that PowerPoint understands. If the program creates files that end in .bmp, .cgm, .dib, .eps, .gif, .jpeg, .jpg, .pcd, .pct, .pcx, .png, .tga, .tif, or .wpg, then PowerPoint can read them. (If you can pronounce that last sentence in one breath, give yourself a pat on the back!) If you have files that aren't in those formats, there are translation programs (such as Graphics Workshop) that may be able to take your file and turn it into a file type that PowerPoint can read.

Techno Talk

Which Format Is Best?

Many programs let you choose which format to save a file in. If you have a simple drawing with only a few different colors, the Graphics Interchange File Format (.gif) is the best. If you have more colors and want an exact reproduction, use the PC Paintbrush format (.pcx). If you have a lot of colors (particularly if you're working with a digitized photograph) and you're worried about how much space your file will take up, use the Joint Photographic Experts Group format (.jpg or .jpeg).

Copycat-Scans: Using a Picture from Outside

If you have a drawing, a photograph, or any sort of document that isn't in computer format (you still have paper? How old-fashioned!), you can put it onto the computer using a *scanner*. A scanner takes a picture of your picture and stores it on the computer. You can usually get scanners starting at about $100, with feature-laden ones heading into the thousands.

If you already have a scanner, you don't have to start another program in order to do your scanning. Just click on the **Insert** menu, select **Picture** and then from the sub-menu select **From Scanner**, and PowerPoint will start your scanner software. (How your scanner software works depends upon what scanner you have. Check your scanner's manual for details.)

Getting the Picture: Get the Picture?

In order to get an existing picture from disk and put it on the slide, select the **Insert** menu and from the **Picture** submenu select **From File**. The Insert Picture dialog box will open up, showing you a list of files. Click on the drop-down arrow at the end of the Look In field, and select the disk with the file from that list. A list of folders and picture files appears. If your picture files are in a folder, double-click on the folder. Keep navigating until you find your files. Then click the file you want and click the **Insert** button.

Now, if you're perfectly organized, your files probably have all these nice long names that tell you exactly what they are, and you can find the folder easily. For the rest of us (and we are in the majority folks, so don't let those goody-goody types get on you!), you'll find yourself faced with a list of filenames like test3.gif, feb273.jpg, and other.pcx, without a clue as to what pictures they contain. PowerPoint was made for we imperfect people; click on the file name, and the picture that's in the file appears to the right of the file list. (If the picture doesn't appear, click on the **Preview** button.)

Click on a picture file, and the picture will be displayed. Make sure you don't have pictures of me in your directories (like this one by Ted Slampyak), as they may scare small children and pets.

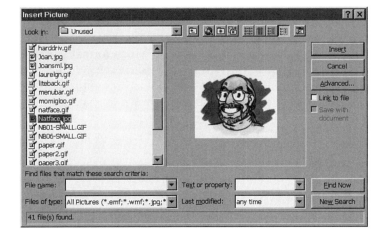

Sizing Up the Scene

The size of computer pictures are measured in *pixels*, the small squares that make up the image on a computer screen. The computer picture is made up of a gridwork of dots, and PowerPoint assumes that you want your picture to be displayed at its *natural* size, one picture dot per screen dot. But that might not be the size that you want it.

When you insert the picture onto your slide, it has sizing handles (white squares) at all four corners and the center of all four sides. Just drag one of those handles to change it to the size you want. Drag a handle in the center of a side to change that side, or drag a corner to change two dimensions at once.

The white squares along the edge of the picture can be dragged to resize the picture.

Sizing Handles

The Picture Toolbar: A Row of Pictures for Working on Pictures

If you want to make major changes to the picture such as drawing a moustache and glasses on everyone in the shot (or, in the case of a picture of me, erasing the moustache and glasses), PowerPoint is not the place to do that. Start up your favorite art program and work on it there before you add it to your slide.

Natural is Good Pictures look best at their natural size. Shrinking the picture means there won't be room to display some of the picture dots, and detail gets lost. Enlarging it means that picture dots are stretched to cover several screen dots, which makes the picture grainy.

However, if you just want to trim the picture or adjust the colors, there's no need to reach for another program. Most of the tools you need will be found on the Picture toolbar. To see this toolbar, just right-click on the picture and select **Show Picture Toolbar**.

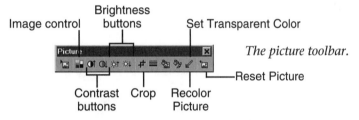

The picture toolbar.

Picture Diet: Trim Your Picture Down

When a farmer uses the word *crop*, it means something he grows. When a graphic designer uses the same word, it means he's shrinking something down. Microsoft must figure that more graphic designers than farmers will be using PowerPoint, because its cropping tool is used for shrinking rather than growing. Cropping is what you use when you have a picture of a whole donut and what you want is a picture of a donut hole.

To do this, click on the **Crop** button on the Picture toolbar. Your pointer will change to match the picture on the button. Use the pointer to drag one of the sizing handles towards the middle of the picture. When you release the handle, all of the picture that is outside the new rectangle disappears. (This missing picture parts are off in the same invisible land as the dirty words that they cut out of movies on TV.) By cropping from all four sides, you can isolate the one part of the picture that you want.

Scheming to Change the Color Scheme

PowerPoint gives you a number of ways to mess with the colors to get them more like you want them. Sometimes, colors that look good when a picture is standing alone don't look so good when it's sitting in the middle of your slide, surrounded and harrassed by other pictures, shapes, and backgrounds.

One of the keenest color changes that you can do is to make one color from your picture invisible (or, as Microsoft calls it, *transparent*). Now, why would you want to do this? If you have a picture that's so ugly that you don't want to see it, you just don't put it on the slide, right?

That's not what it's for. The main reason to make some color invisible is that it lets you have a picture that doesn't look rectangular. If your picture is of a donut, and everything outside the edge of the donut is red, you can make that red invisible by clicking on the Set Transparent Color button, and then on a red part of the picture. Suddenly, you don't see the red anymore; wherever the red was, you see through to the next thing on the slide! You can only make one color invisible on each picture, and only those pixels that exactly match that shade disappear.

With the white color turned invisible, the picture loses its rectangular border. However, because the same color is used elsewhere in the picture, my teeth and my eyes are knocked out as well (ouch!). If I wanted to lose just the border, I'd have to open this picture up with a paint program and repaint the border some color that isn't used elsewhere.

If you think there's too much color overall in the picture, try clicking on the **Image Control** button. That will bring up a menu of different coloring styles. By clicking on **Grayscale**, you can get rid of all those pretty colors and turn the picture into a black, white, and gray version. If even gray is too fancy for your liking, try **Black & White**. Or, if you just want something a lot lighter, select **Watermark**, and you'll get a pale version of your picture. (Watermark is really useful if you want to use the picture as a backdrop for words or other images, since the pale colors aren't likely to distract from what you put in front of it.)

There are four other buttons on the Picture toolbar that let you fiddle with the picture to your heart's content (not to be confused with your heart's *contents*, which would be blood):

➤ More Brightness: Makes all the colors in the picture brighter

➤ Less Brightness: Makes all the colors darker

➤ More Contrast: Makes the bright parts of your picture brighter while making the dark parts darker. This can make some things stand out better.

➤ Less Contrast: Clicking on this button decreases the contrast. If you want to increase the brightness or decrease the contrast (or whatever) a lot, you have to keep clicking the button—you can't just keep it pressed down.

Framing Your Picture

Framing your picture in PowerPoint is easy, and it costs a lot less than framing the picture of a purple cow your kid painted for you at summer camp! The following buttons on the Drawing toolbar can help you perfect your picture presentation:

➤ Use the **Line Style** button to put a border around the picture

➤ Use the down arrow to the right of the Line Color button to select the color for the border. However, the line will always be rectangular. (The line doesn't know whether you set one of your colors to be invisible.)

➤ On the other hand, if you use the Shadow button to create a shadow, only the visible portions of your picture will cast a shadow. The shadow knows!

➤ You can also use the Fill Color button and Fill Effects command to replace the invisible color with another color, a texture, or a pattern. The tools work the same as they do with shapes.

Rotating Your Picture

You can't. Pictures don't rotate. However, you can open some images in a program that supports rotation, like the Microsoft Photo Editor that comes free with Office 97, and do your rotating there.

Clip Art: Resizable, Reusable, but Not Refundable ('Cause It's Free!)

With PowerPoint, Microsoft gives you a bunch of already-made pictures, which they call *Clip Art*. However, when Microsoft says Clip Art, they mean something a little more specific than when other people say Clip Art. Clip Art is generally used to refer to any piece of art that you're allowed to use in your work. Microsoft uses it to refer to pieces of art in a certain special format, one that is quite useful.

Microsoft Clip Art pictures are not defined as a series of dots. Instead, they are defined by mathematically defined lines and curves. Because of this, a Clip Art picture doesn't have a natural size. You can take a Clip Art picture and make it any size you want, and the computer will draw the lines and curves to that size. This way, the picture doesn't look grainy, and unless you make it fairly small, it doesn't lose details.

Clip Art, Oh Clip Art, Where Art Thou?

To find the Clip Art, click on the **Insert ClipArt** button. The Microsoft Clip Gallery 3.0 dialog box opens, with tabs not only for Clip Art, but also for pictures, sounds, and videos. If you've been paying attention to the topic at hand, you can probably guess that you want the Clip Art tab, and you would be right!

The Clip Art tab lets you see all the pictures and pick the one you want.

Web button

At the left of the dialog box is a list of subjects. Click on any of these, and the box at the right will display the pieces of Clip Art that have to do with that topic. Not only is this free art, it's organized!

84

You can scroll through the images if there are too many to be displayed at once. When you find the piece that you want, just double-click on it. Boing! It appears on your slide, ready to work with.

Clip Artery

Once the Clip Art is on your screen, you can do most of the same things to it that you can with other pictures. Oh, there is a price to pay: you can't make any color invisible, but then again, most Clip Art already has an invisible border area!

Free Clip Art on the Web If you have a Web browser and an Internet connection, try clicking on the Web button in the lower right of the dialog box (the button with a picture of the Earth). It'll take you to a Web page where you can get more Clip Art!

There is one thing you gain, and that is that you can change the colors on the picture. Click on **Recolor Picture** button. The Recolor Picture dialog box appears with a drop-down button for each color. Open a drop-down list to see a menu of colors that you can replace it with. (You can select **More Colors** from this menu to see more colors if none of the listed ones please you.) A preview window lets you see how the colors effect things. Once you've got the colors you want, click on the **OK** button.

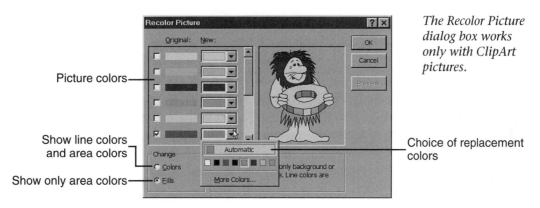

Picture colors

Show line colors and area colors

Show only area colors

Choice of replacement colors

The Recolor Picture dialog box works only with ClipArt pictures.

The Least You Need to Know

➤ PowerPoint can put pictures from most computer art programs onto your slides.

➤ To get the Insert Picture dialog box, pull down the **Insert** menu and select the **Picture, From File** command. On the Insert Picture dialog box, click on the name of a file to see the picture in that file. If it's the right file, click on the **OK** button.

➤ Right-click on the picture and select **Show Picture Toolbar** to get the Picture Toolbar.

➤ Use the buttons on the toolbar to crop your picture and change the colors in various ways.

Chapter 10

The Art of the Chart 101: Numerical Charts

In This Chapter

➤ Enter numbers to chart on a chart

➤ Chart the numbers you entered

➤ Change the chart of the numbers you entered

➤ Assign a design then refine it 'til it shines!

Charts are Mother Nature's way of making numbers look pretty. By putting your figures into a bar chart, a graph, a pie chart, or any of a dozen other types of charts, you can turn a bunch of boring numbers into a quickly understood image. Plus, a graph can show you patterns in your numbers that might otherwise go overlooked. Also, they're great fun at parties.

The chart capabilities of PowerPoint are very powerful. A few years ago, the chart part alone could've been sold as a separate program, and would have been considered a very good one. There are so many chart-enhancing tools that a whole book this size could probably be written on the chart program, and we would offer that book if we thought we could con you out of the mon…er…if we were convinced that there was a real need for one. Luckily, you can make charts pretty quickly, which is what this chapter covers. After that, you should explore the various features on your own, to see what more you can find.

The Part Where You Start the Chart

 Starting the chart is easy: just click on the **Insert Chart** button on the Standard toolbar.

Entering Chart Information in Formation

When you start work on your chart, a grid that looks like a spreadsheet appears. It's not actually a spreadsheet—it can't calculate anything for you. It's just a grid to hold numbers and words. But the amazing thing is that the grid already has all the information needed for a chart, and the chart is automatically put on your slide! The computer must be psychic! You don't have to enter anything.

There's places in the data sheet for all the information that you are charting.

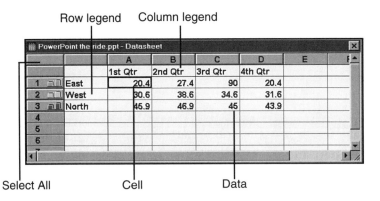

And then you realize that the figures that you see aren't for your chart. They're just for an example chart. Your dreams of having the computer do everything for you while you head down to the video arcade to play *Deluxe Space Bunnyball* are shattered.

The grid has a bunch of numbered rows and lettered columns. The numbers and the letters are on buttons at the start of each row and column. The buttons on the rows with numbers in them have colored bars on them, which show you what color each respective row of data will be on your chart.

The top row and the first column are unlabeled. Use the top row to give each column a name (this will be the legend that goes across the bottom of your chart) and the first column to give each row a name (this will be the legend for each different item that you're charting). Just replace the sample text that's there by selecting a cell (click on it) and typing.

Get This Example Out of My Face

To clear the datasheet so you can start entering your own data, click on the **Select All** button, which is the unmarked button where the row-numbered buttons and column-letter buttons meet. All of the *cells* (the rectangles where the rows and columns meet) will turn into white letters on a black background, to show that they are selected. Right-click on the selected area to bring up a shortcut menu, and choose **Clear Contents**. The example numbers and legends will disappear faster than cookies in a kindergarten!

Entering the Information

Now it's time to put your own data into the cells. To pick the first cell to work with, just click on it. Then, type the information that you want in that cell. To move to the next cell, just use the *cursor keys* (the four arrow keys on your keyboard), or select the cell of your choice by clicking on it with the mouse.

Changing the Look of Your Data

If you want to change the lettering style, just use the standard Font and Font Size drop-down lists and the Bold, Italic, and Underline buttons on the formatting toolbar. Be careful that you don't pick a font that's hard to read at a small size (unless, of course, this presentation is about how you single-handedly messed up the company's finances, in which case the harder to read, the better).

If you want your numbers to look a certain way, such as to be shown as a percentage or with a fixed number of decimal points, click on the **Select All** button to select all the cells. Then:

➤ Use the **Currency Style** button to have the numbers appear (both on the datasheet and on the chart) as dollars and cents.

➤ Use the **Percent Style** button to have them be percents.

➤ Click the **Comma Style** button to put commas into long numbers (like 3,769,400 donuts).

➤ The **Increase Decimal** button increases the number of digits to the right of the decimal point.

➤ The **Decrease Decimal** button decreases the number of digits to the right of the decimal point.

So Where's the Chart Already?

Once you've got your datasheet in shape, it's time to work on the chart that represents the data. Click on the datasheet window's **Close** (X) button to make the datasheet disappear. (If you want to bring it up again, click on the **View** button and select **Datasheet**.) If there is no Datasheet command on the View menu, double-click on the chart and then look for it again. (The View menu changes when the chart is selected.)

When you're working on your chart, it looks like you're in slide view, but you see different toolbars and menus.

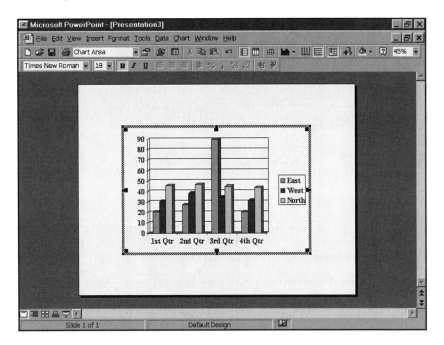

Choosing a Chart Type: So Many Choices, So Many Wrong Ones

To pick a chart type, pull down the **Chart** menu and select the well-named **Chart Type** command. A dialog box appears. Down the left is a scrollable list of chart types. When you select the type of chart you want, pictures of several sub-types of that type appear to the right. Click on the one you want.

This dialog box also has a great button marked **Press and hold to view sample.** Point to and hold this button down to see what your data would look like in sub-type of chart that you selected! It will look a little squooshed because it only has a small area to show it in, but it really gives you a sense of what to expect.

Once you've found a chart type and sub-type you're happy with, grin a little grin and press the **OK** button.

Give Me My Usual Chart

If there's one chart sub-type that you use most of the time, you can tell PowerPoint to make that your default, so you won't have to pick it every time. Select that sub-type in the Chart Type dialog box, then click on the **Set as default chart** button before clicking **OK**.

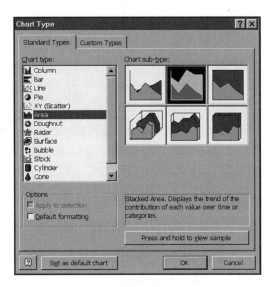

The pictures of chart sub-types don't reflect your data, but press down on the Press and hold to view sample button, and you'll see your numbers in action.

There are about as many different types of charts as there are types of donuts, and, like donuts, the wrong chart type won't communicate anything. (Of course, even the right type of donut doesn't communicate anything, as donuts are silent—but dang, they taste good!)

Bar and Column Charts

A *bar chart* is one where there are bars, and their length indicates some quantity—the bigger the number, the longer the bar. Where PowerPoint says bar chart, it specifically means a chart where the bar goes side-to-side. When the bar goes up and down, it's a *column chart*. PowerPoint also offers bar charts with different shapes instead of a bar, called *cone*, *cylinder*, and *pyramid charts*.

A bar chart.

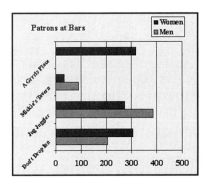

Bar charts are very good for comparing the quantity of a number of things. For example, one bar might represent how many chocolate donuts you've sold, another raspberry-filled, and a third for glazed. If you have totals to compare as well as types that make up the total, you should try the *stacked bar* chart. On a stacked bar chart, you might have one bar for each of the five donut stores in your chain, showing total donut sales. Each store's bar would be broken into different-colored sections, showing how much of that store's total was chocolate, how much was glazed, and so on. If you want to make one of these, don't bother entering the totals in your datasheet; the chart will automatically show the totals just by stacking the individual components.

(In case you hadn't guessed, this chapter is underwritten by *The Hole-sale Warehouse*, a top-notch donut shop at the corner of Third and Main. They're paying big bucks to get me to mention donuts until you get hungry enough to buy some. Okay, it's not big bucks, but they did give me a dozen donuts.)

Line Charts

Line charts have a series of points that show the quantity of something in different conditions, and those points are connected by a line. Line charts are probably the most misused charts yet devised. They should *only* be used when your different conditions have some natural order, such as when you're showing how long a piece of metal gets over a range of temperatures, or how many donuts you're selling each month. In those cases, you can expect some sort of pattern to emerge in the order (sales go up in the summer and down in the fall, for example).

You shouldn't use a line chart for how many donuts are sold in each of a list of stores, for example, because that list doesn't have a natural order. You could totally rearrange the orders the stores are listed in, and the line would end up looking very different without meaning anything different. People will try to look for meaning in the line, and will be distracted from the real information.

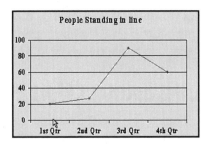

A line chart.

If you're using something that's right for a line chart, but you also want the totaling effect of the stacked bar chart, try *stacked area* charts, which you'll find under the Area type selection.

Pie Charts

Pie charts show a circle broken up into pie-piece-shaped sections. They're used for comparing a fairly small number of quantities. Pie charts are very popular, although some people find it hard comparing the size of the pie slices, because each slide is at a different angle.

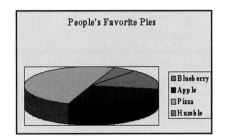

A pie chart.

A pie chart can only show one column of data from your datasheet. If you want to show the same sort of breakdown for several columns, you can either have several pies, or you can try a (believe it or not) *doughnut chart*, which has a series of nested circles, broken up into wedges. However, most people aren't accustomed to doughnut charts, and may have trouble understanding them.

Fancier Chart Types

PowerPoint can make a lot of cool-looking chart types that you may never have heard of before, with names like *radar chart* or *bubble chart*. A good rule of thumb is that if you're unfamiliar with a type of chart, you shouldn't be using it! This isn't because you wouldn't be able to figure out how the chart works—you probably could do it fairly quickly. But if you don't know about the chart, your audience probably won't know about it either! You'll end up spending a lot of time explaining how the chart works, rather than discussing the information that you made the chart to present.

The Top 5 Chart-Busting Chart Features

There are a number of quick enhancements that you can make to your chart. You don't always want to throw all these things in, but it's nice to know that they're there. To find these enhancements, right-click on the chart and select **Chart Options**. A dialog box with a number of tabs appears. The exact tabs shown differ depending on the type of chart, since some of these features are only for certain types of charts. This dialog box has a small picture of your chart, and will show you the effect of your changes as you make them.

The Chart Options dialog box lets you set all sorts of options and see their effect on the chart.

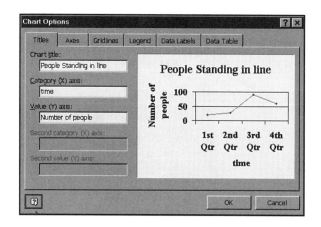

Titles

A chart with just colored bars and numbers doesn't really tell you anything—you have to know what it's a chart of! Pick the **Titles** tab, and you'll be able to enter three titles. The name that you put in the **Chart Title** field is a title for the whole chart, and it goes at the top. For most charts, what you type in the **Category (X) axis** field goes across the bottom of the chart, and names what the different points across the chart mean. For example, if you have a column chart of donut sales by month, a good thing to put in here would be month. The **Value (Y) axis** field is the place to name the values you are measuring, such as number of donuts sold. (3-D charts and some of the fancier chart types make different use of the Y axis and even have a Z axis.)

Gridlines

If you've got a big chart with a lot of things on it, it can be hard to quickly see across and tell which points stand for which values. That's why PowerPoint offers you *gridlines*, lines that go across and/or up and down your chart, making it easier to see how things line up. On the **Gridlines** tab you'll find two checkboxes for the **Category (X) axis**. Checking **Major gridlines** gives you horizontal lines, and checking **Minor gridlines** as well will double the number of lines. Similarly, the same two checkboxes in the **Value (Y) axis** area set up vertical lines.

Legend

The *legend* of your chart is not a tale about how your chart slew five dragons, only to die in its lover's arms, killed by a poisoned donut. Instead, it's a guide to what each of the colors in your chart means. Click on the **Legend** tab to not only be able to turn the legend on or off, but also to pick where around the chart the legend will appear.

Legendary Speed
To quickly turn the legend on or off without opening up the dialog box, just click on the **Legend** button!

Data Labels

Data Labels lets you put the value you're charting or the name of the column right by the point. Usually, this is used to give the value, which allows the viewer to see the exact number in addition to the visual representation. On the **Data Labels** tab, check **Show value** to show the value, or **Show label** to show the name.

Data Table

You put all that work into filling in your datasheet, and now all you have to show for it is this chart. Don't you want people to see all the work you did? Well, if you do, then **Data Table** is the tab for you. Click on **Show Data Table**, and your datasheet will appear with your chart, showing your audience all of the raw figures. If you have the Data Labels on, then you shouldn't also use the Data Table, since it just ends up giving the same information twice.

Data Table in Double Time
To quickly turn the Data Table on or off without opening up the dialog box, just click on the Data Table button!

The second option, **Show legend keys**, makes your datasheet double as a legend. If you turn this on, then you should turn your legend off.

Once you've made all your changes using the dialog box, click on the **OK** button and they will be applied to your chart. (Click **Cancel** instead if you decide not to make the changes.)

A Fine Tune on the Charts

Now that you've got the pieces of your chart basically in place, you could sit back and be pleased with what you have accomplished. Or, you can be paranoid about it and spend a ton of time fine-tuning the chart. But there is something worthwhile about paranoia; if there wasn't, why would everyone but me be paranoid? (It must be a conspiracy!)

Every little piece of your chart has a name, and each part has a control panel that lets you meddle and fuss with it. You can change the fonts of the text areas, change the colors of just about anything, turn lines into dotted lines, make them thicker or thinner.

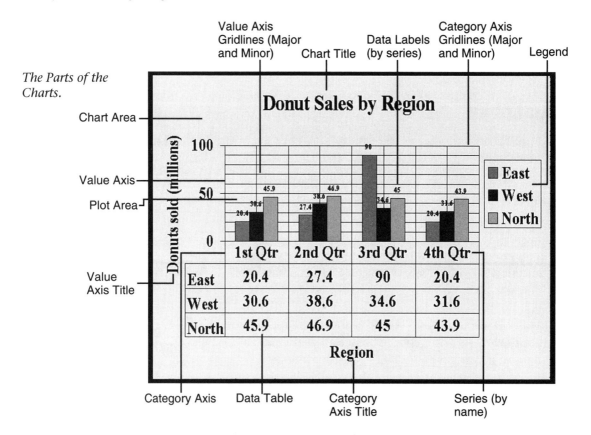

The Parts of the Charts.

To choose the part of the chart that you want to change, click on the down arrow button at the end of the **Chart Object** field. (It's the drop-down list, next to the Print button.) A list of parts of the chart appear. Click on the one that you want to work on. Square dots appear on the ends of the part of the chart that you selected, so you can tell what you're working on.

 Once you've selected the piece, click on the **Format** button, and a dialog box appears that lets you change the attributes of that item. Depending on what object you've selected, you'll have a number of tabs that you can select to change all sorts of things. Explore this a bit, and see what you find! (If the Format button is grayed out, this means that there aren't any attributes you can change about the item.)

Also, while selected, some parts can be resized by using the black boxes as sizing handles, or moved by dragging the whole object!

Section Selection

You can double-click on any part of the chart to bring up its dialog box. This can be trickier than it sounds, because there are so many pieces overlapping that it can be hard to tell just what you're pointing to. However, if you rest the pointer on something for a second, a box will appear telling you what you're pointing to.

Gettin' Outta Here... and Gettin' Back

To leave the chart editing mode, just click outside of the chart, and you'll go back to the usual PowerPoint slide view mode. In slide view mode, you can resize the entire chart using the sizing handles.

If you decide that you want to change anything about the chart later, just double-click on the chart. You'll be brought back into the chart editing mode.

The Least You Need to Know

➤ Charts let you visually display numeric information.

 ➤ To start making a chart, click on the **Insert Chart** button.

➤ Enter column and row names and data values by clicking on one cell of the datasheet, typing in the information, then using the cursor keys to get to the next cell.

➤ To select a chart type, pick **Chart Type** on the **Chart** menu. Select a chart type from the left column, and a sub-type from the pictures at right, then click on the **OK** button.

➤ Avoid using chart types that you're not used to seeing. They'll just confuse your audience.

➤ Once you're done working with the chart, just click outside of the chart area to go back to normal PowerPoint editing.

➤ To return to editing your chart, double-click on it.

Chapter 11

The Art of the Chart 102: Organization Charts

In This Chapter

➤ Build an organization chart

➤ Enhance the chart with fancy lettering and purty colors

➤ Rearrange the chart so that you're the boss!

Organization charts are used to show who reports to whom in a company. They tend to be loved by the people whose names are near the top of the chart ("I may be just a paper folder, but I report directly to the Assistant Vice-President In Charge Of Origami!") and snickered at by those who dwell at the bottom. However, if you're the one making the chart, you can arrange it so that you're near the top. (Of course, your boss may wonder why the Deputy Presentation Assistant ended up above him....)

Charting the Path to Success

To get the whole thing rolling, find the slide that you want the chart to appear on in slide view, then pull down the **Insert** menu and from the **Picture** submenu select the **Organization Chart** command. PowerPoint will open up a new window with the beginning of an organization chart in it. This window is actually a completely separate program designed just for organizational charting.

Organization Chart Program
The charting program is a version of a program called *Org Plus for Windows*, put out by Banner Blue Software. If you find you want to do more advanced, complex organizational charts, look into buying Org Plus, which has a number of features that were not included in the PowerPoint version.

The chart that you start with has four boxes, one top box for a boss (the program refers to bosses as *managers*, but employees usually call the bosses, and so will I), and three boxes for people working for him (they say *subordinate*, but I'll call 'em *employees*, just like real people do). The boss box looks different from the others, with the first line in red and four lines of text (so much that it overlaps the box below it). It doesn't look different *because* it's the boss box, but because it's currently selected for editing. You can change what's in each box, and in fact, you will have to unless everyone in your company is named *Type Name Here*.

In this shot, the chart program has been expanded to take up the whole screen, which you can do by clicking on the **Maximize** *button.*

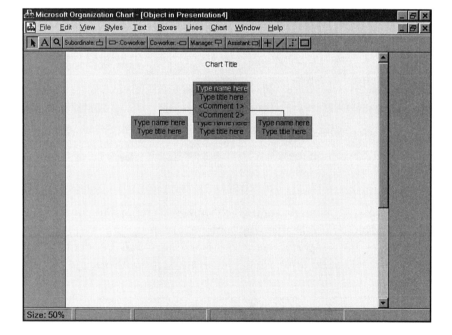

Editing a Box: More Fun Than Boxing with an Editor!

To edit the contents of a box, first you have to select it. That's as simple as clicking on the box. In fact, it *is* clicking on the box. When you do this, the text in the box will turn to white on a black background.

Now that you've got a black background, press **Enter**. The first line gets a red background, meaning it's ready to be edited. The first line is for the name of the person. Type in the name to make the words "Type name here" disappear.

When you're done typing the name, hit **Enter** again, and the red highlight moves to the next line where you can enter the person's title, such as *President* or *PowerPoint Ride Designer* or *Deputy Donut Eater*. After that, hitting **Enter** again takes you to the first of two lines for comments, which you can use for whatever you want. Use it for further descriptions of people's jobs, or for their phone extension, or for comments on their hairdo. ("Nice blonde hair, why are the roots dyed black?")

Grow Your Company by Adding Boxes

If your company has only four people, then you might never have to add any boxes. Then again, if your company has only four people, then you probably don't really need an organization chart to begin with!

To add a box, first click on one of the five buttons at the top of the window (**Subordinate**, **Co-worker** with the box on the left, **Co-worker** with the box on the right, **Manager**, or **Assistant**). When you do this, the pointer will change to a little box with a line coming from it. Then click on the box that you want to connect the new box to. For example, if you want to add the Assistant To The Deputy Donut Eater, click on the **Assistant** button, then on the box for the Deputy Donut Eater.

The two **Co-worker** buttons will create new boxes next to the box that you click on, and connected to the same boss. The difference between the two buttons is that the one on the left adds the new box to the left of the existing one, and the one on the right adds the new box to the right of the existing one.

When you add a box, it is automatically selected, and you can hit **Enter** to start filling in the name and position.

At the Top of the Chart Is... a Title!

When you start a new chart, it says Chart Title at the very top. Leaving that there would be a certain sign that you rushed through your work. To get rid of it, select the text by pointing to the start of the text and dragging to the end of the text. Then, type the title that you want to give it.

Frank Lloyd Chart: Fancier Structures

There are a number of different ways to change how boxes connect to other boxes—some let you reflect cases where employees have more than one boss, while others are there just to make the chart look more organized.

If you click on the **Styles** menu, you'll see a group of buttons with different chart diagrams on it. The top few are for groups, then there is one for assistants and one for co-managers.

The style menu.

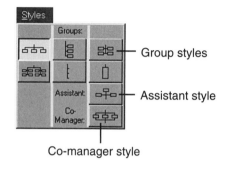

Group styles

Assistant style

Co-manager style

Groups

Selection in a Snap To select a bunch of boxes all at once, point above and to the left of the bunch, then drag below and to the right.

A group is a set of employees with the same boss. Using the buttons under the Style menu, you can group these employees so that they are all next to each other, or all stacked vertically, or even are all in the same box. To do this, first select all the boxes you want to organize (you can do this by clicking on the first one, then holding down the Shift key and clicking on the rest), then pull down the **Style** menu and click on the button that shows how you want the group to appear. (Pick one of the six buttons toward the top; the lower two are used for other things.)

Assistants

To change a subordinate into an assistant, invite him into your office and say, "Stop subordinating to me, and start assisting me!" To reflect this change on the chart, select the employee's box, then pull down the **Style** menu and click on the Assistant style button.

Co-Managers

Co-managers are what you call the bosses when a group of employees have two or more equal bosses. To get the chart to show that these employees have this group of bosses, select all the bosses' boxes, then pull down the **Style** menu and click on the **Co-manager** button. The lines coming down from the co-managers' boxes will join and go to the employees group.

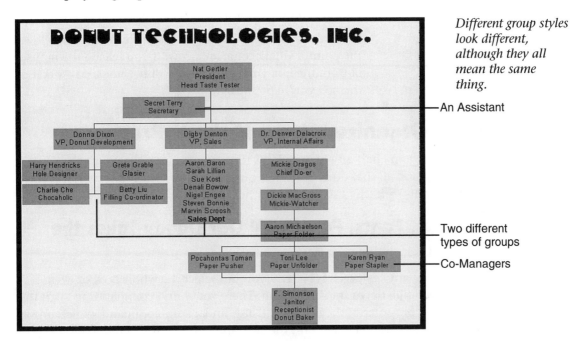

Different group styles look different, although they all mean the same thing.

— An Assistant

— Two different types of groups

— Co-Managers

The Job Shuffle: Rearranging the Chart

An organization chart is going to keep changing. People join the firm, quit, or are promoted, and that means that the chart has to be changed. Since you made the chart, you're going to be the one stuck rearranging it, until *you* quit or get promoted.

To get rid of someone, just select their box, then hit **Delete**. If they had anyone working under them, the chart will now show that they are working for the deleted person's boss.

Check This Out...

Demotion Dilemma If someone's position changes so that his old employee is now his boss, just dragging them down won't work. Instead, move the old employee up to whoever he's now reporting to, then drag the old boss into his new position.

To move a person from reporting to one boss to reporting to another, drag that person's box (a red outline will follow as you drag) until your pointer is below his new boss's box, and then slide it up. When the pointer turns into the diagram on the Subordinate button, release the mouse button. The box will be moved over there, and any employees of the person in the box will also be moved, so they are still his employees.

If you drag the box in from the side instead of from below, the pointer will become an arrow. If you release the mouse button, the box you're dragging will become a co-worker of the box you're pointing to.

You've Got It Organized, Now Make It Pretty

Now that you've got your chart all organized, it's time to mess with the colors and fonts and line thicknesses and all that other stuff that can make your presentation more attractive. Some of this stuff can also help make the chart more informative.

We'll Have Fonts, Fonts, Fonts ('Til Our Daddy Takes the Text Bar Away)

To change the look of any text, select the text (you can select the whole box, or even multiple boxes), then pull down the **Text** menu. There you'll find commands to align the text at the left, right, or center of the box. You'll also find a **Font** command, which brings up a dialog box that lets you pick the font, the size, and whether it's a bold, italic, or normal. Plus there's a **Color** command that brings up a dialog box showing squares of various colors—double-click on any of them to make the text that color.

Every Company Needs a Colorful Background

Pull down the **Chart** menu and select the **Background Color** command (which shouldn't be hard to find, since it's the only command on that menu). This brings up a dialog box displaying various colors. Double-click on the color you want, and it will fill the chart background.

However, this only lets you have one of a handful of colors. The chart program does not have the wide range of colors or the nifty fill tools that the main PowerPoint program has. If you want something fancier, don't set the background color. Instead, after you're done making the chart, select the chart in PowerPoint, then use the PowerPoint fill tool to set the background. (If you've already set a background color in Chart and decide that you want to use a PowerPoint fill instead, double click the chart to get back into the chart program, choose the **Chart, Background Color** command, and select the rightmost square on the bottom row. This will reset the background color, and the PowerPoint fill will now work.)

Colorful Co-Workers

Changing the color of the boxes can be more than just decoration. For example, you might want to have all of your administrative people (accountants, secretaries, and so on) show up in blue, your sales people in green, and your technical people (donut bakers advanced donut design engineers, and folks like that) show up in purple. To do this, select the boxes that you want to change, then pull down the **Boxes** menu and select **Color**. You'll get the same sort of color dialog box that you get with fonts and with the background color, except this one controls the box background.

Also in the Boxes menu are commands that let you add a shadow under the box, and to change the color and style of the border line around the box.

Define the Line

You can change any line to any thickness and style you like. To change the look of a line, first you have to select the line. You can select any single line by clicking on it. The line will change color when you do so, although the color change is minor and can be hard to see. You can select a bunch of lines at once by pointing to a spot on the chart's background and dragging diagonally. A rectangle appears, with one corner where you started dragging and the opposite corner wherever the pointer is now. When you release the mouse button, everything within in the rectangle gets selected. (Don't worry about the fact that boxes have been selected as well, since the Line commands won't affect them.)

The selected lines turn gray. However, with the standard thin line, this color difference can be hard to see.

The commands on the **Line** menu let you set the thickness, style, and color of all the selected lines. The **Thickness** and **Style** commands let you just pick one from a submenu, while the **Color** command brings up the Organization Chart program's Color dialog box.

Again, these aren't merely decorative. For example, dotted lines are good for showing proposed changes to the organizational chart.

Adding New Lines

Sometimes, you need more lines than just the ones from bosses to employees. You might want to use a different color line to show how information runs through the organization, or you might want to draw a big rectangle around a branch of the chart that makes up a single division.

If you press **Ctrl+D**, four additional buttons are added to the toolbar. The first, with a plus sign on it, is the Horizontal/Vertical Line button. The second (with a diagonal line on it), is the Diagonal Line button, used for drawing lines at any angle. Both of these work by clicking on the button, then dragging the mouse from the line's starting point to the line's ending point.

The Draw buttons.

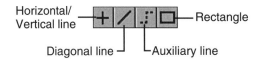

The third button is the Auxiliary Line button. This is the most useful one, as it lets you add new lines from one box to another. Click on this button, then point to the edge of one box and drag the pointer to the edge of another box. The program will automatically route the line around the boxes to connect the two edges. Better yet, this line will keep the two boxes connected even if you move the boxes! (You can adjust the path of this line by grabbing hold of one of its edges and dragging it.)

The fourth button, Rectangle, lets you make new boxes. Using this, you can make boxes that aren't connected to anything, and you can make them any size you want. (Normal boxes are designed to fit tightly around the text they hold.) You can use this tool to put a title or a legend in a box, or to create a square highlighting one area of the chart. This box will always appear *behind* other boxes and lines, so it won't cover them up.

Text to Go

You can put text anywhere you want on the chart, to let you annotate things beyond what's said in the boxes. To do this, click on the **A** button, then click on the chart where you want the text to appear. Then, type! (To edit the text later, just double-click on it.)

Other Little Chart Tricks

The Organization Chart program has a number of other features that you can take advantage of. Because it is a separate program, it doesn't have all of the same features as the main program (it doesn't have the animated Office Assistant, for example), but it does have its own tools to meet your needs (it still has Help information, which you can get by hitting the **F1** key).

Zooming in a Zoom

You can change how close a look you get at your chart. You can shrink it down so that you can see the whole chart at once, or you can zoom in on it, so that you get a really close look at each dot in the dotted line. Change your view by hitting **F9**, **F10**, **F11**, or **F12**, with **F9** being the furthest view and **F12** making it so close that you'll think someone glued the chart to your eyeglasses.

Selection Shortcuts

You can quickly select all of something (all the lines, all the boxes, all the co-manager boxes, and so on) by pulling down the **Edit** menu and selecting the **Select** submenu. There you'll find 10 different quick selection possibilities (such as **Group** or **All Co-Managers**), which is handy if you're making big changes all at once.

Chart Trivia

Pull down the **Help menu** and select **Chart Info** to get a display telling you how many boxes are on the chart, how many are currently selected, and other information about your chart.

Returning to Uncharted Territory

When you're done working with your chart, click on the **Close (X)** button. A dialog box will appear, asking you if you want to update the object in your presentation. Click on **Yes**, and you can go back to working on your PowerPoint presentation, where you'll find the chart on a slide.

If you want to make changes to the chart after it's on the presentation, just double-click on it, and you'll be back in the Organization Chart program. If you find that your boss keeps asking you for changes, just change his title to Executive Bunnybrain and see how long it takes for him to notice! You'll be chuckling about that one while standing in the unemployment lines!

The Least You Need to Know

➤ To start making a chart, pull down the **Insert** menu, and from the **Pictures** submenu, select **Organization Chart**.

➤ To select a box on the chart, click on it. To select additional boxes, hold down the **Shift** key and click on them.

➤ To add a box, click on the button for the sort of box you want to add (**Subordinate**, **Co-Worker**, **Manager**, or **Assistant**), then click on the box you want to connect it to.

➤ Change who a subordinate reports to by dragging his or her box below a different boss's box, and then dragging up onto the box.

➤ Text can be added by clicking on the **A** button then clicking where you want the text.

➤ Once you're done working with the chart, just click on the **Close** (**X**) button for the Organization Chart window and select **Yes** from the dialog box that appears.

➤ To return to editing your chart, double-click on it.

Chapter 12

Backing Up Your Words: Beautiful Backgrounds

In This Chapter

➤ Use a background designed by genuine Microsoft employees

➤ Design your own background

➤ Create a look for your presentations

"Behind every great man is a great background." Truer words have never been said. Well, *certain* truer words have never been said, but a lot of words that have been said have been truer. You can't expect deep philosophical insight from a computer book. What you *can* expect is to learn how to give your words and pictures a nice backdrop, and to pick the basic design look for your presentation. What could be more fun than that?*

The Lazy Way: Using a Pre-Made Design

PowerPoint comes with an assortment of designs, which have nicely designed backgrounds and layouts all ready for you. These are good for saving you time and effort. The one risk is that everyone else who has PowerPoint has the same templates, so if you use one of these, there's a reasonable chance that members of your audience will have seen them already, and will somehow relate your presentation to the one they'd seen before.

*Answer: Dropping a thousand superballs off of a tall building.

To start a new presentation using one of these backgrounds, pull down the **File** menu and select the **New** command. A dialog box appears, with four tabs. Select the second tab (**Presentation Designs**), and you'll see a list of different designs.

View each file
as an icon

View a list of
file names

View full details
about each file

*The three buttons
above the image
change the way that
the list of designs is
organized.*

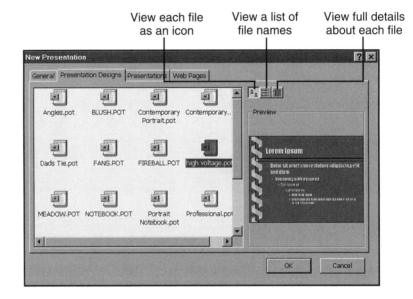

Click once on any one of the designs, and you'll see a small version of what a typical slide would look like in the Preview area at the right of the dialog box. The slide won't look very good. This isn't because the design is bad, but because the colors are simplified for the preview display, and the resolution is low, so just about any design will look bad. Still, it should give you some idea of what the slide will be like.

When you find one you like, click on the **OK** button. PowerPoint will start the new presentation for you, and the New Slide dialog box appears, from which you select an AutoLayout for the first slide. If you choose the slide from the New Slide dialog box that's highlighted by default, you'll find that it's arranged visibly differently from the one you selected. It probably has the same pieces, but in different places. This is because every design actually has *two* background designs. This design is used just for the title slide, the one you saw earlier is used for all the other slides.

Doesn't Look So Good?

If the design you opened up doesn't look so good, click the **Close Window (X)** button on the menu bar to get rid of it, then start again.

Color My World, Differently!

If you like the basic look of the background, but you aren't happy with the color, change it! You can change the color for all of the slides, or you can change just one to make it stand out.

To do this, pull down the **Format** menu and select the **Slide Color Scheme** command. A Color Scheme dialog box appears, showing a series of little slides. Each slide has a title in that color scheme's default title color, some bulleted text in the scheme's bulleted text color, a shape in the scheme's shape colors, and a chart using the scheme's chart colors. Click on the scheme you like, then click the **Apply** button to make it the color scheme for the current slide, or **Apply to All** to make it the color scheme for all of the slides in this presentation!

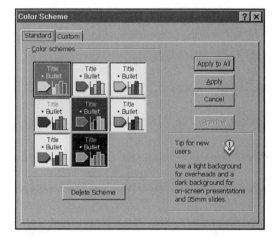

Use the Standard tab in the Color Scheme dialog box to choose one of the pre-designed color schemes, or use the Custom tab to create your own.

Design Yourself a Rainbow

If you want to roll your own color scheme, pick the color scheme that's closest to what you want, and then click on the **Custom** tab. This will display the 8 colors that make up the scheme, each labeled for what this color applies to (such as Backgrounds or Shadows). Double-click on any one of these colors, and a Color dialog box appears that lets you select a new color for it.

Once you've selected a new color, click on the **OK** button to close the Color dialog box and return to the Color Scheme dialog box. After you've changed at least one color, an **Add as Standard Scheme** button becomes available. Clicking on this will add the color scheme to the list on the Standard tab, so you can use it on other presentations. What could be a better lasting legacy than that?*

*Answer: Finding a cure for hangnail.

As you change the various colors, you'll see the colors on the sample slide in the lower right of the dialog box change. Once you've changed the color scheme to what you want, click on **Apply** to apply it to the current slide, or the **Apply to All** button to change your whole presentation at once.

Coloring for Clarity

For on-screen presentations, bright letters on a dark background look best. For overheads and slides, use dark letters and bright backgrounds.

The Less-Lazy Way: Design Your Own Background and Slide Style

Some people like to design their own backgrounds. This won't come as a surprise to people who work in the Personnel department, who are used to getting resumes that show people redesigning their own backgrounds. For example, they might say that they were a serviceman stationed in the gulf, when really they were a man at a Gulf service station. But, of course that's not the sort of background we're talking about.

If you want to design a background, it should probably be the first step in building your presentation. After all, what color you make everything else depends on what they will appear against. To get started with a new, thoroughly blank presentation, pull down the **File** menu and select **New**. From the dialog box that appears, select the **General** tab and on there double-click on the file named **Blank Presentation**. The New Slide dialog box will appear, asking you to choose a layout. Click on the **OK** button to pick the default (Title Slide), and a basic title slide form will appear, in plain black text on a white background. (Make sure you're in Slide View to see it.)

Master View: No, It's Not for 3-D Reels

Pull down the **View** menu and select **Master**, and then select **Slide Master** from the sub-menu. A new slide will appear in your Slide View, this one with five boxes of text, including descriptions of what each box is for. This is your *Slide Master*, the basic format that will be used to build all the other slides. Anything you add or change here will be added or changed on all your slides.

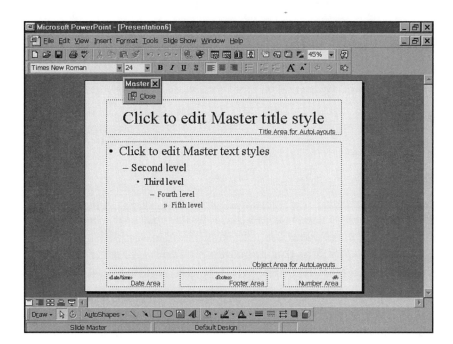

The text in the master on each box tells you what that box is used for on the slides.

Changing the Text Styles

Changing the text styles on the Master will change the automatic styles used on all the slides in the presentation. For example, if you click on the text that says Click to edit Master title style and then click on the **Italics** button, not only will the text on that line of the Slide Master be in italics, but so will the titles on all the slides you make. You can adjust the font, the size, and the color all in the same way you'd change text in a text box, as you saw in Chapter 5, "The World of Words."

There are five lines of text in the biggest box. The first of these affects the main list on each slide. The second (which says Second level) affects sub-lists, the third affects sub-sub-lists, and so on. (If you're actually using fifth level on any of your slides, it's time to rethink your presentation! You don't need sub-sub-sub-sub-lists!)

Each level's style can be changed separately. You can even change the bullet style for each, by right-clicking on the line and selecting **Bullet** from the pop-up menu, just like you would with text on a normal slide.

Check This Out...

WordArt Won't Work

You cannot make your default text style WordArt. If you select the Master style area and then click on the WordArt button, all you'll end up doing is putting a fancy WordArt presentations of the words Click to edit Master text style on all of your slides!

Changing the Text Areas

If you click on any of the Slide Master's five text areas, sizing handles will appear. At this point, you can re-size or move any of the areas just like a normal text box. This will affect all of the slides created with the AutoLayout tool. For some AutoLayouts, the main text area is divided in half, and this will still be true no matter how you re-size it. You can even delete an area by selecting it and pressing **Delete**, but you shouldn't delete the title area or main text area. It's okay to delete the smaller areas, though, such as the Date or Footer area, if you don't want them on your slides.

Changing the Basic Slide Color

The first step in designing your background is to choose the basic background color to fill up the slide. (Actually, the first step is to read this section of the book, but I would guess that you're already doing that.) Pull down the **Format** menu and select **Background** to get the Background dialog box. Click on the drop-down button and select one of the colors from the list that appears, or select **More Colors** to go to a standard Color dialog box, or **Fill Effects** to go the standard Fill Effects dialog box that you learned about in Chapter 7, "WordArt: Your Logo-Making Low-Calorie Friend." You can fill it with gradients, textures, patterns, or pictures, just like with anything else.

Decorations: Deck the Slides!

To decorate your background with pictures, boxes, logos, whatever, do it in just the same way that you would decorate a regular slide. When you put that stuff on, it may appear to overlap the text on the master slide, but don't worry; the text on the actual slide will go in front of everything that you add.

Even so, you may want to be careful of adding things that overlap where the text is, since things that you add there can end up distracting from the text, and making the text hard to read. It's usually better to add highlights at the edges of your slide, where you won't have text. You don't want something so busy that you can't see it, otherwise trying to read your slides will be as hard as trying to listen to someone while people stand right behind you, whispering. If you're going to use light text, keep all of your background elements fairly dark, and vice versa.

How'd They Do It?

If you see something you like in one of the pre-packaged backgrounds, just load up that background, select the Slide Master View, and see what pieces they used. (You may have to select the background and Ungroup it to see what the individual pieces are.)

How to Earn the Title "Master Title Masterer"

If you only make the one Slide Master, then your title slides will have the same background as the rest of your slides. To make a separate master for the Title Slide, pull down the **View** menu and click on **Master**. If the command **Title Master** is selectable, there already is a Title Master for this presentation, and selecting that command will let you edit it.

If Title Master is grayed out, however, select **Slide Master** instead. Then pull down the **Insert** menu and select the first item, **New Title Master**. This will copy all the background elements you added to your Slide Master onto a new Title Master for you to work with.

Title Masters have different text boxes than Slide Masters. You can make your Title Master a bit busier than your Slide Master. After all, the text will be bigger, making it easier to read.

Once you've made the Title Master, you can pull it up at any time by pulling down the **View** menu, selecting **Master**, then selecting **Title Master** from the sub-menu.

Save and Save Again!

Once you've designed a background for your presentation, you should save it twice. The first time you save it, you're saving it as a template, so you can reuse it with other projects, and the second time, you're saving it in a normal presentation file for this project. You could save it a few more times if you wanted, but why would you waste time like that?*

First, pull down the **File** menu, and select **Save As**. The Save As dialog box appears. Click on the drop-down arrow at the end of the Save As Type field, and select **Presentation Template (*.pot)** from the list. A list of folders will appear in the dialog box. Double-click on the one marked **Presentation Designs**. A list of files appears. Type a name for your background design into the File Name field, then click on the **OK** button.

*Answer: Because you're getting paid by the hour!

The Save As dialog box lets you save your backgrounds as a template as well as letting you save your presentation.

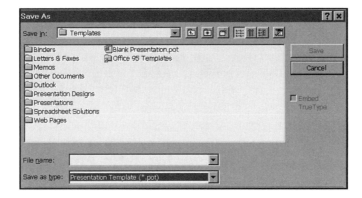

Quick Save

In the future you can save the additional work just by clicking on the **Save** button.

Now that you saved it, you'll be able to reuse your own design in the exact same way that you use the Microsoft-provided designs.

Now, it's time to save your presentation for the first time. Give the **File, Save As** command again and select **Presentations (*.ppt)** in the Save As Type field. Then, type a name for this presentation into the File Name field, and click on the **OK** button. Now your presentation has a name!

Now that you're done working with your slide master, click on the **Close** button on the Master toolbar to resume working on the individual slides in your presentation!

Slide Iconclast: Making One Slide Different

Some time, you might find yourself needing just one slide that's different, one slide that doesn't have the same background as the rest of the slides in that presentation. You don't know if there's some mystical command that will remove the background, or perhaps a mystical incantation which will cause it to disappear. You're faced with the problem of just how you make the background go away.

You don't make it go away. Instead, you do what you used to do when you had to clean up a big mess in the five minutes before your parents got home. You cover it up. Just draw a big rectangle over the whole background, and fill it with whatever you want the background of this slide to look like. This is a much more effective cover-up than the time you threw the tablecloth over the grape juice stain in the rug.

Does "Footer" Mean It's More Foot Than Something Else?

A *footer* is just some information that goes at the bottom of something, below the main content. For example, in this book the page number is a footer.

You can easily set up to three footer items on any presentation (assuming that you didn't delete the boxes for them while designing your master). You can put a date on them, a slide number, and one other piece of text that can be anything you want.

To do this, pull down the **View** menu and select **Header and Footer**. When the Header and Footer dialog box appears, make sure that the **Slide** tab is selected.

The dialog box says Header and Footer, but for slides, it only has Footers. That's the best place for things on a slide anyway.

The dialog box has three checkboxes in the Include On Slide area to let you choose which footers to show. If you check the **Date** checkbox, then you have to choose whether you want the current date to always appear (**Update Automatically**), or whether you want to set a **Fixed** date. If you pick Update Automatically, then the date on the slides will be the same day that the person is watching the computer-based slide show, or the date the overheads were printed. When you pick Update Automatically, pull down the menu below it and pick the format for the date (such as choosing between April 30, 1997 or 4/30/97 or any of a dozen different formats).

To get the slide number to appear, just click the **Slide Number** check box. Do you want a slide number? If you're doing a computer-based presentation, probably not, since that will just be additional information to clutter up the screen. However, if you're producing overheads, real slides, or printed handouts, you do want the numbers. Who out there hasn't at some time accidentally dropped a pile of papers or a tray of slides, and watched them scatter in various directions with little hope of ever getting them back in order?*

*Answer: My mother. She's too perfect for something like that.

➤ To get the whatever-text-you-want footer, just click on the **Footer** checkbox and type the text you want into the field.

➤ If you don't want the footer information on the title slide (and you probably don't), check the **Don't show on title slide** checkbox.

➤ Once you've set it all up, click on the **Apply to All** button, and the footer will be added to all the slides!

The Least You Need to Know

➤ To choose a pre-made background, use the **File**, **New** command, select the **Presentation Designs** tab, click on the design you want from the list, then on the **OK** button.

➤ To start with a new, totally blank design, use the **File**, **New** command, select the **General** tab, and double-click on **Blank Presentation**.

➤ To create your own background design, start with a blank design, then select the **View**, **Master**, **Slide Master** command.

➤ Any drawing, shapes, or text that you add to the Slide Master will appear on all the slides as background, behind anything you add on the slide.

➤ The Title Master starts with all of the elements that you put on the Slide Master. However, changing them or removing them does not change the Slide Master.

➤ To save your design as a template, choose the **File**, **Save As** command, pull down the **Save As Type** menu, and select **Presentation Template**. Then double-click on the **Presentation Designs** folder, type a name for your design, and click **OK**.

➤ To add footer information (including date and slide number), select **View**, **Header and Footer** to get the Header and Footer dialog box.

Part 3
Fancy, Flashy, Fabulous Features

Sound and movement are very important. Without them, we wouldn't be able to tell real flamingoes from the plastic ones. Without sound and motion in your presentation, it could be a flaming (or even flamingo) failure.

In this part, you'll learn about putting sound and motion in your presentation, plus interaction. With properly set-up interaction, the user can skip over all the material you spent so long putting together!

BRAD'S LIFE TOOK ON NEW MEANING WHEN HE DISCOVERED THAT HIS SOUND CARD MADE REALLY DISGUSTING NOISES.

Click Here for Interactivity

Interactivity is very useful in an on-screen presentation. With an interactive presentation, the user can choose which information he wants to see, which means you can put a lot more information in without boring the people who don't want to see it. And even if you don't need interactivity, proper use of it can keep the viewer feeling involved in your presentation, making it more enjoyable for him. Why, if people liked things without interactivity, then television would be popular!

You Can Click on Anything!

Any object on your slide can be made interactive, so that something happens when the user clicks on it. Your words, your pictures, your shapes, your logos, and even your lines can be made clickable.

To do this, right-click on the item in Slide View. It will become selected, and a shortcut menu will appear. Select **Action Settings**, and the Action Settings dialog box will appear. (If you haven't saved the presentation yet, a dialog box will appear first, offering you the opportunity to save your file. You can click **Yes** to save it or **No** not to.) The **Mouse Click** tab of the Action Settings dialog box has what you're looking for.

Interact with this dialog box to make your interaction work.

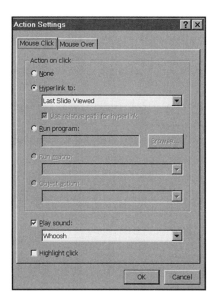

Going to Another Slide: The Playground Hop

Most of the time, you'll probably want to create a place to click that takes you to another part of your presentation. PowerPoint calls a way to get from one slide to another slide (or to a Web page) a *hyperlink*. To me, that sounds like an overactive breakfast sausage, but it's Microsoft's word, do we'll go with that.

The most common type of hyperlink you'll want to make is on that takes the viewer to another part of your presentation. To do this, click on the **Hyperlink to** radio button. The field below it will become active. Click on the drop down menu to see a list of the sorts of links you can create. Most of them take the viewer to another slide when the object is clicked. There are choices to let you go to the Next Slide, Previous Slide, First Slide, Last Slide, Last Slide Viewed, and one that says Slide… and nothing else.

If you just want the user stepping through your presentation, you'll probably be using the Next Slide and Previous Slide buttons. However, if you're looking for real interaction, letting them pick their path, Slide… is the one that you will use the most.

Select **Slide...**, and you get a new car and a trip to Jamaica. Oh, okay, I lied. You just get a dialog box, but it's a very nice dialog box. On the left is a list of the slides in your presentation. Slides that have titles will list the titles, while slides that don't have titles have the slide number listed. Click on the slide that you want to link to, and an image of the slide appears in the lower right, so you can make sure that it's the slide you want. Then click on the **OK** button to set the link.

Tight Links
When you create a hyperlink to a specific slide, the link stays to that slide even if that slide is moved and changes slide number.

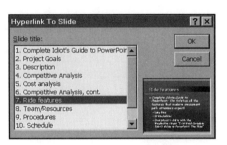

A new car and a trip to Jamaica.

Pop Your Peepers on Plural PowerPoint Presentations

Sometimes, you'll want a hyperlink into *another* presentation. That way, you don't have to build everything you ever want to say into one huge presentation.

To do this, select **Hyperlink To** from the Action Settings dialog box. From the menu below it, select **Other PowerPoint Presentation**. A list of your presentations appears. Double-click on the presentation you want. Another dialog box appears, with a list of slides in that presentation, but this isn't a very good one, because it doesn't show you a picture of the slide, so you just have to go by the titles. Double-click on the title of the slide you want.

Welcome to the World Wide Web; Look Out for the World Wide Spider

You can create a link from your presentation to a page on the World Wide Web. This makes a lot of sense if you're publishing your presentation on the Web (I'll show you how to do that in Chapter 21 "Putting It on the Web"). It lets the user go from the information in your presentation to relevant stuff on another Web site.

However, it can also work when someone is seeing your presentation on-screen directly, rather than over the Web. When you do it this way, it isn't nearly so elegant. The system that the presentation is running on needs to have a copy of Microsoft Internet Explorer (a Web browser), and it needs a connection to the Internet. When the user clicks on the hyperlink to the Web, Internet Explorer starts up. If the Internet connection is a dial-up one, the user will have to tell the Internet Dialer to make the connection. Then the linked-to Web site appears on the Internet Explorer screen, but the viewer may not know Internet Explorer and may not be comfortable with it. All in all, linking a non-Web presentation to the Web is probably a bad idea.

Having a Web browser suddenly appear can be confusing to someone who was not on the Web, or who may not be used to the Web.

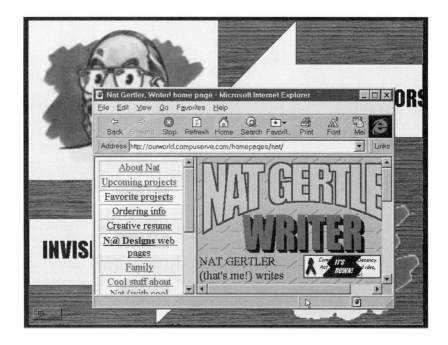

To create the link, select **Hyperlink To** on the Action Settings dialog box, pull down the menu below that, and select **URL**. Now, *URL* here does not refer to the Dook Of Url of song fame. Instead, it means *Uniform Resource Locator*, which makes it sounds like a catalog telling you where to find cub scout pants, doctors' jackets, and police hats. What it really means here is the Web page address, that big long string that starts with an "http:" and tells people where to find your Web page. (For example, http:// ourworld.compuserve.com/homepages/nat/ is the URL for my Web page.) When you select URL from the menu, a dialog box appears asking you for the URL. Type it into the space provided and hit **Enter**, and the hyperlink will now point to that Web page.

Starting a Program

You can create a link that starts another program on your computer. This can be useful if your presentation is about the program, or if you want to give people an easy way to start Solitaire while the boss isn't looking.

To make this choice, instead of picking Hyperlink To from the Action Settings dialog box, select **Run Program**, then click on the **Browse** button that's under it. A file navigator opens. Click on the drop-down button at the end of the Look In field and select the hard disk with the program from the menu that appears. A list of folders on the hard disk appears below. Double-click on the folder the program is in (if it's a folder within a folder within a folder, you'll have to do this several times to get to where the program is). When you find the program file, click on it, then click on the **OK** button. Voilà! You've now got a program linked in.

Putting a Sound with the Click

You can make it so that, when you click on something, it makes a noise. It can make that noise along with linking to another slide or program, or it can just make that noise. This way, you could have them click on a picture of a car to hear it go vrooom, or a picture of a duck to hear it go quack, or a picture of Leonardo DaVinci to hear him go quack.

In order for the sound to work, the presentation will have to be viewed on a computer that has a sound card and speakers. Most computers sold these days have these things, but some don't, mostly ones bought by companies. A lot of companies think that sound systems have no business application (wrong), and that having them only encourages people to spend their time blowing up aliens when the boss isn't looking (less wrong). So if you're creating a presentation for people to view on their own machines, you may not want to rely on sound.

To add a sound, on the Action Settings dialog box, click the **Play sound** checkbox. Click on the drop-down button under it to see a list of standard available sounds, then select the one you want. If you don't want one of the prepackaged sounds, you can select **Other Sound** to get to the Add Sound dialog box, which contains a list of sound files you can use—but you probably won't find anything *interesting* there unless you've put it there yourself. (I'll tell you about making your own sounds in Chapter 17 "Sound Advice on Sound.")

Flash That Thing!

Under the Play Sound checkbox is another checkbox that you can only use if you select Play Sound first. Check off this **Highlight click** checkbox, and your object will flash when someone clicks on it, which helps them to know that they clicked on the right thing.

Flash Without Sound If you want the object to flash but you don't want a sound, check off **Play sound** but select **[No Sound]** from the list beneath it.

Done with the Dialog Box

Once you've set what the link goes to and chosen the sound if you want one, click on the **OK** button at the bottom of the Action Settings dialog box. To test out your new hyperlink, you can click on the **Slide Show** button to see the slide in action, click on the hyperlink to see it work, then right-click and select **End Show** to return to your work. Look out, though—you'll now be at the slide you linked to rather than the one that you linked from, and you'll have to find your own way back!

Clickless Actions

If you check the other tab on the Action Settings dialog box, you'll find it has the exact same contents as the Mouse Click tab. The difference is hidden in the *name* of this other tab, which is Mouse Over. The action you select on this tab is what happens when the pointer passes over the object. Why would you want to have an interaction without clicking? Three good reasons come to mind:

➤ You're making an interactive presentation for little kids. Pointing without clicking is both simpler to understand and easier to do, since most mice aren't designed for their little paws.

➤ You're making a *kiosk*, an information center like you might see in the middle of your local shopping mall. If you don't need a click, you can create a presentation that can be entirely controlled by a trackball without any buttons, which is easy for shoppers to figure out and leaves fewer parts to worry about breaking.

➤ You want to have a sound or have the object flash when the pointer passes over it, and then take another action when you click on it. For example, when the pointer passes over the picture of a flying sheep, the user could suddenly hear "Click here to learn more about flying sheep!" Then when the sheep is clicked on, a slide about famous flying sheep in history is displayed.

As the third reason suggests, you can set separate actions for passing over the object and clicking on it. Just set one action on the Mouse Click tab and one on the Mouse Over tab. However, make sure the action on the Mouse Over tab isn't a hyperlink, because if a new slide appears when the pointer is on the picture, the user will never have a chance to click on it!

Missing Link: Getting Rid of an Interaction

To get rid of hyperlink, just right-click on the object, select **Action Settings**, then select **None** from whichever tab you set the link on. This will clear the hyperlink. To get rid of a sound action, just click on the **Play sound** checkbox so that the checkmark goes away, and your presentation will be that much quieter!

Click Pick: Shaping Your Clickable Area

The clickable area for a shape is that shape. If you make a circle and link it to a sound, then the user can click anywhere on the circle to hear the sound. (This is true even if the circle has no fill; you can see through the center, but if you click there, PowerPoint knows you're clicking on the circle.) The area outside the circle but inside the circle's box is not clickable.

When you make a text box clickable, the user has to click on the text itself. Even if it's filled in, the rest of the box is not clickable.

The clickable area for most other objects is rectangular. For example, if you have a picture on your slide, and you give it an interactive action of some sort, then the user can click anywhere on the picture. This is true even if the picture has an invisible edge color—they can click on the invisible edge and it still works the same as if they'd clicked on the visible part of the picture.

How it Stacks Up

If the user clicks somewhere where you have several objects stacked up, what happens? The answer is that whatever's on top where they click controls what happens. If it's an object with some interaction, the interaction takes place. If it's an object with no interaction, then nothing happens, even if it's on top of another object that has an interaction. As with many things on life, whoever's on top gets control.

There is, however, an exception (in PowerPoint, if not in life). If you put a shape with no fill and no action on top of a shape with action, and the user clicks inside the shape, then PowerPoint looks down to the next level and does that action. If the outline of the shape is visible, and the user clicks on the outline, nothing happens. It only happens where you can see down to the next level.

If you have an unfilled shape with an action on it, and someone clicks on the unfilled interior, then the action does take place. This is a handy feature, useful in one of my favorite tricks.

Nat's Nifty, Patented, Pick-Parts-of-a-Picture PowerPoint Trick

Let's say you have a picture of you and your dog, standing side by side. (No, you don't have to say it out loud!) And you want to make it so that when someone clicks on you, they hear the sound of a laser, and when they click on a your dog Ralphie, they hear a whoosh. Now, it's one picture, so it's one object, so you can only have one click action on it, right? Right.

But let's say you use the circle tool to draw a circle over your dog. You don't want to hide Ralphie at all, so you select **No Fill** for the circle's fill, and **No Line** for the outline. Now we have a completely invisible picture. Nobody even knows it's there!

Right-click on the invisible circle, select **Action Settings**, and set the sound played when the circle is clicked on to **Laser**. Make another shape to cover you, and set the sound for that picture to **Whoosh**. Voilà! The user *thinks* he's clicking on you, but he's really clicking on the invisible shapes. (You can use any AutoShape this way. Most picture items are easily covered by a circle or rectangle, but if you need something that carefully follows the outline of an item, pick one of the freeform drawing tools in the AutoShapes Lines menu.)

Setting the Shape

Placing an invisible shape is hard, since you can't see where the edges are. Instead, when you draw it, you should use a thin, visible outline. That way, you can see where you're putting it. Once you've got it in place, then you click on the drop down button next to the Line Color button and select **No Line**.

Links Within Text

A text box links the same way as any other object, so long as it has a background fill. Just select the text box, right-click on it, select **Action Settings**, and so on.

However, you can also make individual parts of the text have their own link. To do this, first select the text box, then select the text in the box that you want to link. Right-click on the selected text to get the pop up menu. Then set that action just like you'd set any other.

These Buttons Were Made for Action

There's a nice set of pre-made button shapes designed just for interactivity, lurking there under the **AutoShapes** button. When you click on that button, select the **Action Buttons** command, and you'll get a menu full of buttons. Put these buttons on your slide like you would any other AutoShape—just drag to draw on the slide where you want the button. You can make them any size. Once you place an action button, the Action Settings dialog box will automatically open up. Some of the Action Buttons are specially designed for going to the next slide, previous slide, first slide or last slide, with pictures on them that look like the controls on a VCR or a CD player. When you place one of these, the right hyperlink is already set for you in the Action Settings dialog box. Just click **OK** to accept the hyperlink.

The action buttons look a little different from most AutoShapes, because they have a built-in sticking-out button appearance. An action button, by default, appears in the color you have set for Fill Color, but you can change its color like any other drawn object (see Chapter 7, "WordArt: Your Logo-Making Low-Calorie Friend"). Whatever color you select for the object, the edges will look shaded to create that effect. Because of this effect, action buttons look best without an outline.

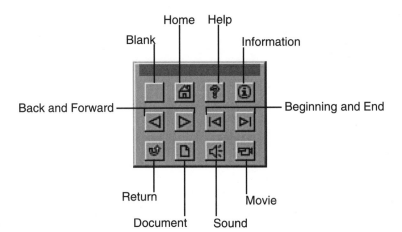

Having a Web browser suddenly appear can be confusing to someone who was not on the Web, or who may not be used to the Web.

Action Master: Interactivity on Your Slide Master

By putting interactive elements on your Slide Master, you can easily have them on every slide of your presentation. This is a good place for action buttons such as the VCR-style buttons and the Help button.

If you don't want one of the buttons on an individual slide, just cover it up with some other object!

The Least You Need to Know

➤ Interactivity lets you make it so that some action occurs when you point to or click on certain objects.

➤ To give an object an action, right-click on that object in Slide View, and select **Action Settings** from the shortcut menu.

➤ Selecting **Hyperlink To** in the Action Settings dialog box lets you select what is linked to from the menu below.

➤ Clicking **Play Sound** in the Action Settings dialog box lets you pick a sound to play from the menu below. You can play the sound whether or not you're also doing another action.

➤ The Action Buttons on the AutoShapes menu are designed specially for interaction.

Chapter 14

Look Up in the Sky: Flying Text and Pictures

In This Chapter

➤ Add animation to your presentation

➤ Make words and pictures appear and disappear when you want

Motion is the greatest invention of all time. Before motion, life was pretty dull. Nothing happened. Everything stayed as it was. All you could do was sit there and watch TV all day, and you couldn't even change the channel.

Now that motion exists, life has improved a lot, because now we can change channels. You can bring that same sort of motion excitement to your on-screen presentations, with text, pictures, and shapes moving all over the place! Used well, it's a real eye-catcher for your key points.

A Presentation with Animation Is Your Destination

The animation capabilities of PowerPoint control how an object is brought onto a slide. Instead of appearing immediately when the slide appears, the object that you animate comes in afterward, appearing in some special fashion. You can have the object appear automatically, or wait until the user clicks a button before appearing. If you've got more than one animated object on a slide, you can control the order that they appear in. The object always ends up wherever you've placed it.

The Quick Way: Animation for Lazy Folks

You can animate any object quickly, if you're willing to settle for one of a number of basic, useful animations. To do this, get into Slide View, and select the object that you want to animate. On the Slide Show menu, select **Preset Animation**, and a sub-menu will appear with a list of different animations that can be performed on this object.

Certain animation styles only work only with text, while others work only with pictures and shapes so you won't ever see all of the styles on the submenu at once. Each style includes an appropriate sound that goes with the animation, such as a *whoosh* sound when you bring an object flying onto the screen. The animation styles include:

➤ *Off* removes any animation from the object.

➤ *Drive-In* makes the object move into place from the right side of the screen.

➤ *Flying* makes the object move in from the left side of the screen.

➤ *Camera* makes the center of the object appear first, then it grows in a circle until it reaches the edges.

➤ *Flash Once* makes the object appear, disappear for a moment, then reappear.

➤ *Laser Text* makes the letters in a text box appear one at a time, flying in from the upper right corner of the screen.

➤ *Typewriter* makes the letters in a text box appear one at a time, in place.

➤ *Reverse Order* makes the bottom item on a list appear, then the item above it, and so on up to the top of the list. (This is good for Top Ten lists, where you can count down to the top.)

➤ *Drop In* makes text appear one word at a time, coming down from the top.

➤ *Wipe Right* makes the object appear, in place, from side to side, as if a piece of paper that had been covering it up is pulled to the right.

➤ *Dissolve* treats the object as a bunch of little squares, making the squares appear one at a time until the object is complete.

➤ *Split Vertical Out* shows the center, fully top-to-bottom, of the image first, then spreads that out to the edges. (For text, it does this one word at a time.)

➤ *Appear* makes the object just appear.

➤ *Fly from Top* brings the object down from the top of the screen.

All of these animations require clicking the mouse button (or hitting a keyboard key) to start them. This is very good for when you're showing the presentation to someone, allowing you to control when each new item appears. It's not so good if the viewer is in control, because it encourages them to just keep clicking the button, and next thing you know, they're skipping over slides altogether!

Big, Slow, and Clunky

It takes a lot of computing power to animate a large object, particularly if the object is moving (Fly or Crawl) rather than just appearing in place (Wipe, Dissolve, and so on). Because of this, large objects will move jerkily on slower computers. If you've got a Pentium running at 100 megahertz or more, with a good graphics card, you shouldn't worry about it. If your presentation is going to be seen on slower machines, don't move the big stuff.

Animation Demonstration Station

There are two ways to check your animation. One is to go into Slide Show mode, and actually see your show at work. However, for those looking for the quick and lazy way to do it, pull down the **Slide Show** menu and select **Animation Preview**. A small Color window will appear over the slide view, showing the animation (without waiting for your click to start each bit of animation). If you want to see the animation again, just click on the window.

Animating for Control Freaks

If you want to have more control over your animations, you can use a lot more animation effects, pick the sound that goes with each animation, pick the order that animations take place in, and set the amount of time to wait between animations. It takes a little more work (ugh! Work!), but it can give you so much more than the quick method.

To start, pull down the **Slide Show** menu and select **Custom Animation**. A dialog box appears, with a list of all of the animated objects on the slide, and four tabs of animation-related settings.

The Custom Animation dialog box is your one-stop, 24-hour animation station!

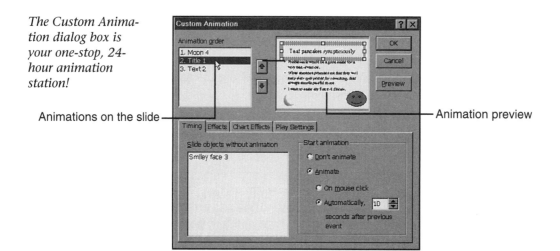

Animations on the slide ——

—— Animation preview

Putting the Order in Order

The upper left-hand corner of the dialog box has a list of all the animations on the current slide, in the order that the animation takes place. They are named pretty simply, so just by looking at the list, there is no easy way to tell two text boxes apart—they're both called *text*, followed by a number. This is about as handy as naming all your kids *Charlie*. However, if you click on an item in the list, the object will appear selected in the preview box at right, so you'll be able to tell which one it is.

To rearrange the order of these events, select an item whose order you want to change. Click on the up arrow button to move it earlier in the list, or the down arrow button to move it later on the list.

Animati-on and Animati-off

To turn an animation off, so the object won't be animated, first select the animation in the order list. Then, click on the **Timing** tab and select **Don't Animate**. The item will be moved off of the order list, and onto the Slide objects without animation list, which is on the Timing tab.

To take an object that doesn't have animation and make it animated, select the **Timing** tab, click on the name of the item, then click on **Animate**. The object will be added to the bottom of the Animation Order list.

When?

The timing tab also lets you select whether an animation should happen automatically, or wait for a button push. If you select **On Mouse Click**, it will wait for the push, but if you select **Automatically**, that animation will take place immediately after the previous one finishes. You can choose how long to wait by typing a number of seconds into the field next to Automatically. This time can be anywhere from 0 seconds to 9999 seconds—although if you set it to 9999 seconds, the viewer probably won't stick around to see the animation happen. (That's over two and a half hours!)

What?

Choosing an object and turning animation on is like telling a child "Go do something!" You haven't told it what to do, and it probably won't think of something by itself. (And if it did, you probably won't like it.)

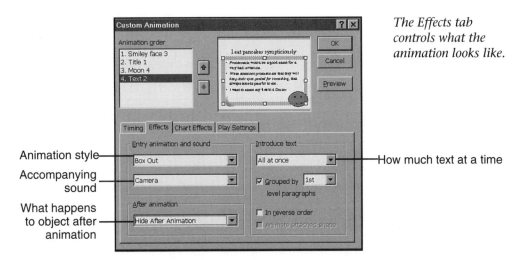

The Effects tab controls what the animation looks like.

Animation style — How much text at a time

Accompanying sound

What happens to object after animation

The **Effects** tab has all the settings you need. In the Entry Animation and Sound area are two drop-down lists. The top one has the style of movement. Click on the drop-down button for it, and you'll see a long list. Most of these have a type of movement and a direction, such as letting you choose whether something flies in from the left, right, top, or bottom. The types of movement are:

➤ *Appear* makes the object just appear into place.

➤ *Fly* makes the object move into place quickly.

➤ *Blinds* reveal the object as if you were opening venetian blinds in front of it.

➤ *Box* shows the object from the edges to the center (*in*) or from the center to the edges (*out*).

➤ *Checkerboard* treats the object as a bunch of little squares and wipes each square into place.

135

➤ *Crawl* is the same as Fly, only slower.

➤ *Dissolve* treats the object as small squares, which appear in random order.

➤ *Flash* makes the object appear, disappear, and reappear in the same spot.

➤ *Peek* moves the object in from the edge of the object's box.

➤ *Random Bars* puts up lines from the object until it is whole.

➤ *Spiral* brings the object moving onto the screen along a spiral path, getting larger as it does.

➤ *Split* starts showing the object in its horizontal or vertical center, then spreads out to the edges.

➤ *Stretch* starts with the object squished small and grows it until it's full size.

➤ *Strips* reveals the object starting from one corner and heading to its opposite corner.

➤ *Swivel* causes the object to repeatedly grow and shrink from side to side, making it look as though it was a flat item suspended by a string.

➤ *Wipe* starts revealing the object from one edge and spreads to the opposite edge.

➤ *Zoom* makes the object grow (*in*) or shrink (*out*) into place, making it look like it's moving toward or away from the viewer.

There are two other choices on this menu. Choosing **No Effect** means that no animation takes place, and choosing **Random Effects** means that the computer gets to pick which effect is done, and may choose differently each time the slide is shown.

Action Words

Folks in the presentation business refer to animations where the text is moving as *moves* and animation where the text appears in place as *reveals*.

What Does a Dissolve Sound Like, Anyway?

The field below the Effect field lets you pick the sound that goes along with the animation. If you want it to be silent, pick **[No Sound]**. Otherwise, you can pick one of the sounds listed, or you can pick **Other Sound** (the last option on the list), which will display a list of sound files for you to select from. However, unless you've created your own sound file, there won't be anything interesting for you to pick. (I'll tell you about creating your own sounds in Chapter 17, "Sound Advice on Sound.")

After the Thrill Is Gone

Eventually, the animation is over, and the object is where it's supposed to be. Now, you can just leave it lying there, you can make it disappear, or you can change its color. The After Animation field on the **Effects** tab lets you pick what happens.

To just leave the object lying there, like wrapping paper on Christmas, click on the drop-down menu and select **Don't Dim**. To make it disappear immediately, select **Hide After Animation**. To have it wait until the next mouse click and then disappear, select **Hide On Next Mouse Click**.

Also on the menu is a bunch of colors, and a choice to let you pick even **More Colors**. Choosing these will make your object change color after the animation.

Changing the object's color sounds like a pretty weird thing to do, and in many cases, it is. If you choose a color, the whole object changes to that color. If you do this to a picture, you end up with just a rectangle of color—unless the picture has an invisible color, which will stay invisible, so you are left with a picture-shaped blob.

But changing the color of text after it appears can be pretty cool. If you are animating a list (and I'll get to how to animate text in a second), this lets you bring up one point, show it, then make it dim while the next point comes up. This way, the current point is always brightest on the screen, while the previous points are still visible!

Nifty Disappearing Tricks

If you want the disappearance of an object to be an event, don't make it disappear at all! Instead, cover the object with a rectangle the same color as the background. Animate this rectangle into place just after you animate the object into place. For example, if you Dissolve the rectangle, it looks like the object is dissolving away!

By changing black text to gray after animation, the most recently animated text stands out.

Moving Words: Words of Motion (Not Emotion)

There are a number of special settings that apply only to objects with text, whether they are titles, text boxes, or text that's connected to a shape or picture. These are available in the Introduce text area of the Effects tab on the Custom Animation dialog box.

The Introduce Text list revealed!

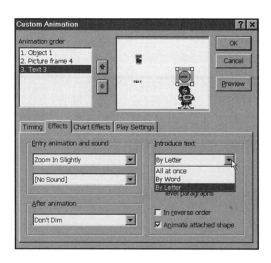

The first field here is a drop-down menu that lets you select how much text is introduced at a time. Your choices are:

➤ *By Letter* animates on the first letter, then the second letter, then the third, and so on.

➤ *By Word* brings on the whole first word in one animated step, then the second, and so on.

➤ *All At Once* sounds like it should bring the text on all at once, right? Well, that's true if your text is only one paragraph. It really should be called *By Paragraph*, since it brings on the first paragraph, then the second, and so on.

If you check the **In Reverse Order** checkbox, the final letter, word, or paragraph will appear first, then each preceding one until it reaches the first. If you have people in your company who think backwards—Admit it! You do!—then this is good for giving presentations to them.

The **Grouped By** field is used with the All At Once option to decide whether you display sub-lists (a list under a paragraph or list item) as separate paragraphs, or as part of the main paragraph. If you want to treat them as part of the main paragraph, use the up and down arrows to select **1st**. If you want the sub-list treated as their own paragraph, choose **2nd**. If you want sub-sub-lists treated separately, choose **3rd**.

Check the **Animate Attached Shape** checkbox if the text is on a shape object, and you want the object zoomed in just as the text is. Otherwise, the shape will be on the slide from the very beginning, waiting for the text to appear.

Moving Up the Chart: Chart Effects

In the world of PowerPoint objects, charts are the privileged class with their own tab on the Custom Animation dialog box. This is for graph-type charts; lowly organizational charts need not apply.

Select the **Chart Effects** tab to decide which parts of the charts get animated. If you check the **Animate Grid and Legend** checkbox, the grid and legend appear at the start of the animation, and the datasheet appears at the end. If you don't check either, those things are on-screen from when the slide first appears.

Chart Animations
The ability to animate the elements of a chart is new for PowerPoint 97.

The things that really get animated on your graph are the bars, points, lines, or however you present your data. The drop-down **Introduce Chart Elements** list lets you pick what order the data appears in. The choices are:

➤ *All at Once* animates them all at once.

➤ *By Series* animates all the same colored data at once.

➤ *By Category* animates the data from left to right, a group at a time.

➤ *By Element in Series* animates each of the first color, from left to right, then goes on to the next color, and so on.

➤ *By Element in Category* animates each piece of data, from left to right, one at a time.

The other settings on the Chart Effects tab are the same as settings on the Effects tab, letting you pick the animation style, sound, and what happens to the data after being animated.

Chart Choices

Bar-style charts look good using a Wipe in the direction that the bar is going (right for bar charts, up for column charts). It makes it look like the bar is growing to the data point. Similarly, line charts look best with a Wipe Right, making it look like the line is being drawn.

This chart is being animated by series, with a Wipe Up. The East series has already appeared, and now the West series is growing to its points.

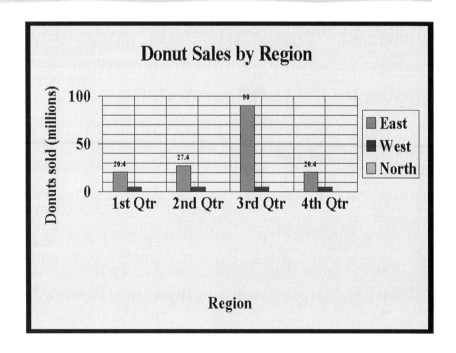

Checking the Animation

To test your animation while still using the Custom Animation dialog box, just click on the **Preview** button. The preview box will show all the animation for the slide, straight through, without waiting for any mouse clicks.

When you're happy with what you've got, click on the **OK** button to make the changes official, then go into the Slide Show View to see it at work full size.

Hey! What about the other tab?

The Play Settings tab on the Custom Animation dialog box is used when displaying video (movies) in your presentation. As such, the information on that's just down the block a few pages, in Chapter 16, "Movies in PowerPoint: Like TV, Only Smaller."

The Least You Need to Know

➤ To quickly animate an object, select it in Slide View, pull down the **Slide Show** menu, and select one of the animation styles listed in the **Preset Animation** sub-menu.

➤ The **Slide Show, Animation Preview** command opens up a small window on your screen. Click on this window to see the slide's animation.

➤ PowerPoint can animate only one object at a time.

➤ To get more control over animation effects, select **Custom Animation** from the **Slide Show** menu to get the Custom Animation dialog box.

➤ To select what object's animation you're working on, click on the object name in either the Animation Order list (if it's already animated) or the Slide Objects Without-out Animation list (if it isn't). The latter list is on the Timing tab, and you should click the **Animate** radio button to move the selected item up to the Animation Order list.

➤ When viewing a Slide Show, you may have to click the mouse button after an object is animated to start the next object. The lower right of the Timing tab is used to set if the slide show waits for a mouse click before animating, or if it waits a fixed period of time.

➤ The left side of the Effects tab lets you select the animation style, the accompanying sound, and what happens to the object after animated. The right side has special controls for text animation, letting you pick the order in which the text appears.

Chapter 15

Tricky Transitions and Terrific Timing

In This Chapter

➤ Pick how one slide disappears and the next one appears

➤ Set a sound to go with the slide change

➤ Set the slides to change automatically after a fixed amount of time, thus saving much wear and tear on the mouse button

➤ Twiddle your thumbs like a professional

You see transitions all the time on television, it's how they get from one scene to another. Sometimes you just see one shot, then the next shot. That's a transition, although a boring one. When the commercial ends and the screen is black for a moment before the Enterprise fades into view, that's a transition. When the Love Boat anchor slides up the screen and suddenly we're in the Captain's quarters, that's a transition. When a checker-board pattern comes over Ralph Malph's face and when the pattern goes back, we're at Pinky Tuscadero's demolition derby, that's a transition. When Tom Hanks puts on a dress to masquerade as "Buffy," that's… well, actually, that's transvestitism, which is different.

Transitions: What They Are, Why You Want Them, and How You Get Them

Each slide on a presentation has a transition associated with it, which tells PowerPoint how to change the display *from* the previous slide *to* this slide. If you want to set the transition *from* this slide *to* the next slide, do it on the next slide!

When it comes time to work out your transitions, use the Slide Sorter view. This way, you can see the slide you're working on as well as the next slide, and you can easily hop from slide to slide to set the transitions.

From Slide Sorter view, right-click the slide whose transition you want to set, and select the **Slide Transition** command on the shortcut menu. A Slide Transition dialog box appears, full of all sorts of meaningful things, plus a dog (or, at least, a picture of one).

The Slide Transition dialog box. The dog, like most dogs, doesn't mean anything.

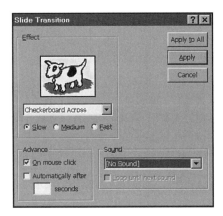

Transition Decision

The menu to select the type of transition that you want is directly under the dog, which may not be the cleanest of places to be. Click on the arrow, and you'll find a list of different transition styles, many of which have a choice of direction (such as Cover Up and Cover Right, which are the same style with two different directions). Some of these styles are similar to animation styles. The styles available are:

➤ *No Transition* means that the slide just appears in place, with no special effects.

➤ *Blinds* replaces the slide as if the new slide was on opening venetian blinds behind the old one.

➤ *Box* replaces the old slide from the edges to the center (*in*) or from the center to the edges (*out*).

144

➤ *Checkerboard* treats the slide as a bunch of little squares and wipes each square into place.

➤ *Cover* makes it look like this slide is being slid across in front of the old one.

➤ *Cut* is the same as No Transition.

➤ *Cut through Black* replaces the old slide with a black slide for an instant, then puts up the new slide. The black isn't really visible, but this may look a little better than just Cut on projection screens.

➤ *Dissolve* treats the new slide as a lot of little squares that it displays one at a time.

➤ *Fade through Black* makes the old slide fade away until it's completely black, then the black fades into the new slide. (This is a good way to mark the end of one topic and the start of another one.)

➤ *Random Bars* puts up short lines from the slide until it is whole.

➤ *Split* treats the new slide as two halves, wiping in opposite directions.

➤ *Strip* is a diagonal wipe.

➤ *Uncover* makes it look like the old slide is being pulled away to reveal the new one.

➤ *Wipe* replaces the slide a bit at a time, moving from one side to the other.

➤ *Random Transition* will randomly pick a style and direction each time the transition takes place.

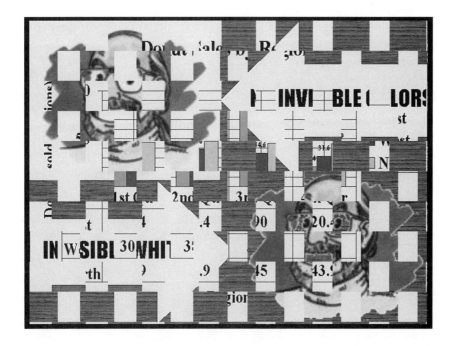

The Checkerboard Across transition is starting to reveal a slide with a graph.

When you select the transition you want, the picture of the dog turns into a picture of a key, allowing you to preview the type of transition that you selected. Exactly what this presentation is that involves a dog and a key, I cannot tell you. Select another transition, and the dog replaces the key.

Handy Transition List

The Slide Sorter toolbar has a handy drop-down list of the transition types, letting you pick the style of transition for a slide quickly. If you don't see this toolbar, pull down the **View** menu, and from the **Toolbars** menu select **Slide Sorter**.

Slow Change or Fast Change

Below the transition style field is a set of radio buttons, which let you choose between **Slow**, **Medium**, and **Fast**. This sets how quickly the transition takes place. When you select one of these, the dog/key transition takes place again at that speed.

Something Not to Use

Below the transition Effect area is a set of checkboxes that let you set whether the program waits for the user to click before showing this slide, or whether it just waits until a selectable number of seconds after the last slide is done. You can set these things here if you want—but you don't want. Leave it set to waiting for the mouse click. I'll show you a better trick for setting the waiting time later in the chapter. (I'm teaching you all the powerful tricks. Remember to use them for good, not for evil.)

Listen to the Transition

Using the Sound area of the dialog box, you can pick a sound to accompany the transition. Click on the drop-down arrow and select a sound from the ones listed, or select **Other Sound** to bring up a file browser that will let you find the sound file you want. (For information on creating your own sound files, see Chapter 17, "Sound Advice on Sound.")

Once you've selected a sound, the **Loop until next sound** checkbox becomes clickable. If you click it, the sound will repeat like a kid wanting to know if he can get an ice cream cone, please please please please please please please? It will stop when another sound appears. (If you don't click it, the sound just plays once.)

(Dialog) Box Out

When you're done picking your transition settings, you can click the **Apply** button to use them on the selected slide, or you can pick **Apply to All** to use them on all the slides. Using the same settings on all the slides is not that bad an idea. Watching one different transition after another can get tiresome after a while and even distracts from the point you are presenting.

Sound Ceaser
All of the sound selectors include a choice called **Stop Previous Sound**. This lets you stop a repeating transition sound without starting a new one!

When you do this, the transition will quickly be displayed on the selected slide in the Slide Sorter view.

This symbol means this slide has a transition set.

Transition time

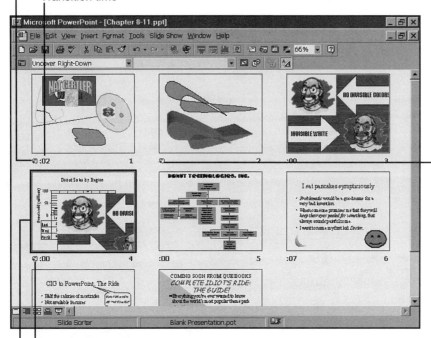

The Slide Sorter view gives you handy transition information at a glance.

This symbol means the slide has animation.

Slide has a transition, but no timing

Transition being demonstrated after closing dialog box.

Time for Timing!

Estimating time is not a human being's greatest ability. How many times has someone said to you "I'll be with you in a minute," only to take a vast number of minutes, combined into a large block of time? How many times were you supposed to get a date home by 11, but when you checked your watch, it had suddenly become next Tuesday? How many times have you opened the door just as someone was about to knock? That has nothing to do with the topic at hand, but man, is that spooky!

Trying to estimate how long it will take you to present a slide, or how long you need between animations on a single slide, is tricky when you're just staring at some dialog box. That's the main reason for the *Rehearse Timings* feature. (That, and they wanted a feature name that's an anagram for *Her Steaming Sire*, which is what you often have to face if you say you're going to bring your young date home at 11 and bring her back next Tuesday instead.)

Running the Timer

To set your timings, pull down the **Slide Show** menu, and select **Rehearse Timings**. The slide show will start from the beginning. However, once the first slide is up, you'll see one difference from a normal slide show: a Rehearsal control panel.

Rehearse Timings mode.

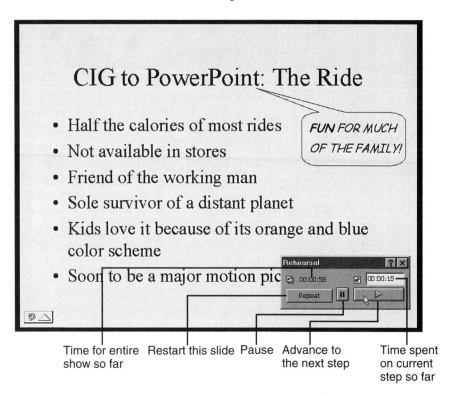

Time for entire show so far   Restart this slide   Pause   Advance to the next step   Time spent on current step so far

When your slide comes up, stare at it for as long as you want it to appear in your show, then click on the **Advance** button. If you're planning to talk while you show your presentation to people, give your talk while doing this—that will let you know how long to wait. If you're counting on someone else seeing the presentation and reading the content to themselves, try reading it yourself, out loud, slowly, and use that to determine when it's time to move on.

Make a Whoopsy?

If you mess up in giving your speech, reading it out loud, or you want to restart the slide for some other reason, just click on the **Repeat** button. The timing will start over from the beginning of the slide, so you can keep doing it until you get it right.

When Your Good Time Is Over

When you've run through the entire presentation, the Rehearsal control pad goes away. If your last slide is still showing, click once on it. A dialog box will appear, telling you how long your whole presentation was, and asking Do you want to record the new slide timings and use them when you view the slide show? Click on **Yes**, and all the transition and animation timings will be set!

You will then get a dialog box asking you if you want to review the timings in the Slide Sorter view. Click on the **Yes** button to return to the slide sorter view.

Mixing Untimed in with Timed

If you want most of your presentation to be timed, but a few things to wait for a mouse click, go ahead and use the Rehearse Timings feature, then go back and reset the slides you want to pause by selecting.

The Least You Need to Know

➤ A transition is the method used to move from one slide to another. Transition settings include the way the replacement is animated, the sound that accompanies it, and whether it takes a mouse click or waiting a period of time to trigger it.

➤ To set the transition settings for a slide, go into Slide Sorter view, right-click on the slide, and select **Slide Transition**.

➤ Pull down the drop-down menu under the dog to select a transition style. The transition style will be displayed using the dog picture and a key picture.

➤ It's best to leave the **On Mouse Click** checkbox checked, and set the screen timings using the Rehearse Timings feature.

➤ To set the time lags on all of your slides, as well as on the animations, select the **Slide Show**, **Rehearse Timing** command.

➤ Step through your slide show using the **Advance** arrow button on the Rehearse control panel. However long you wait before advancing, that's how long the wait will be when the slide show is playing.

Chapter 16

Movies in PowerPoint: Like TV, Only Smaller

In This Chapter

➤ Get (or even make) a movie clip to put on your slide

➤ Move the movie clip you got (or even made) onto your slide

➤ Start and stop the movie clip you got (or even made)

Movies are very useful. These on-screen bits (often referred to as *video*) are great for showing things that move, like trains or chimps. Or, if the camera making the movie moves, you can use it to show all the sides of something that doesn't move, like mountains or Uncle Oswald. You could hold the camera still and shoot video of something that doesn't move, but then you'd probably be better off just using a normal photograph or, in the case of Uncle Oswald, not using anything at all.

Some Warnings About Movies

Before you start gearing up to fill your presentation with movies, you have to be aware of the problems with it. These won't be big problems if you're doing this on your own computer, but they will be big problems if you want to use this presentation on someone else's.

Problem One: Moving Movies

Even though the movies in presentations seem small, only taking up a part of the screen and a few seconds of time, they're very big on your disk. One ten second clip can sometimes fill up a floppy. Five minutes of video that only take up a tenth of the screen will take someone using a modem over an hour to download. The files are big. This can be a problem even if you aren't trying to move it to someone else's machine, since your hard disk may only have so much space on it.

Problem Two: Projector Problems

In the same way as a Beta tape won't fit in a VHS player, or a 35 millimeter film won't fit in a 16 millimeter projector, or a new trick won't fit an old dog, your movie may not be

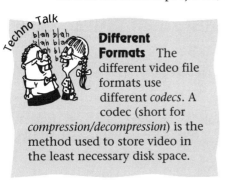

Techno Talk

Different Formats The different video file formats use different *codecs*. A codec (short for *compression/decompression*) is the method used to store video in the least necessary disk space.

able to play on someone else's machine. This is because they don't have the computer equivalent of the "right projector," which would be the right *driver*. A driver is a program that tells the computer how to deal with a certain device or a certain type of file. In this case, the driver tells the computer how to understand the movie file. Since there are many different movie file formats, there are many different drivers, and most computers won't have them all installed. If you use the Video For Windows format, most PCs that are set up for multimedia will be able to understand it. (You can recognize a Video For Windows file because of the .avi at the end of the file name.) If your file uses one of the other formats, however, the odds are good that someone else's PC won't have a driver for it.

Slow-Go Is a No-no

Computers with slow processors or without high-quality video cards can process video very slowly. This can mean either a movie that looks like it's in slow-motion, or a movie that looks very jerky because a lot of the individual pictures that make up the movie (the *frames*) are being skipped over. If you have such a machine yourself, you'll see the problem quickly. If you have a good machine but share your presentation with someone who has a bad machine, then he'll see the problem.

Mommy, Where Do Movies Come from?

The stork doesn't bring movie files, unfortunately. Even if he did, it would probably just be movies about things that interest storks, such as migrating, eating fish, or the New York Stork Exchange. If you want people-interesting movies, you have basically three choices: buying them, getting them for free, or making them yourself.

Buying Movies for Less Fun and Less Profit

Just as there are clip-art disks full of pictures, there are also disks full of movies (and ones with some movies, some pictures, some sounds—a multimedia smorgasbord). There aren't as many of these out there, however, and they are of limited usefulness. Check out the contents of any such disk before you buy it to make sure that it has what you need on it; because movies take up so much room, they can't put something-for-all-occasions on it the way they *try* to do with some of the picture disks.

At best, though, this can only get you a fairly generic shot. You may be able to get a short clip of planes flying, or a flower growing, or an animation of the earth rotating, but if you want a specific plane, or a specific flower, or a specific earth, your odds of finding it are slim.

Free Movies: Two of My Favorite Words, Together

Movies are digital files, and if there are ones to be had, you'd figure they would be out on the Internet. You'd be right, but there aren't nearly so many movies as you might expect. People aren't using a lot of movies in their Web pages, because they're so slow to transfer. There are only two sorts of movies that are really plentiful out there, and you can't really use either of them. The first type is, umm, "adult" movies, and while those do get attention, they're generally not appropriate in presentations. The other is clips from TV shows, movies, and music videos, and these are frequently made by people who have the equipment to make them, but not the legal rights to them. Don't use these—your *presen*tation might turn into a *prison*tation!

Microsoft offers some useful ClipArt movies that you can get over the Web. Pull down the **Insert** menu, and from the **Movies and Sounds** submenu, select **Movie from Gallery**. The Clip Gallery dialog box will open, with the Videos tab already selected for you. Click on the button with the picture of the Earth. (If a message appears letting you know that you're going to be using the Internet; click OK to answer it.) Your Web browser will open bringing up Clip Gallery Live, a site for free pictures, sounds, and videos. There will be a link there offering first-time users help on using this Web site. Click on this link, and you'll be guided through finding and getting what you want based on the type of media you want (video, of course) and the category.

> **Shortcut to the Gallery** Click on the **Insert Clip Art** button on the standard toolbar to open up the Clip Gallery.

You'll only be able to see smaller, simplified versions of the videos before downloading them. The Microsoft videos are mostly short cartoons, good for humorous highlights that you can use with business topics.

The Videos tab of the ClipArt gallery displays the first frame of each movie in the gallery.

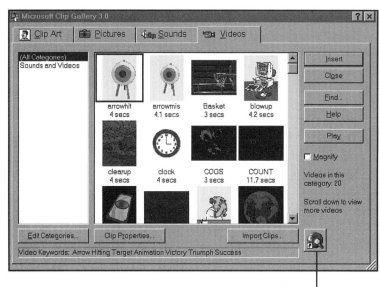

Click here if you want to get clips from the Web.

Once you've downloaded the clip, it will be added to your ClipArt gallery on the Videos tab, handy for not only PowerPoint but also other Microsoft applications.

Movie Making: You Can Become You-Nited Artists!

If you have a camcorder, you can shoot whatever movie you need. So you've got the perfect movie that you want, but it's on video tape, not in the computer. How do you get it in there? Well, you could tear the tape out of the cartridge and stuff it into your floppy drive slot—but all you'll end up with is a stuffed-up floppy drive.

What you really need is a *video capture card*, a device you install in your computer that you can connect to your VCR. The card takes the signal coming from the VCR and converts it into a movie file. Video capture cards cost anywhere from a couple hundred dollars up into the thousands. The cheaper ones can only make smaller movies that use up a small part of the screen, but that may be all you want anyway!

If you just want to make movies of things around your desk, particularly if you want to show yourself talking to the presentation viewers, you can get by with a simple digital video camera. For about $100 for black and white, $250 for color, you can get a Connectix QuickCam, which connects to your printer port and lets you create small movies. These little cameras are a lot of fun, particularly if you like watching yourself on the screen while you work! (They're also really handy for video teleconferencing.)

Self-portrait: a QuickCam digital video camera films itself in a mirror.

Compu-Toons

You can also create your own computer animated movies! Most of the time people talk about computer animation, they are talking about things like *Toy Story*, where entire 3-D worlds are designed on a computer, and then the computer generates films of things moving in that world. This sort of animation is called *modeling*, and to do it you will need some modeling software with animation capabilities (such as *TrueSpace* or *Ray Dream Studio*). Don't expect to do anything as complicated as *Toy Story* unless you have a lot of computers, a lot of friends, a lot of time, and a lot of talent, but there are plenty of examples of nice short pieces done by one person with some spare time.

Another type of computer animation is *morphing*, which involves changing the shape of things on a picture or turning one object into another. If you've seen one of those ads where a cow turns into a glass of milk, or an unshaved man turns into a shaggy dog, or a car turns into an alley, then you've seen morphing at work. It's not that hard to learn to use a morphing program well enough to take a photo of yourself and give yourself pointed Spock ears, and it's only a little harder to use it to make a movie of your ears growing the points on them.

Finally, there are a number of programs that let you use the computer to create more traditional animation, combining a series of individual drawings into a movie.

Adding a Movie

To insert a movie onto your slide, go into Slide View and slide the view where you want the movie to start. (As you'll see soon, you can have a movie run over several slides.) Pull down the **Insert** menu and select the **Movies and Sounds** submenu. There, you'll see two commands that let you insert movies. **Movie from Gallery** opens up the ClipArt gallery to the Videos tab, where you can select any movie that's already on the Videos tab by double-clicking on it. **Movie from File** opens up a file browser, letting you pick any video file from any of the disks in your system. Double-click on the file name to add it to your slide.

When you do this, the first frame of your movie appears on your slide. As with any box, you can click on it to see the sizing handles or to drag it.

Resizing Your Movie

Don't.

As with a picture, the movie appears at its *natural size*. Making a movie larger won't make it any more detailed, it will just look grainy and may display more slowly. Making a movie smaller will lose detail and won't speed it up at all.

Having said that, you can resize it if you really want to. Just use the sizing handles.

Roll the Picture: Interactive Activation

There are three ways that the movie can start playing. You can have it start playing when the viewer clicks on it, when the mouse passes over it, or automatically. ("Mouse passes over" should not be confused with "mouse's passover," which is a holiday for Jewish mice.)

To have a click or a mouse pass-over start it, right-click on the movie and select the **Action Settings** command. The Action Settings dialog box appears, with separate tabs for Mouse Click and Mouse Over settings. Select **Object Action** on the appropriate tab. The drop-down menu under that option will now be usable, but since **Play** is the only choice on that menu, it will already be selected for you.

Go to the other tab and make sure that **None** is selected, so that you don't have conflicting settings.

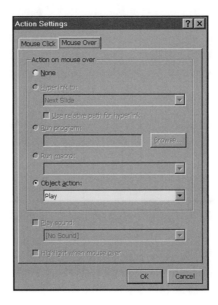

Most of the action settings are designed for other types of objects. Your choices for movies are to either play or not play.

Roll the Picture: Activation Automation

As if the overworked Custom Animation dialog box didn't already have enough to do, it's stuck with the automatic control of movies. To bring up the dialog box, right-click on the movie and select **Custom Animation**. The dialog box opens, with the Play Settings tab selected for you.

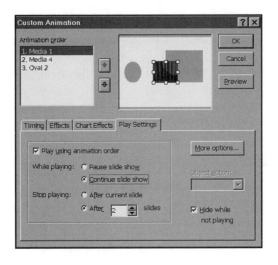

Use the Timing tab to set when the animation starts, and the Play Settings tab to set when it stops.

Click on the **Play Using Animation Order** checkbox to show that you want the animation controls to start the movie. Click on the **Timing** tab, and you can select **On Mouse Click** (which starts the movie on the next mouse click after the previous object was animated), or **Automatically**, which starts the movie a fixed number of seconds after the last object was animated. To see more about how these work, check out Chapter 14, "Look Up in the Sky: Flying Text and Pictures." (That chapter also tells you how to arrange the animation order, which it affects when your movie starts if you also have animated objects on the page. It also has moving prose, scintillating illustrations, and lots of punctuation!)

Animating Movies Works... Sort Of

You can use the Effects tab to set how the movie appears onto your slide. However, only the first frame gets animated. When the animation is done, then the movie starts playing.

When Will It Ever End?!

Clicking back on the **Play Settings** tab lets you set how long the movie keeps playing. If you select **Pause Slide Show**, the next slide won't show up until this movie is done. (Animations can still continue while this goes on. If you want, you can animate pieces of popcorn flying at the screen while the movie is showing, just like a real movie! However, anything you animate will pass *behind* the movie area, never *in front* of it.)

Choosing **Continue Slide Show** lets you pick one of two Stop Playing choices. Choosing **After Current Slide** means that the movie is stopped when it's time for the next slide. If the slide isn't over, tough luck for it! Choosing **After (number field) Slides** will wait until not only this slide is finished, but however many more slides you enter into the number field. That's right, the slides will go away, but the movie will just keep playing, like some demented dinner guest who decides to stay for the week whether you like it or not!

After the Movie Is Over

The Play Settings tab has a **Hide While Not Playing** checkbox which will make the movie appear only once it starts playing, rather than having the opening frame displayed while waiting for it to play.

There's also a button marked **More Options**, which is about as uninformative as a button name can possibly be. Click on it, and the **Play Options** dialog box appears.

*If kids had a Play Options dialog box, you could turn on **Go play outside** and turn off **Play video games**!*

This dialog box has two checkboxes. Check on **Loop Until Stopped**, and the movie will repeat over and over until something stops it (such as moving to the next slide). This is handy if you have a movie that's designed to repeat, like a cartoon of someone juggling where repeating it makes it looks like he keeps juggling. It's also good for driving the viewer nuts, if you have a movie that is annoying or distracting.

Play Options Shortcut To get to the Play Options quickly at any time, right-click on the movie in Slide View and select **Edit Movie Object**.

The **Rewind Movie When Done Playing** checkbox has a goofy name. After all, the movie is a file, so what is there to rewind? Is it going to make your hard disk spin backwards? No, actually if you check this, the first frame of the movie will be shown after the movie is over. If you don't check it, the last frame shows.

Movie by Design: Slides with Built-In Movie Space

There are a couple of AutoLayout slide designs that include a place for a movie. You'll find these designs by clicking on the **New Slide** button and scrolling toward the bottom of the AutoLayout display. These layouts have a picture of a movie *clapper*, that hinged board that someone claps in front of the camera before they shoot each scene of a movie. (The purpose of this is to scare the bejeebers out of anyone on the set who isn't paying attention.)

If you double-click on the media clip area of the slide, PowerPoint will act the same as if you issued the **Insert, Movies and Sounds, Movie from File** command, and when you select your movie, it will appear in the Media Clip space.

This slide suggests you double-click to insert a media clip, but it really means "movie."

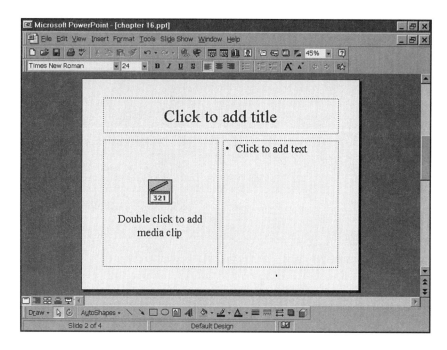

The Least You Need to Know

➤ PowerPoint can play movie files of a number of different formats, but if you want your presentation to run on other machines, you're best off with the Video For Windows format (.avi files).

➤ There are a lot of existing movies in formats that PowerPoint can read. You can also transfer movies from video tape using a *video capture card*, or record movies directly onto your hard disk using a *digital video camera*. There is also software that lets you make computer-animated movies.

➤ To insert a movie file onto your slide, use the **Insert, Movies and Sounds, Movie from File** command. To use a movie file from the ClipArt gallery, use the **Insert, Movies and Sounds, Movie from Gallery** command. Click the Earth button in the ClipArt gallery to copy free movies from Microsoft's Web site into the gallery.

➤ To have a mouse click start the movie, right-click on the movie in Slide View, select **Action Settings**, pick the **Mouse Click** tab on the dialog box that appears, and select **Object Action**.

➤ In the Custom Animation dialog box, selecting the **Timing** tab lets you select when the movie starts, and the **Play Settings** tab lets you set when the movie ends.

➤ On the Play Settings tab, choosing **Pause Slide Show** means the slide won't be over until the movie ends. Choosing **Continue Slide Show** lets you choose between stopping the movie when the slide ends, or continuing the movie on to other slides.

Chapter 17

Sound Advice on Sound

In This Chapter

➤ Record your own sounds

➤ Add sound effects to your animations, transitions, and button presses, until your presentation is cacophonous!

➤ Record a narration to accompany your presentation

➤ Play sounds right off of a CD to accompany your presentation

Sound can take many forms, and serve many purposes. There's music, whose charms have been noted for their savage beast-ensoothement properties. There is the spoken word, which is so powerful that it can cause a war, or stop one. There are the sounds of nature, like the whipping of the wind, the crackling of the fire, and the chirp of the cricket, all of which reminds us of the beauty and wonder around us. And there is the din of the loose computer fan which has been rattling for sixteen chapters now and it won't go away, no, won't go away until it's driven me mad! But I won't let it, for my invisible friend Jojo and I have crafted a plan...

Things to Spend Money On: Your PC Sound System

In order to use sound in your presentations, you're going to need a computer that can play sound. Otherwise, all you hear is the unending torture of the rattling computer fan that we can prove, yes prove, is under the command of the CIA.

These days, most PCs are sold as being *multimedia ready*, which means that the sound system is already built in. If you're not so lucky, you can add one. What you need is a *sound card*, which the computer uses to create and shape the sound, plus some computer speakers (or, if you don't want everyone to hear, a pair of headphones will do fine). You can get these things as a kit for under $100, and then all you need is a few spare hours to install the card and its software, much of which will be spent cursing because while it's supposed to be easy to do, it rarely works out that way.

If you're recording your own sounds, you'll also need a microphone. There's a microphone connector in the back of your sound card. There's also a *line in* connector, which you can connect to your stereo if you want to record something from there.

If you're going to be playing CD audio, you'll need a CD-ROM drive, and it will have to be properly connected to your sound card—which it probably is if you bought a multimedia system. (If you install your own sound card, you'll just have finished putting your whole system back together when you first notice the cable that's supposed to connect the CD-ROM drive to the sound card.)

Recording: Yes, You Really Do Sound Like That

To record your own sound, whether it be a short speech extolling your product or capturing the sound of a whirring fan to use as evidence of a CIA plot, you're going to have to tell PowerPoint that you're inserting the sound onto a slide. This might be a lie; you might be using the sound as part of an animation or transition, which is different than making it part of the slide itself. However, PowerPoint doesn't get mad if you lie to it.

To start off, pull down the **Insert** menu, and from the **Movies and Sounds** submenu, select **Record Sound**. The Record Sound dialog box appears, with a simple set of recording controls.

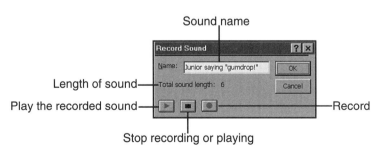

The recording buttons have a triangle, a square, and a circle—simple, yet meaningless symbols.

Sound name

Length of sound

Play the recorded sound

Stop recording or playing

Record

Get your microphone in position and click on **Record** to start the recording. When you're done, click on the **Stop** button, then on the **Play** button to check your sound. If you don't like it, click on **Cancel** and start over (but you'll never sound as good as you do in your own head). If you do like it, type a name for your sound into the name field, then click on the **OK** button.

A sound icon, a little picture of a speaker, will appear on the slide. If you keep this picture in your presentation, when the user clicks on it, he will hear the recording. (In fact, if you double-click it in Slide View, you'll hear the sound.) There are other ways you can start the sound playing in the slide show, which I'll show you soon. And you can hear the sound while you're in slide view just by double-clicking on this!

Check This Out...

Sound Sound Bad?

Adjust how loud and how good your recordings will be by clicking the **Start** button and selecting **Control Panel** from the **Settings** submenu. Double-click on the **Multimedia** icon in the window that appears. The lower half of the **Audio** tab controls recording. The higher the sound quality you choose, the more disk space is used. Telephone Quality is the lowest quality, and Radio Quality is better. Even setting it to **CD Quality** (the highest setting) won't make up for the fact that you're recording on a cheap microphone in the middle of an office, though.

Slammin' Down That Slide Sound

There are a number of ways that you can set up the sound to start playing. You can have it so that the user clicks on a sound icon to hear it, or the user clicks on something else to hear it, or it plays automatically during the transition, animation, or some other point during the display of the slide. You can make it play all of those times, causing an awful and annoying din!

Click on the Speaker Picture

To have the user click on the picture of the speaker to hear the sound, you really don't have to do anything except move the picture where you want it to be. It's already set up to wait for the mouse click.

You can do anything to that speaker picture that you can do to a normal picture, including resizing it.

Sound Tricks You've Already Learned

If you've read certain earlier chapters of this book, you've already seen a drop-down list of sound effects that you can select sounds from in certain cases. The sound you have just recorded is automatically added to that list, so you can select it when choosing your sound.

These uses include:

➤ Having the sound go off when a certain object is clicked on, or having it go off when the mouse passes over that object. To see how to do this, read Chapter 13, "Click Here for Interactivity."

➤ A sound effect accompanying an animation. This information is in Chapter 14, "Look Up in the Sky: Flying Text and Pictures."

➤ A transition sound effect. Check out Chapter 15, "Tricky Transitions and Terrific Timing."

If you're using the sound for any one of these, you aren't going to need the speaker picture. Click on it and hit the **Delete** key to get rid of it!

Playing the Sound Automatically

You can use the animation features to trigger the sound automatically, as part of the slide's sequence. To do this, you need to still have the speaker picture... but dagnabbit, you really don't want the speaker showing up on your slide! Is there some bizarre incantation or arcane ritual that will rid you of it?

No need to switch to some antique religion! Just drag the speaker off the slide, and leave it either to the right or the left of the slide. You'll still see it in slide view, but it won't show up on the Slide Show!

To set when the sound will appear, right-click on the speaker picture and select **Custom Animation**. That's right, this all-purpose command can trigger your sound as well!

Click on the **Timing** tab on the Custom Animation dialog box, then select **Animate** and **Automatically**. Use the up and down arrow keys to move the sound through the order of things being animated.

On the **Play Settings** tab, click on the **Play using animation order** checkbox, and the options below it will become selectable. This lets you set when the sound ends. The sound will end automatically when the sound is over, of course, but you can tell the sound to shut up before that! Choosing **Pause Slide Show** means that the next slide will not automatically appear until after the sound is over. Choosing **Continue Slide Show** lets you choose between **After Current Slide** (which means that when this slide is over, the sound will stop) or **After (number field) Slides**, which means that the sound can keep going for the number of slides that you enter into the number field, and will then stop.

164

The Timing tab lets you select when the sound begins.

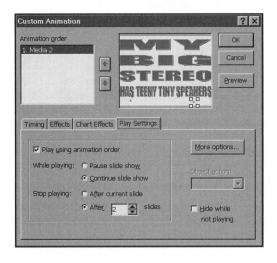

The Play Settings tab lets you select when the sound ends.

If you want the sound to keep repeating, click the **More Options** button on the Play Settings tab, click the **Loop Until Stopped** button, then on the **OK** button.

Using a Stored Sound

Sounds abound in this world, and you can't record them all yourself. Luckily, you can use any sound file on your system, or even one from your Clip gallery, as an automatic sound, giving you access to many more sounds.

To use a sound from a file, select **Insert, Movies and Sounds, Sound from File**, and then select the sound file using the file browser. To select a sound from the Clip gallery, select **Insert, Movies and Sounds, Sound from Gallery** and then double-click on the sound

165

you want. (And yes, you can click on the Earth button to download sounds from Microsoft's Web site into the gallery! You can get free boings, free clicks, free music... everything but free speech! It works much the same as downloading video clips, as described in Chapter 16, "Movies in PowerPoint: Like TV, Only Smaller")

All sounds look alike. Luckily, they have their names and their lengths under them, so we can tell them apart.

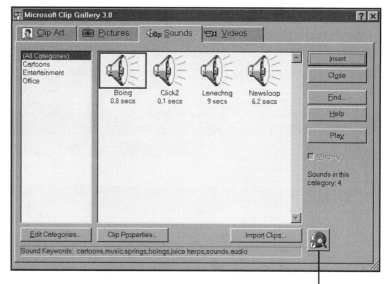

Click to get sounds from Microsoft Web site

CD: OK 4 U!

Your CD-ROM drive can be used for more than just a retractable donut caddy. It can also be used to play audio CDs, and PowerPoint takes advantage of that. You can play audio tracks in your presentations.

Check This Out...

No "Chipmunking" Your Music
Your CD-ROM drive may be double speed, quadruple speed, even 12-times speed... but audio CDs will still play at the normal speed (doggone it!)

Mostly, you'll be using this to add music to presentations. The CD-ROM drive may be quick, but it's a little too slow for use with things like sound effects. While many good sound effects CDs are available, the lag between the effect-triggering event and when the effect would actually start is just too long.

To add CD playing to a slide, first put the CD in your drive. Make sure that it's the CD you're going to have when you do the actual presentation; if you meant to have Wagner's "Flight of the Valkyrie" and instead use Grungemunch's new hit, "I Fell Off of Complete Idiot's Guide to PowerPoint the Ride and Fell in Love," it's not only going to confuse your audience, it can confuse your computer.

It will also confuse your computer if the CD is playing while you're trying to set this up. If you've got your system set to automatically start playing CDs when they're inserted, just hold down the **Shift** key while inserting it.

Once your CD is safely inside the CD-ROM drive, yank down the ever-popular **Insert** menu and, from the **Movies and Sounds** submenu, select the **Play CD Audio Track** command. The Play Options dialog box will appear. When we've seen this box before, most of it has been grayed out, but that won't be the case now.

The CD controls in the Play Options dialog box are usable when you want to control a CD. Of course.

You get to pick where on the CD to start playing, and where to stop. Every CD is broken down into numbered tracks, usually one track for each song. The fields here let you pick which number track to start on, where on that track to start (in minutes and seconds), what track number to end on, and where to end it. You can type in these numbers, or you can use the up and down arrow buttons at the end of each field to adjust them.

Always set the track number before you set the time, because whenever you change the track number, the time is reset, either to the beginning of the track (for the start time) or the end of the track (for the end time). You can set the time either in minutes and seconds, with a colon in between (such as 2:35) or just as seconds, with no colon (155). If you want to play a complete single track, just enter that track number as both the starting track and ending track.

You can have the selection repeat by clicking **Loop until stopped**. Once you're done setting things up, click on the **OK** button, and you'll see a CD picture on your slide. If you want to change the settings (if, for example, you set a time incorrectly), right-click on this picture and select **Edit Sound Object** to bring back the dialog box. (If you set *both* times incorrectly, that makes you a no-good two-timer!)

Starting the CD

You can cause the CD to be started by clicking on an object, passing over an object, or automatically. These things are done using the same instructions you use when using a sound.

Remember, you can't play more than one thing off of the CD simultaneously. You *can* play a CD track and a sound file at the same time. And, of course, the sound of a rattling, Illuminati-controlled fan can accompany any other sound, and haunt you no matter how far you get from the computer.

Narration: Sharing Your Snide Comments with the World

You can record a narration to go along with your presentation. This is really useful if your presentation is meant to be personally presented, but you need to make copies for people who aren't there. This way, they can get the advantages of your comments, your insights, and your ill-concealed belches.

There is a down side to using narration, however. Because PowerPoint can only handle one sound at a time, the rest of the sounds in your presentation won't be played when the narration is. Only the narration will be heard.

To record a narration, pull down the **Slide Show** menu and select **Record Narration**. This will pop open a Record Narration dialog box that will warn you about how much space you have left on your hard disk, and how much narration that will allow.

The Record Narration dialog box lets you know how long a narration you can store on your hard disk, so you know if you have to talkrealfast.

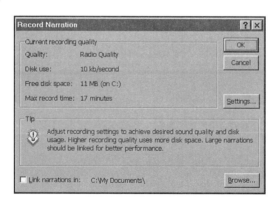

Now, your narration may not take up a lot of time, but it could eat up your disk space very quickly. There are two ways to deal with this: changing the quality of your recording, or storing your narration on a separate disk.

Degrade Yourself: Lowering the Audio Quality

To change the narration quality, click on the **Settings** button. This will bring up the Sound Selection dialog box, opened to the Audio tab. Open the Name drop-down list box and select one of the following options: CD Quality, Radio Quality, or Telephone Quality.

Now, CD Quality sounds like it's a good choice, but it takes up a lot of disk space. It really doesn't sound that much better than Radio Quality for voice recordings, and it takes up *twelve times* as much disk space. If you have enough disk space for half an hour of Radio Quality, it will hold less than three minutes of CD Quality. Practically, it's not worth it.

Radio Quality is good, and probably the best choice if people are listening on the same computer as you're recording it on. However, if you're hoping to send this presentation out on floppy disks, you'll want to use Telephone Quality... or be prepared to use a lot of floppies. While Radio Quality is noticeably better than Telephone, it takes up twice as much disk space.

Disk-o Dancing

PowerPoint tends to put everything into one big presentation file, which is really handy when it comes to moving the presentation from one system to another, but not really handy when it comes to making the most efficient use of a multi-disk system.

If you click on the **Link Narrations In** checkbox, PowerPoint will store your narration in separate files, one file for each slide. Click on the **Browse** button, and you'll see a standard file browser where you can select the disk drive and folder for the narration to be stored in. The identity of this location will be stored in the presentation file, so PowerPoint will know where to find it. (The file names will start with the presentation name, then have additional info, then end with a .WAV extension.)

Plenty of Disk Space? Link Anyway! Your narration will be read more smoothly if it's stored in a separate file.

Recording the Narration

Once you've settled on your settings, click on the button marked **OK** (which, as we all know, is short for Oklahoma, where narration has been honed to an art form). The Slide Show will start.

Record your narration by speaking into the microphone, clicking to advance the presentation as appropriate. Keep going through the entire presentation. Remember to breathe occasionally.

You may want to practice your narration a few times before recording, since if you mess up, you have to start all over again. However, you can pause the recording by right-clicking and selecting **Pause Narration**. Grab your lunch (or whatever you're pausing for), then right-click again and select **Resume Narration**.

Skip the Talk If you want to show your slide show without the narration that you recorded for it, select the **Slide Show, Setup Show** command and select the **Show without Narration** option.

Once you've gone through the entire presentation, a dialog box appears, letting you know that the narration has been saved, and asking you if you want to save the timings also. This is a great way of setting the timings for your slides, so that they go along well with the narration. Click the **Yes** button if you want to save them, and the **No** button if you don't.

If you choose **Yes**, another dialog box will appear, asking if you want to go to slide sorter view to view the times. Choosing Yes or No is up to you. You have free will. After all, the aliens aren't brainwashing *you* using subliminal messages hidden in the rattling of your computer fan.

The Least You Need to Know

➤ To record a sound, use the **Insert, Movies and Sounds, Record Sound** command. Press the **Record** button, record your sound, then press **Stop**.

➤ To use a pre-made sound from the Clip Gallery, use the **Insert, Movies and Sounds, Sound from Gallery** command, then double-click on a sound in the Gallery. The speaker picture appears on the slide.

➤ To use a pre-made sound file that's on your disk, use the **Insert, Movies and Sounds, Sound from File** command. Select a file using the file browser, and the speaker picture will appear on the slide.

➤ You can use sound on a standard CD by putting the CD in your CD-ROM drive and giving the **Insert, Movies and Sounds, Play CD Audio Track** command. In the dialog box, select which track to start playing, where in that track to begin, which track to finish with, and how far into that track to go, then click **OK**.

➤ To have the sound play automatically as part of the slide, drag the picture off the side of the slide, right-click on it, and select **Custom Animation**. Click on the **Play Using Animation Order** checkbox.

➤ To record a narration to go with your presentation, use the **Slide Show, Record Narration** command. A Record Narration dialog box appears. Click on the **OK** button when you're ready to start your narration. Speak into the microphone, while clicking the mouse to advance through your presentation.

Part 4
Sharing the Presentation with Others

A presentation is like Kissing Disease—it's not much fun until you share it with someone.

In this part, you'll learn to prepare your presentation for display, whether it's in print form, for computer display, for a real slide show, or even to put it out on the Web. And once you start showing it to others, you'll learn a lot, like how quickly other people can spot mistakes you miss.

Chapter 18

On Your Own Screen

In This Chapter

➤ Display the presentation on the computer that you set it up on

➤ Mark up the slides as you present it

➤ Show the slide show in a window

➤ Idiot-proof your presentation so you can leave it running as a kiosk without people messing up your computer

You've already designed the presentation. That's the fun part. You don't actually have to show it to anyone. You can take pride in your own work rather than seeking outside confirmation.

But then again, if you don't show it to anyone, then your boss doesn't pay you, or your customer doesn't buy your product, or the Complete Idiot's Guide Ride never gets built and you never make royalties off of it. Let's face it, pride is nice to have but so is money. It's hard to walk into a donut shop and say "I've got a lot of pride, so give me a dozen glazed."

Speaker Mode: Full-Screen Show-Off

It's your presentation, you're showing it to people, and dadgummit, you want to have full control over it. This is the time to show it in Speaker mode.

To tell PowerPoint you want this presentation to appear in speaker mode, yank down that **Slide Show** menu and select **Set Up Show**. The Set Up Show dialog box appears. Stare intently at it. You're going to get to know this dialog box quite well over the course of this chapter. Some day, it may save your life. But probably not.

Your control over how the Slide Show runs starts here in the Set Up Show dialog box. All those animations, narrations, and timings you spent time setting up, you can disable here!

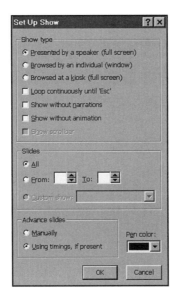

The very top selection in the dialog box is **Presented By a Speaker (full screen)**, and that's the one that you want to pick. Odds are that it is already selected, since that's what PowerPoint defaults to if you haven't selected anything else.

At the bottom of the dialog box under Advance Slides is a choice between advancing to the next slide Manually or Using Timings, If Present. When you're giving a presentation, odds are that you'll want to choose **Manually** (which means waiting for a mouse click), since you're there talking to people about each slide.

Click on the **OK** button, then pull down the **Slide Show** menu again and select **View Show** to get the show rolling!

The (Poorly) Hidden Menu

While the slide show is showing, the slides all look perfect and pristine, just the way you designed them... until you move the mouse. Then, not only does the pointer appear, but a little arrow design appears in the lower left of the screen. This is the hiding spot for the hidden menu. Click on it, and the menu appears. (You can also bring up the menu simply by right-clicking anywhere on the screen.)

The hidden shortcut menu has a wealth of tools for the presenting speaker.

Slipping Slideways: Moving to Another Slide

You don't need the menu to move you to the next slide; just click anywhere that doesn't have anything designed to be click on, and you'll move to the next slide.

To back up one slide, select **Previous** from the hidden menu. To go ahead to any other slide, select **Go** and, from the sub-menu, select **By Title**. Another cascading menu appears, listing the titles of your slides, and you can select the slide that you want there.

Doodle Diagramming: Writing on Slides

Sometimes, it's handy to be able to mark up your slides while you're showing them. You may want to circle something to highlight what you're talking about, or draw lines showing how one item is connected to another item, or scribble over the name of the person who just stormed out of the room on the corporate organization chart.

PowerPoint lets you do this, but don't expect it to look great. Mice are not the world's greatest drawing tools, and trackballs are even worse. The ability is there if you want it.

To start, just select **Pen** from the hidden menu. Your arrow pointer will turn into a pen, and when you drag the pointer, it will draw a line.

You can change what color the pen is by selecting **Pointer Options, Pen Color** and selecting a pen color from the list. You can erase everything you drew by selecting **Screen, Erase Pen** or type the letter **e**—but you don't have to worry about erasing the slide when you're ready to move on. The pen is automatically erased when you move on to the next slide, so if you come back to this slide, it won't be there. (The pointer also stops being a pen and resumes being an arrow when you advance.)

The mark-ups show the development department's planned blitz against the administrative branch, aiming to tackle their quarterback and steal their coffee mugs.

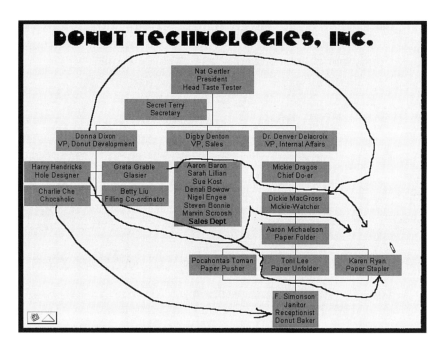

But what if you want to draw a full diagram, without all the stuff on the slide getting in the way. Well, you could take a pen and slowly and carefully cover up everything on the slide with one color, much like the way you once sat there and scraped all of the silver stuff off of your Etch-a-Sketch so that you could see the inside. Or you could do it the easy way: select **Screen, Black Screen**. The whole slide will go black, and you can select **Pen** and start drawing on it. When you're done, select **Screen, Unblack Screen** and you'll be back to working with your slide.

Avoiding Invisible Ink
You can set a default pen color on the Set Up Show dialog box. Pick a color that shows up against the background you're using.

You can return to using the arrow pointer at any time just by selecting **Arrow**. Even if you don't, the pointer will turn into the arrow when you move on to the next slide.

A Slide up Your Sleeve

What if there's a slide you're not sure you want to show? Perhaps it has the answers to a question that you think someone is going to ask at a certain point, but you don't want to show it unless they ask. The answer is easy: hide the slide!

In Slide Sorter view, select the slide that you want to hide, then pull down the **Slide Show** menu and select **Hide Slide**. Then, when you're showing the slide before the hidden one, and you suddenly want to show the hidden one, just select **Go, Hidden Slide**. The hidden slide will be displayed. If you don't purposefully go to the hidden slide, the slide will be skipped right over in order. You can have as many hidden slides as you want in your presentation, so long as you don't hide them all!

Show's Over!

To quit the show at any time, just select **End Show** from the hidden menu or press the **Esc** key. Otherwise, the show will end when you try to advance past the last slide.

A Sly Innuendo... Er, a Slide in a Window

You can show your slide show in a resizable window on your screen, which is really handy if you're trying to play Space Bunnies of Death in another window. To do this, pull down the **Slide Show** menu and select **Set Up Show**. Then, in the dialog box, click on the **Browsed by an Individual(Window)**. Click on the **OK** button, then issue the **Slide Show, View Show** command. The window will open up, and the show starts.

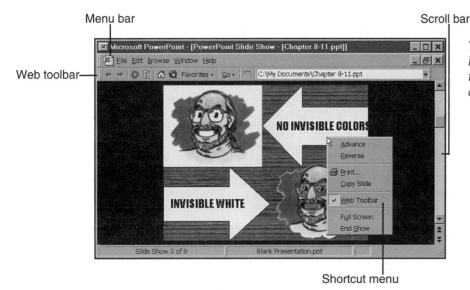

Menu bar

Scroll bar

Web toolbar

The slide is shown as big as it can be in the window without changing the ratio.

Shortcut menu

Menus: Hidden No More!

Windows have menus. It's as sure a thing as dogs having fleas, or computer manuals having obfuscating terminology. As such, the slide show doesn't need a hidden menu in this mode. It still has one, but everything on there is also on the standard menus.

And while they're there, you might as well use them. Your window may well have a Web-related toolbar showing, and if your presentation doesn't link to the Web, there's no need for it. It's just additional screen clutter. To get rid of it, pull down the **Window** menu and select **Web Toolbar**.

Sliding Ahead

As usual, if you're using the timing feature, the slides will advance automatically, and if you aren't, you can click to move ahead. You can move more quickly through the presentation by using the scroll bar at the right of the window. And if you want to see the names of the slides so you can pick which one to leap to, pull down the **Browse** menu and, from the **By Title** submenu, select the slide you want to go to.

Finishing Up

When you're done with the slide show, just click on the **Close** button on the end of the menu bar, and away it goes!

Kiosk: Accident-Proof, Idiot-Proof, Safety in a Can!

Letting someone else use your computer to view a presentation is just asking for trouble. The next thing you know, they've stopped the Slide Show, and in an attempt to restart it have somehow managed to reformat your hard drive, and you smell the faint but telltale scent that lets you know that someone has stuck a slice of individually wrapped, processed American cheese food into your CD-ROM drive.

This is not good. This is something to be avoided, unless you have your computer heavily insured and wish to collect. However, if you start the presentation running in Kiosk mode, you can avoid worrying about this. Why? Because you can hide away your computer and the keyboard somewhere where cables can reach but prying hands cannot. All the user needs is the mouse and the monitor, and they can't even stop the presentation using the mouse. All they can do is advance to the next slide, or click on a hyperlink. If they hit the end of the presentation, it starts all over again.

It's referred to as *Kiosk Mode* because it can be used to set up a *kiosk*, a stand-alone unit like you might see in the mall, a big wooden box with a monitor showing and a trackball sticking up through a hole. The computer is all locked inside, away from prying hands (unless the prying hands have a crowbar).

Attractive Trackball

If you're trying to quickly throw together a kiosk-like setup that younger kids or the elderly may be using, consider getting Microsoft's EasyBall trackball. It's got an oversized ball that's better for those who are not so nimble, and it only has one button, which reduces confusion.

Setting Up a Kiosk Show

Pull down the **Slide Show** menu and select **Set Up Show** to bring up everyone's favorite dialog box (well, it's probably someone's favorite, at least). Click on **Browsed at a kiosk (full screen)** option, then on the **OK** button to set kiosk mode. Finally, pull the menu down again and select **View Show** to get it rolling.

Viewing Slides

You can't back up, you can't select a slide to go to, you can't pull off any of those nifty tricks. There is no hidden menu to help you. You can just wait for the timing feature to take you forward, or follow a hyperlink built into the presentation. Idiot-proof and powerful do not mix.

COMING SOON FROM QUE BOOKS

COMPLETE IDIOT'S RIDE: THE GUIDE!

➤ Everything you've ever wanted to know about the world's most popular theme park attraction.

➤ See how 107 tons of steel, 15 miles of cables, and 30,000 Pixie Stix were used to build this thrill-ride

➤ Tricks and Tips to getting the most out of your Complete Idiot's experience!

There are no menus, hidden or otherwise, in kiosk mode, as this ride guide slide shows.

You can't even click to go forward, unless there is a hyperlink to the next slide. This would be a good place to include a hyperlink to the next slide on the background, because if you're not doing a time-based presentation, you're going to need to give the user some way to move ahead.

Kiosk Planning

It's a good idea to have all but the transition from the first to second slides timed. That way, if someone walks away from the kiosk, the show will keep showing until it reaches the first slide, and then it will stop, waiting for someone to click on a hyperlink to continue the presentation.

Finishing the Show

When the show is over and the viewer has viewed the last slide, the show automatically starts all over again, ready for the next person! Then how do you stop the show when you want your computer back? Just hit the **Esc** key!

Simple Show-Starting

You can save a copy of your presentation that automatically starts showing when you double-click an icon on your desktop. This can save time, and make things a lot easier for anyone who wants to look at it without having to learn about PowerPoint.

To do this, pull down the **File** menu and select **Save As**. A file navigator appears. Click on the drop-down button for the **Save in** drop-down menu, and select **Desktop**. This tells PowerPoint that you want an icon for the file on the desktop. Then, pull down the **Save as type** drop-down menu at the bottom of the navigator, and select **PowerPoint Show** (*.pps). This tells PowerPoint that you're saving it as an automatically starting show.

A PowerPoint Show icon.

Click **OK** and the icon for this presentation will appear on your desktop!

The Least You Need to Know

➤ Pulling down the **Slide Show** menu and selecting **Set Up Show** gives you the Set Up Show dialog box, which has many functions for controlling how your show appears.

➤ Selecting **Presented by a Speaker** gives the most control over the presentation when you present it. When running a slide show in speaker mode, hidden menu can be brought up by pointing at the arrow symbol in the lower left of the slide, or by right-clicking.

➤ In speaker mode, select **Previous** from the hidden menu to back up one slide, or select **Go**, **By Title** to go to any slide of your choice.

➤ In speaker mode, you can draw on a slide by selecting **Pen**, change the pen color by selecting **Pointer Options, Pen Color**, and erase your drawing by selecting **Screen, Erase Pen**.

➤ If you select **Browsed by an Individual** on the Set Up Show dialog box, your presentation will be shown in a resizable window with visible menus (window mode). In window mode, you can see whichever slide you want by selecting **Browse, By Title.** Finish a windows mode slide show by reaching the end, or by clicking on the **Close** button on the end of the menu bar.

➤ To view the slide show in kiosk mode, select **Browsed at a kiosk** on the Set Up Show dialog box.

Chapter 19

Sending the Presentations to Others

In This Chapter

➤ Make a presentation that is easy to send to others

➤ Send your presentation through e-mail

➤ Put your presentation on a floppy disk and send it through real mail

You've created your presentation, and there are people all over the country, all over the world even, who you want to have see it.

You could send them all plane tickets and fly them in to see the presentation on your computer. Or, you could pack up your computer and fly it to every place that they are, dedicating the next few years of your life to spreading your presentation.

Unfortunately for the airlines, there is another option, one which doesn't involve you giving them a lick of money. You can just send the presentation, either via e-mail or on floppy disks through the regular mail. And, unfortunately for Microsoft (and they have no one to blame but themselves), you don't even have to give everyone their own copy of PowerPoint, because you'll also be sending them a program that lets them see the presentation for themselves.

Preparing Postal-Possible Presentations

So you've created this great presentation, filled with lights and sounds and video clips of the entire run of the *Mr. Peepers* TV show. And you start to put it on a floppy disk. And another floppy. And another. Seventeen thousand five hundred and thirty-six floppies later, you've got your presentation stored and ready to ship. Where are you going to find a box big enough?

But hey, it would be worth it. Just imagine the look on the recipient's face when he gets it! And the days of fun he'll have installing it on his own PC so he can view it!

Obviously, this is something you want to avoid. If your goal is to send your presentations to others, you'll want to try to keep it lean and make sure it isn't too big.

That doesn't mean that you can't have a lot of slides. A slide with just text on it takes up very little space, and you could fit dozens of them on a single floppy. No, the culprit in creating a bloated presentation is more likely to be all those nice little multimedia touches.

That video presentation of you reading the Declaration Of Interactivity is a prime culprit. Video eats up disk space really fast. A minute video, even in a small window, can easily take up ten megabytes, which would add seven floppy disks to your presentation. That same ten megabytes could take an hour to transfer to someone's computer via e-mail, if that person has a dial-up connection to the Internet.

After video, the next big culprit is audio. Small sound effects here and there don't eat up that much, but if you're using narration, you'll fill disks quickly. You can cut down how much space the narration takes by reducing the audio quality of your recording (as discussed in Chapter 17, "Sound Advice on Sound").

Finally, pictures can take up a lot of space. Highly detailed, high-resolution photographs eat up disk space very quickly. You may want to try using your graphics program to store the pictures with fewer colors, or a lower-quality, higher-compression JPEG mode.

Pack It Up

You've got your presentation all ship-shape and ready to pack up for its trip. If you're putting it on floppy disk, you'll want to run a special program called the Pack and Go Wizard which will lead you through the steps of this process. You also want to use this Wizard if you're going to e-mail the presentation.

To get the process rolling, load the presentation into PowerPoint, then pull down the **File** menu and select **Pack and Go**. The Pack and Go Wizard appears, listing the 4 steps you need to go through. Click on the **Next** button to get to the first step.

Packing steps —

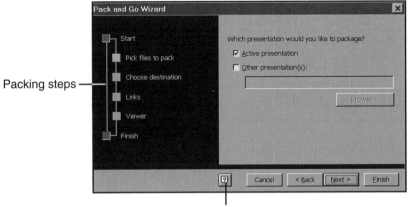

The Pack and Go Wizard: Not just a fly-by-night magician!

Click here for help.

Step One: Pick to Pack

The first step asks you to pick the presentation that you want to pack. By default, Active Presentation is already checked off. Since that's the one you want, just click on **Next** to move on to the next step!

Step Two: Stick This on Your Disk

The next step that appears lets you choose which disk drive the presentation is going to be stored on. There are radio buttons listing all of the floppy drives on your system, and one more marked Choose Destination. If you're putting the presentation on a floppy, click the radio button for the right floppy drive. Stick a formatted floppy into the drive.

> **Check This Out...**
>
> **Pack for Two**
> You can send several presentations at once. Just check **Other Presentations**, click on the **Browse** button, and select the other presentations you want to add in.

185

Opt for a floppy, or find a folder.

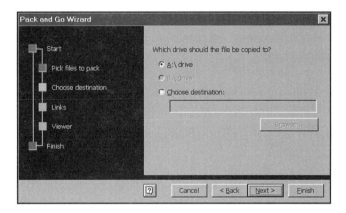

If you're preparing this to be e-mailed, you'll want to store it on your hard disk. Click on the **Choose Destination** button, and then on the **Browse** button, and a file browser will appear. Select the disk drive and folder where you want the presentation stored, then click the **Select** button to show you've made your selection.

Once you've selected your disk drive, click on the **Next** button.

Step Three: Include Linked Files

The dialog box now asks you if you want to include your linked files. Of course you do! Linked files are pictures, video, and sound files that are used in your presentation, but haven't been built into the main presentation file. It's a silly question to ask! Check off the check box for this.

Don't create the missing link! Include everything!

There'll also be a checkbox asking if you want to include your font files. Check this one as well. Otherwise, all of those fonts that you carefully picked because they look just right will be replaced by other fonts on other people's PCs.

Once you've put a check in all the checkboxes here, click on the **Next** button to move on to the next step.

Step Four: Pick to Pack a Player

The final step of the Wizard is choosing whether you want to include the Viewer program with your presentation. This program will play the presentation for others even if they don't have PowerPoint. If you're not sure whether the person has PowerPoint 97, include it. Even if the person doesn't have PowerPoint 97, they will need a system that's running Windows 95 or Windows NT in order to watch your presentation. These days, that includes most of the people you are likely to send the presentation to.

Send the Viewer along if you are not sure the recipient has PowerPoint.

In order to include a copy of the player program, you're going to need a copy of the program. If you have the CD-ROM that you installed PowerPoint from, stick that in your CD-ROM drive. That's where the system will look for it. If you didn't install PowerPoint from CD-ROM, you can get a copy of the program from the World Wide Web. To do this, pull down your PowerPoint **Help** menu, and from the **Microsoft on the Web** submenu, select **Free Stuff**. Your Web browser will start up, and will load up a page listing free utilities for PowerPoint. You should be able to find the player (called Viewer for PowerPoint 97) there.

Stall the Install

To keep your computer from trying to run the PowerPoint or MS Office installation program when you stick the CD-ROM in, just hold down the **Shift** key as you close the CD-ROM drawer.

When you're finished with this step, instead of clicking on the **Next** button, just click on the **Finish** button. The packing process will start.

The Computer Packs Like a Thing That Packs Very Well

The computer will start packing the files away, while showing you a status dialog box letting you know what is happening. The first file that it creates is pngsetup.exe, which is the program that the person who gets the presentation will run to unpack it onto his machine. This only takes up about one tenth of the space on a standard floppy disk.

Next it creates pres0.ppz, which has the presentation information in it. If you're writing to a floppy and this file fills up the disk, PowerPoint will ask you for another floppy disk. It will then create a file on this one, with more of the presentation in it. If this one fills up, it will ask for another one, and so on. Make sure that you number the floppy disks in the order that you put them in! Otherwise, the user will have to keep guessing which one is which, and will probably throw a large weasel at you the next time he sees you.

Once the packing is complete, PowerPoint proudly shows you a dialog box, letting you know that the job has been completed successfully.

Make sure you tell the recipient that to unpack the presentation, he has to run the pngsetup.exe program, which he can do by clicking on the **Start** button, selecting **Run**, then clicking on the **Browse** button and finding where the file is (either on the floppy or wherever his e-mail gets stored). If you're sending it via e-mail, remember to send both files! (Also remember that if you make changes to the presentation, you will have to re-pack it.)

And write your mother, while you're at it.

CD-ROMming Your Presentation

If you do have a large presentation full of sound and video to share, you may want to consider making your own CD-ROMs. CD-R recorders, which can make CD-ROMs, have dropped to a few hundred dollars, although the individual blank disks are still around $10 each.

If you do put your presentation onto a CD-ROM, don't use Pack and Go to put it on there. Packing it just means that the recipient will have to unpack it onto his hard disk, and you'll take up a lot of unneeded room there. Instead, copy the Viewer program, your presentation file, and any linked files onto the CD-R disc. (You may have to copy some of your hard disk directory structure, to make sure that linked files are found in the right place.) Then the recipient can view the presentation directly from the CD-ROM.

Shoo! Send It Away Quickly

If you're using Microsoft Exchange to handle your e-mail, and you just want to send off the presentation without packing it (which is fine if you're sending it to someone who already has a player or has PowerPoint 97), you can do it really quickly.

Open the presentation you wish to mail, then pull down the **File** menu, and from the **Send To** submenu select **Mail Recipient**. Microsoft Exchange will appear to find out who you want to send it off to. Tell it that information (this is no time to keep secrets from your computer), and it will ship the file right off. If you want everyone in your organization to be able to get it, use the **File, Send to, Exchange Folder** command, and select a public folder to put it in.

The Least You Need to Know

➤ To keep your presentations small enough to be easily sent on floppy or via e-mail, avoid using video and high-quality audio in them.

➤ If you want to send your presentation, use the Pack and Go Wizard. Pull down the **File** menu and select **Pack and Go** to get it started.

On the Pack and Go Wizard dialog box, click on the **Next** button to get it started, then fill in each piece of information each screen asks for and click **Next** to move to the next one. When you're done, click **Finished**, and the packing will take place.

➤ If you do include the presentation player, you'll need either the CD-ROM that PowerPoint came on, or the player file downloaded from the Microsoft Web site.

➤ As your presentation gets packed, PowerPoint will tell you when you need to stick another floppy disk in the drive. Make sure to number them all.

➤ If you're e-mailing the presentation, you will need to send two files: pngsetup.exe and pres0.ppz.

Be sure to tell the person you're sending the file to that they will need to run pngsetup.exe to unpack the presentation so they can run it.

➤ To use Microsoft Exchange to send your presentation file to another PowerPoint user, just use the **File**, **Send To**, **Mail Recipient** command.

Chapter 20

Reaching a Crowd: Slides, Overheads, Projection Screens, and Network Presentations

OLD OVERHEAD PROJECTOR

OLD OVER HEAD PROJECTIONIST

In This Chapter

➤ Make slide-projector slides of your computer slides

➤ Create overheads

➤ Use computer screen projectors to make your image huge

➤ Convince your boss that you need two computers: one to run the show, and the other to show the show

➤ Run your presentation over a network, at a safe distance from your audience

With your standard computer set up, you can show your presentation to up to 273,000 people. Of course, you can only show it to about 3 of them at a time, but hey, you've got nothing better to do, right?

By projecting your presentation onto The Big Screen (even if it's not a very big Big Screen), you can show it to lots of people at once. Maybe not 273,000 of them (unless you project it on the scoreboard during the Super Bowl), but certainly more than 3.

There are basically four forms of projection you can use. You can use a slide projector, actually making slides out of your slides. You can put them onto clear sheets and project them with an overhead projector. You can use one of several methods of projecting your computer display directly. Or, you can send it out over a network, so that each member of your audience is at their desk, looking at their own PC.

Slides on Slides

Using a slide projector to show your presentation places some strong limitations on what you can do. A slide can't show animation, or play sound, or be interactive. All it can do is project an image, which reduces PowerPoint to a drawing program.

However, it does have some useful advantages that should not be overlooked. A slide projector is very easy to carry around, and you can ship slides off to most corporations and schools and feel confident that they not only have the equipment to see what you sent, but to show it to a large group. Plus, if enemy agents have you cornered, slides are easier to swallow than floppy disks.

Slide-maker, Slide-maker, Make Me a Slide!

If you want to make your own slides, you could try just photographing your screen and telling the Fotofolk that you need them developed as slides. They will look horrible, but you'll have done it on the cheap!

The proper equipment to use is a *film recorder*. This is a device that you attach to your computer using a card and a cable. The computer treats the film recorder the same way as it does a printer, sending the image to the recorder when you tell it to print. You can get film recorders that can turn out a slide in a minute and a half. You just step through your presentation on the computer, and tell it to take a picture when each slide shows up.

The bad news, however, is the cost. It's quite likely that you'll spend more on the film recorder than on the computer that you attach it to. Generally speaking, this is not a device that you get when you want to throw together a quick presentation. This is something that you get for the graphics department of your company, when they need it for this and a number of other things.

Let Someone Else Pay for the Big Stuff

Luckily, you can hire someone else to make your slides for you. There are *computer imaging service bureaus* that specialize in dealing with computer graphics, and they can make the slides for you. You can look them up in the yellow pages, or you can ask whoever does your company's computer graphics.

You'll need to find out from the service bureau what media they take; they are bound to be able to handle floppy disk, but if your file is too big for that, they might be able to take it on tape, on a removable hard disk, in compressed format on a ZIP disk, or any of a number of other possibilities.

This will probably cost you about $10 per slide, which can quickly add up to hundreds of dollars. However, most of these places are using very good quality equipment, so your slides will come out looking sharp.

Service Bureau via Modem

Microsoft made a deal with a company called Genigraphics for them to accept PowerPoint presentations by modem, and have the slides (or full-color overheads, or posters) delivered to you by overnight delivery. In order to use this, your system has to have a modem. The cost ranges from $6.99 to $19.99 per slide, depending on how quickly you need it done. Volume discounts are available.

To send the file to Genigraphics, pull down the **File** menu and select **Send To, Genigraphics**. (If you don't see the Genigraphics option listed, you will have to run PowerPoint Setup again, and tell it to install the Genigraphics drivers.) From there, a Wizard will take you through the process.

Grayed Out?

If the Genigraphics command is grayed out, that means that the Genigraphics Wizard wasn't installed on your computer. Ask the Office Assistant about Genigraphics for information on how to install this Wizard.

Preplanning the Presentation

If you're preparing a presentation for slides, it's best to plan ahead. (It's best to plan ahead even if you're not doing that, but then the plans that you make are different!) When you've first opened up your presentation, but before you've put anything on it, pull down the **File** menu and select **Page Setup**. A dialog box appears, which lets you control the ratio of the page width to the height.

Using the Page Setup dialog box, you can set the height and width separately.

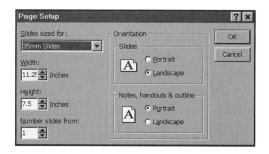

Click on the drop-down button on the **Slides Sized For** field, and select **35mm Slides**, then click on the **OK** button. This will make the slides a little shorter than they were, which is the right ratio of height-to-width for slides. (If you view this show on your screen, there will be black bands at the top and bottom to make it fit your screen, like a letterboxed movie on TV.)

Changing an Existing Presentation

Using Page Setup to change the size of existing slides will squish or stretch the graphic elements. The text won't stretch, but it may get rearranged on the page, so check all your slides to make sure they still look okay.

Preparing the Files for a Service Bureau

The service bureau isn't going to want to handle your PowerPoint presentation. What they'll want is a file all ready for their printer. To get this, call them and ask them what *printer driver* they'll want you to use. (You may have to install this driver from the Windows installation disk, if you don't already have it installed.) Then pull down the **File** menu and select the **Print** command.

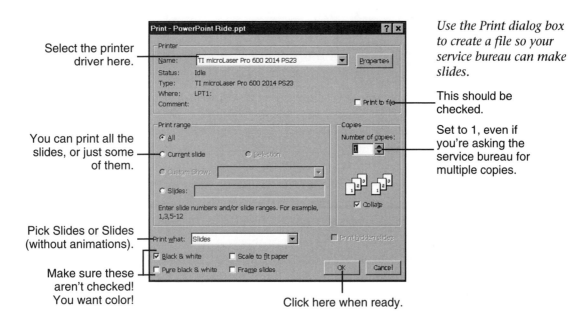

Select the printer driver here.

Use the Print dialog box to create a file so your service bureau can make slides.

This should be checked.

Set to 1, even if you're asking the service bureau for multiple copies.

You can print all the slides, or just some of them.

Pick Slides or Slides (without animations).

Make sure these aren't checked! You want color!

Click here when ready.

Select the printer driver that the service bureau requested in the **Name** field, put a check mark in the **Print to File** checkbox, select **Slides** in the Print What field. If you have a choice between Slides (with animations) or Slides (without animations), pick **Slides (without animations)**. Make sure neither of the black and white options is checked off, and then click on the **OK** button. A file browser will pop up, wanting you to name the file and pick a disk and a folder to put it in. You might as well put it directly on the disk you'll be sending to the service bureau. Once you've selected where it goes, click on the **OK** button, and the file will be created. (Make a copy of the disk to keep for yourself, so if something goes wrong at the service bureau you have a copy.)

I Own a Film Recorder, and Want to Use It!

To send the image to your own film recorder, take the same steps described above for sending it to the service bureau, only select your film recorder in the Print dialog box's **Name** field and *don't* put a check in the **Print to File** field. Click on the **OK** button, and all the necessary information will be sent to the film recorder.

Overheads Over Easy

Overheads (sometimes called *transparencies*), clear sheets that you use with an overhead projector, are kind of keen. Not only are they big, translucent versions of your slides, but if you take a blank overhead sheet and use it to block the cat's favorite path, the cat will try to walk right through it.

Transparencies are a handy way to show your presentation because you can make them yourself without a vast expense, and most places you're likely to want to show your show will probably have an overhead projector (and if they don't, you can get one for $200–$300). If everyone involved is too cheap to buy a projector, you can just show the sheets to people. (You can try that with slides, but people will end up squinting a lot!)

To make your own transparencies, you'll need a printer (either a laser printer or an ink jet printer) and you'll need some transparency sheets. Make sure that you get sheets specifically designed for whichever sort of printer you have, because if you take a laser printer transparency sheet and run it through a color ink jet printer (for example), the ink won't stick to the page and you'll end up projecting psychedelic puddles that used to be your information. This may look cool to people on acid, but if most of your audience is on acid, it's probably time to find a new line of work! On the other hand, if you run an ink jet sheet through your laser printer, the sheet will melt and turn your laser printer into a high-tech lump.

Blank overhead sheets cost between 50 cents and a dollar apiece, and you buy them in packs of 20 or more. You may also want to get some cardboard frames for them, if you're going to be using them repeatedly and want to keep them in good shape. You can also keep them in a 3-ring binder by using clear binder sheet protectors, which is handy because you don't have to take the overheads out of the protectors to project them.

Overhead Set Up (and then follow through with a backhand?)

Setting up for overheads is much the same as setting up for slides, only you select **Overheads** on the Page Setup dialog box, rather than 35mm Slides. However, you have one other choice to make: **Portrait**, or **Landscape**. Now, Microsoft throws these two art terms at you just to confuse those of us who work in words rather than in art, but they're really quite simple. *Portrait* means that the page is turned so that it's tall and narrow. *Landscape* means that it's turned so it's short and wide.

Portrait mode is really nice if you're doing lots of text and long lists of things. However, Landscape has the big advantage of being the same relative dimensions as the computer screen, so you can show your show on the screen or on the overhead projector, and it will look the same.

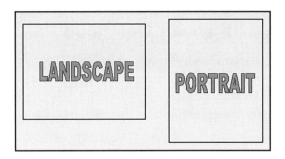

Landscape transparencies are wider. Portrait transparencies are taller.

Clear Thoughts on Transparent Printing

If you're making your slide show for overheads, there are a few things you should remember. Write them on your hand, if you have to (but be prepared to swallow your hand if captured by the enemy).

The first thing to remember is that if your printer is black-and-white, then your transparencies will be black-and-white (well, black-and-clear). All of your fancy colors will be for naught, and if you put one color on top of another, it may be hard to tell them apart. To plan for this, while designing your slides, click on the **Black and White View** button on the Standard toolbar. PowerPoint will now show your slides in black and white, so you know what to expect. (In Slide View mode, it will also show you a color version in a small window.)

If you are using a color printer, you may still want to avoid overlapping colors and using backgrounds. Ink jet inks often smear a bit, and this can cause an ugly, muddy effect if you have large areas of color connecting. Even single colors can come out muddy, because the printer has to mix several colors to make the color you want. Much of this depends on the quality of your color printer and how well it works with the overhead sheets you have. If you want to try color backgrounds anyway, test it out on one overhead first and see how it comes out, before committing to doing a whole bunch that way.

Ink Jet Smear Fear

Make sure you let each ink jet-printed sheet dry thoroughly before stacking them! Otherwise, you'll end up with overheads with smudgy printing on both, not good for anything but harassing the cat.

Color Overheads with Lower Overhead

If you don't have a color printer and want color overheads, or if you want to make sure that the overheads you use are of the highest quality, then you can use a service bureau to print them. You do this by printing them to a file (as shown in the slide section) and taking the file to the service bureau, where they will have high-end color printers to print them on.

This, however, is not cheap. You can expect to pay somewhere around $15 apiece for color overheads. If you're just looking for color, it may be cheaper to go out and buy a color printer. Cheap color printers cost about as much as you would pay for 15 to 20 service bureau overheads.

Two Screens, or Not Two Screens

Slides and overheads are nice, but they can't show all that beautiful animation and those movies that you built into your presentation. Wouldn't it be the nicest thing if you could take what's on your computer monitor and project it on to a large screen?

No, it wouldn't; the nicest thing would be if eating ice cream made us svelte and healthy. The projection thing is nice, though, and there are several ways to do it. You could get a card that converts your computer video into video that TVs can handle, and hook your screen up to a projection television system. The image may be blurred a little, but if you use large fonts, that shouldn't be a problem.

Another way to do it is to use a device designed to project computer information. An *LCD projector* is like a television projector, only it's designed for sharp computer graphics. An *LCD panel* is like the screen of a color laptop computer, only it doesn't have a back, so light can shine right through. If you put the LCD panel on an overhead projector, light shines through the display and projects the image on the screen!

LCD: Little Color Dots

LCD stands for *liquid crystal display*. Such a display is made up of little segments that are normally clear, but become visible when a small amount of electricity is applied to them. Digital watches have LCDs, with 8 segments being used to make up the numbers.

But, if you're using this display, you really don't want to be looking up at the big screen, and you probably don't want to be showing everyone the hidden menus and other things you're doing with the system. A good presentation should look like magic. Wouldn't it be the nicest thing if you could have one display that you're looking at, doing all the work, while the users just see the projection of the slides that you want them to see? No, the nicest thing is the ice cream, remember? But this thing is not only nice, it's possible!

It Ain't Cheap, but Here's How

First, you need two PCs. Both of them have to have PowerPoint installed. Since you're trying to project this, one of them will have to have an LCD panel or projector, and those aren't cheap. You're talking about prices starting in the thousands and going into the tens of thousands. (But you *can* rent them instead! Check the yellow pages under *Computers: Rental.*)

You also need a *null-modem cable*. This is a cable that connects the two computers' serial ports, hooking them up so that the outbound wires of one computer are connected to the inbound wires on the other, and vice versa. Using this cable, the computer you're using tells the projector computer what to do.

Load up the presentation, pull down the **Slide Show** menu, and select **View on Two Screens**. When you do this, PowerPoint will give you further details on how to get your slide show going in this mode.

Network Presentations: Avoiding Your Audience

If you have the PCs at work linked together with a PowerPoint-compatible network, you can run the presentation over that network, so that each member of the audience is at his own desk, on his own PC. This can be handy because it's less disruptive of the workday. It's also really useful if you're delivering bad news or bad puns, since you will be out of the audience's donut-throwing range. You can even run the presentation over the Internet, so you can dial it in from a remote mountain cabin, and no one will be able to track down where you are.

This works a lot like the two screen method, only with a lot more screens. Each computer involved in the presentation needs to be running a copy of PowerPoint 97. This makes Microsoft happy.

Starting the Presentation

To start with, everyone who wants to view the presentation on their screen has to start running PowerPoint. They pull down the **Tools** menu and select **Presentation Conference**. On the dialog box that appears, they should select **Audience** and then click **Next**. This will start a Wizard that will take them, step-by-step, through the process of preparing to receive a presentation.

When your audience has gotten all that going, you should do the **Tools, Presentation Conference** command on your own PC. Instead of selecting Audience, you select **Presenter** and then click **Next**. This will start your own Wizard, helping you with the start-up process.

There is one option along the way marked **All Participants Must Start Now**. This is handy for making sure that no one comes in during the middle of your conference. However, if you select this, make sure that all the audience members click **Finish** on their Wizard before you click it on yours. Any member of the audience who doesn't do this will be locked out of the show, and made fun of in the parking lot after work.

Your Slide Is Everyone's Doodle Pad

The audience can do more in this case than just watch—they can all write on the slides using the pen. All they have to do is click and their pointer will turn into the pen. When anyone writes on a slide, everyone can see it.

Network Presentations Ain't So Great

There are a number of things that you cannot use in a presentation that's going over a network. You can't use video. You can't use any sounds except for the sound effects that are built into PowerPoint; anything that you've recorded yourself won't work. And you can't use anything that uses a program besides PowerPoint.

Now, this last thing may not sound like much. After all, you probably aren't going to use your presentation to start Tetris when everyone else can see. However, there are a number of programs that come with PowerPoint and that seem like part of PowerPoint that you won't be able to use. You will not be able to use charts and graphs, because when you create those you're actually using another program. If you want a chart to appear in a networked presentation, you'll have to draw it yourself using AutoShapes, rather than using the usual chart tools.

A Trio of Tools to Use with Two to Two Hundred Views

PowerPoint has a couple of tools that you can use whether you're running your presentation on one screen, two, or over a network, but that you're more likely to be using when running on more than one screen. That's because they cover up part of the screen, which would ruin the effect for your audience.

Speaker notes give you a text display for each slide. You can put whatever you want into these notes: a little script telling you what to discuss on the slide, a reminder that there's a hidden slide, a dirty limerick, whatever. You don't have to worry about what you put up there, because everyone else is going to be watching the main screen... unless you have one of those weirdos in the front row who tries to watch the presentation's backward reflection in your glasses.

The *Meeting Minder* is used for taking notes during your presentation, and is particularly helpful if your presentation is meant to organize the project.

The *Slide Meter* keeps track of how long your presentation is supposed to take and how long it *is* taking, letting you know if you have to speed up to get done before running over schedule.

Notes on Notes

You can create Speaker Notes either in Slide Sorter View or Slide View. Slide View is better for creating them as you create your presentation, but Slide Sorter View works best if you already have your presentation and are adding notes later.

To add notes to a slide, select the slide, pull down the **View** menu, and select **Speaker Notes**. A Speaker Notes dialog box appears. It's mainly a big field to type your notes on that slide into.

Enter your notes in the big field by clicking inside the field and typing. You can then select another slide to start working on the slide's notes, or click **Close** if you're done working on notes altogether.

Once you've got your notes in place, you can start the slide show. You have to do the slide show in Speaker mode for this to work. Right-click on any slide and select **Speaker Notes**, and the same Speaker Notes dialog box will appear. You can even edit the notes during the show. As you advance to each new slide, the dialog box will show the notes for that slide.

There is no rule that says you have to put limericks in your Speaker Notes, but why not?

If this slide needs notes to appear, setting them up is quite clear.

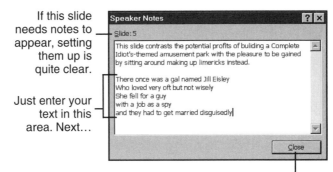

Just enter your text in this area. Next…

…you finish by clicking right here!

Speaker Notes for Non-Two Screeners

You can print out your Speaker Notes to use as cheat sheets or handouts. Just select **File**, **Print** and choose **Notes Pages** in the Print What field.

Use the Meeting Minder, or Never Mind Your Meeting!

There's another notepad you can use during your presentation, the Meeting Minder. This is really designed for tracking feedback and planning during the presentation, but it can also be used for limericks, and perhaps other things.

To pull up the Meeting Minder while showing a presentation in Speaker Mode, just right-click and select **Meeting Minder**. A dialog box opens, with two tabs. The Meeting Minutes tab is used for general notes, while the Action Items tab is used to create a schedule listing things that need to be done and who needs to do them.

Select the **Meeting Minutes** tab, and you'll see it's just one big field, just like the Speaker Notes had. Type whatever you want in there.

Click on the **Action Items** tab, and you'll see fields to enter work assignments, including a description of the work to be done, the name of the person to do it, and the date due. Enter this information and click on the **Add** button, and this info gets added to the list below it. (You can change things on the list by selecting them and clicking on **Edit**, or remove them entirely by selecting them and clicking on **Delete**. These are both handy for making sure that anything assigned to you gets reassigned from you to someone else!) When you hit the end of your presentation, you'll discover that PowerPoint has made a new slide, listing the action items!

Click to enter notes ──┐ ┌── Click to record to-do items

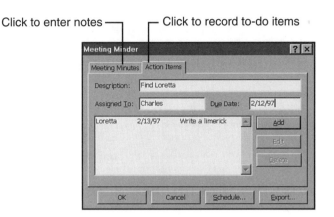

The Action Items tab allows you to schedule items for other people to do. With a little planning, you can avoid doing them yourself.

If you have installed Microsoft Office 97 (not just the standalone PowerPoint product), clicking on the **Schedule** button opens up the Microsoft Outlook appointment calendar/ meeting planner program—which is another complete program of its own. You can have PowerPoint send e-mail to Outlook on every action item you recorded so that it appears on the appropriate person's schedule and to-do list. Clicking on **Export** lets you export all of the Meeting Minder information to Microsoft Word, the word processor part of Microsoft Office. There's not room here to tell you how to use either of these products, but feel free to spend your hard-earned shekels on *The 10 Minute Guide to Outlook 97* and *The Complete Idiot's Guide to Word 97*.

Minding Your Meetings at Other Times

You can pull up the Meeting Minder while editing your presentation. Just pull down the **Tools** menu and select **Meeting Minder**.

Watch Your Speed: The Slide Meter

Presentations shouldn't take forever. It doesn't really take that long before your audience starts feeling that they have better things to do, such as eating, or sleeping, or ironing the parking lot. Caught up in the excitement of big-time presentation-giving, it's easy to lose track of just how long you're taking. The PowerPoint programmers built in a tool to prevent this, probably so that they could be spared from long-winded presentations themselves.

To access it during a show that you're presenting as speaker, right-click on the slide and select **Slide Meter** from the shortcut menu. A Slide Meter control panel pops up, showing you how long you've been on this slide, and how long since the start of the presentation.

The Slide Meter will tell you if you're going too slowly. (So will your audience!)

How long this slide has been running

Slide Meter

☑ 00:00:08 ── Yellow means this is running overtime.

Manual advance

Too slow ☑ 00:00:26 Too fast ── How long this presentation has been running

The green area means you're going the right speed.

The Slide Meter works even better if you've set slide timings, even if you aren't using the timings to automatically advance the slides (which is an option you control in the Set Up Show dialog box). With timings set, the Slide Meter shows you how your speed compares to the speed set with the timings. One display shows how you're doing with the current slide, showing a green meter expanding to the point at which the slide is measured for, at which point the meter turns yellow (you're running over) and then red (you're running way over).

You shouldn't be as concerned about running over on an individual slide as you are on running long for the whole show, which is what the second meter is for. There's a pointer that points to a central green area if you're averaging the right speed, moves to yellow and red areas at the left if you're going too slow, or at the right if you're going too fast. As with the Speaker Notes and the Meeting Minder, only you can see this on your display.

The Least You Need to Know

➤ To set up your presentation with the right dimensions for slide projector slides, use the **File, Page Setup** command and select **35mm Slides** on the **Slides Sized For** command. To send the images to a film recorder, use the **File, Print** command and select your film recorder on the **Name** list.

➤ To set up your presentation with the right dimensions for transparencies, use the **File, Page Setup** command and select **Overhead** on the **Slides Sized For** command. If you select the **Landscape** option, the dimensions will be the same as for an on-screen slide show.

➤ You can show a presentation on two PCs both running PowerPoint by cabling them together with a null modem cable. This is particularly good if you're using one of the screens to project a large image that everyone can see. To start the two screen slide show, use the **Slide Show, View on Two Screens** command on the controlling computer.

➤ To show the presentation to other folks over an in-house network or over the Internet, everyone in your audience has to be running PowerPoint.

➤ Speaker Notes let you create a little on-screen sheet of notes to help you with each slide. To create Speaker Notes, select the slide, then pull down the **View** menu and select **Speaker Notes**.

➤ The Meeting Minder lets you take notes and schedule events for Microsoft Outlook while presenting your presentation. Bring it up by right-clicking and selecting **Meeting Minder** during your presentation.

➤ The Slide Meter lets you see how long you've been taking to present your slide show, and compare that to any timings you set up. Right-click and select **Slide Meter** during your presentation to see it.

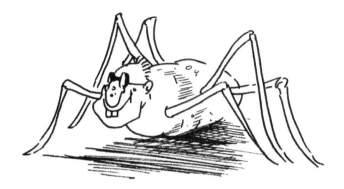

Chapter 21

Putting It on the Web

In This Chapter

➤ Get your presentation ready for publication on the World Wide Web

➤ Set the size and format of your presentation

➤ Pick a better tool for making Web presentations

The World Wide Web is wide indeed. Yes, it is most certainly wide. And it's webulous as well, very webulous, even though that isn't even a word. However, the most important thing about the Web is that it can reach the whole world. Odds are that most of the people you want your presentation to reach are somewhere in the world. By turning your presentation into a World Wide Web site, you make it so that anyone with a connection to the Internet (a world-wide network of computers) can take a look at your presentation. PowerPoint includes the tools to make your presentation ready to be placed on the Web.

Why You Shouldn't Use PowerPoint to Build a Web Site

When you use PowerPoint to make a Web site (a publication on the Web), it doesn't try to make it seem like a normal Web site. Instead, it tries to make the Web act more like PowerPoint. It doesn't really take advantage of the full power of the Web browsers, and it tries to put controls into Web pages that are very different from what Web users are used to using. An example of this difference is that something designed for the Web will automatically adjust the size of its display to fit the user's screen, while a PowerPoint presentation on the Web doesn't change size, meaning it may appear too small on some people's screens (making it hard to read) or too large on others (so they can't see a whole slide at once).

This isn't to say that you should never use PowerPoint to create a Web site. It's very good for one thing, and that's taking a presentation that you created for some other form and making it available on the Web. If you created a presentation for your students on The Rise and Fall of the Designated Hitter, and you want them to be able to refer to it while working on their term papers, you can give them instant access to it over the Web. This way, you don't have to recreate all your work.

If you have Microsoft Office, you already have a better Web designing program. The word processor Microsoft Word has some very good tools for making proper, straightforward Web pages. For more information on using these features, head down to your local bookstore and grab a copy of *The Complete Idiot's Guide to Microsoft Word 97*!

Techno Talk

blah blah blah blah blah bl b

Real Web Site Tools

If your goal is to create the best possible Web site, your best bet is to use a program that's designed just for that. Netscape includes a straightforward page design tool in the Gold version of Netscape Navigator. Microsoft offers FrontPage, a more powerful tool that's a bit awkward for the individual user, but great if you have a bunch of people working together to build a site. For the maximum control over your pages, you should learn HTML, which stands for *Hypertext Markup Language*, the language used to describe Web pages so that the Web browser will know what to display. All of the other tools just take what you want and translate it into HTML for you.

Que offers *Complete Idiot's Guides* to all of these methods. None of them have been turned into amusement park rides yet, though.

Presenting: Web-Presentable Presentations

If you're hoping to put your presentation on the Web, you should keep that fact in mind while you design it. Some things are good for Web design, other things aren't so hot. Planning ahead of time can help you avoid heartache later. (Although if you're one of those people who like heartache, not planning might be a good idea!)

There are some things that work well on the Web, other things that don't work well, and things that don't work at all.

Things That Work Well

Text and pictures work well on the Web. The Web is likely to reduce their size on the screen, so you should keep them large, but other than that, they should be fine.

Hyperlinks from slide to slide work well, and hyperlinks to Web sites work far better on the Web than they do in a non-Web presentation, since those sites get displayed in the same window used for presentation itself.

Things That Work, but Not Well

You should probably avoid animations and transitions. There is a way to get them to work, but it's a pain in the neck—not for you, but for the person who wants to view your presentation. Now, things that make life harder for someone else are not as bad as things that make life harder for ourselves, but this one makes things hard enough that people will probably just skip your presentation altogether.

You see, Web browsers do not naturally support the ability to view PowerPoint animations. When someone tries to view your presentation, their browser will tell them that they have to download a special piece of software that's designed to let their browser see your presentation. They can go to the download site, get the software, and then come back and view your presentation… but with all that work, they'll probably just skip it, particularly since odds are good that they will never again need that software. It's kind of like having a book in a library that you can only read using special glasses available only in a shop on the other side of town.

Plus, that software is available for only certain computers running certain browsers. There's plenty of people viewing the Web using non-Windows computers, and using Web browsers that you've probably never heard of. In order to include animations, you'd have to cut your presentation off from them altogether.

Don't worry if you're converting a presentation that already has animations built in. Later in this chapter, you will learn to tell PowerPoint just to skip the animations in the Web version of it.

Things That Don't Work on the Web

Audio and video do not work on the Web. Don't blame Microsoft (for this, anyway). The Web, as most people use it, is far too slow for quickly responsive audio and video. Trying to deliver full-speed video on the Web is like trying to deliver a new car to someone by passing it piece by piece through a straw: by the time you get enough of it through to be of use, the recipient has lost interest.

Do That Web Magic!

To convert your presentation to a form that can be used on the Web, load it up, pull down the **File** menu, and select **Save as HTML**. That'll start a Wizard (the Wonderful Wizard of Web!) to step you through the conversion process. When the Save as HTML dialog box opens up, click on the **Next** button to get started with the conversion.

Step One: Save Time If You've Done This Before

The first step is to pick whether you're going to use a new layout, or an existing layout. If you've done this before, and you saved your layout (I'll show you how to do this later, because it's too late to show you how to do it earlier!), just click on the **Load an Existing Layout** radio button, then on the name of the layout from the list. Click on the **Finish** button, and the conversion will start!

If this is your first time doing this conversion, you don't have an existing layout, which pretty much limits your choices. Click on the **New Layout** radio button, then on the **Next** button to start describing the layout. You'll then be presented with two radio buttons, one marked Standard and one marked Browser Frames. Select **Standard**, then click on the **Next** button. (The Browser Frames option gives the user a slightly better set of controls over the presentation, but it shrinks the display to do so and it only works with certain browsers.)

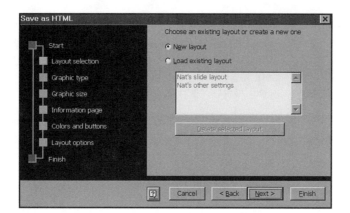

You can jump ahead or back to any step. Just click on the step in the left part of the dialog box.

Step Two: Graphic Format Frenzy

The next selection screen gives you a choice between saving each slide as a GIF file or a JPEG file, or saving the whole presentation in a format that needs the PowerPoint Animation Player. As I explained previously, you want that last choice about as much as you want a jalapeño and peanut butter sandwich on rice cakes.

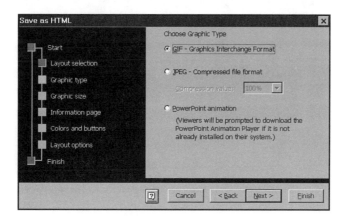

No! Don't click that PowerPoint Animation button! I mean it!

If your slides consist of text, simple graphics, and simple backgrounds, then you should click on the **GIF** radio button, because the viewer will get to see the slide more quickly this way.

If you have backgrounds with complex fades, or full-color, full-detail photographs on your slides, click on the **JPEG** button, and you'll get a wider range of color. If you select this, you can pick how good a picture you want. Click on the drop-down button to select a percentage from 50 to 100. The higher the number, the better your picture will look, but also the longer it will take before the viewer can see it all.

Once you've made your selection, click on that ever-popular **Next** button to move on to the next step.

Step Three: Big Slide, or Little Slide?

The next piece of information is how big your slide should be. Usually, the person viewing the PowerPoint presentation automatically gets to see it at the right size to fill up his screen. However, on the Web, you have to pick a size ahead of time. If you pick the best size for a person with a small screen, it will look small on big screens. But if you pick the best size for a big screen, it will be too big for people with small screens, and they'll have to scroll around to see it all. It's a dilemma wrapped in a conundrum, and served with a side order of enigmas.

The screen size is measured in pixels, *the number of dots that make up the screen image. Most people use 640 by 480 or 800 by 600.*

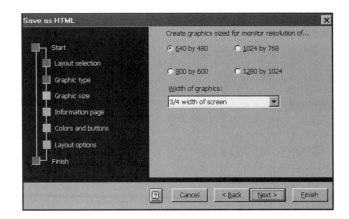

Generally speaking, your best bet is to make it the right size for the smaller screen users. Not only does that assure that everyone can use it, but by keeping the slide reasonably small, you make sure that it can be downloaded to the user quickly. Select the **640 by 480** radio button, then click on the **Width of graphics** drop-down list box and pick **3/4 width of screen**.

Why Not Full Width?

You don't want to pick Full width of screen for your slide, because the Web browser's window takes up some of that width. Even at 3/4 width, people using lower screen resolutions may have to scroll up and down to see the whole slide, depending on their browser option settings.

When you're finished with this step, just click on the **Next** button, and saunter on down to the next one!

Step Four : A Veritable Barrel Full O' Information

The next set of questions ask for information that it can put on the first page. You can decide that this is none of anyone's business, if you want. Then again, you can decide that the whole presentation is none of anyone's business...

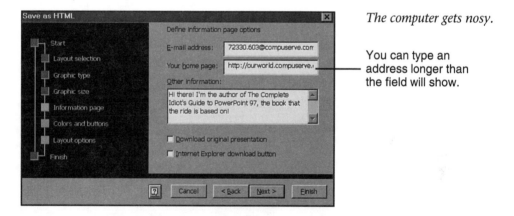

The computer gets nosy.

You can type an address longer than the field will show.

In the **E-Mail Address** field, fill in an e-mail address where people can contact you if they want. Below that in the **Your Home Page** field, add in the address of the main Web site for you or your company (or the National Organization of Weasel Jugglers, if you want). Remember to start the home page address with http: or else it won't work.

Put any other information you want people to know about you or your presentation into the **Other Information** field.

There are two checkboxes at the bottom of the dialog box. Clicking on the **Download Original Presentation** checkbox means that your original PowerPoint presentation will also be put on the Web, so that anyone who has PowerPoint can see the presentation as you originally designed it, with all the audio, video, and animation. Remember, though, that this will take up Web server space, and probably not many people will download it.

Clicking on the **Internet Explorer Download button** checkbox puts an ad for Microsoft's Web browser onto your page. This slows down the viewing of the page slightly. It's not as if the user needs that particular Web browser to look at your presentation, since the presentation looks just as good with the more-popular Netscape Navigator, or with most other modern graphical Web browsers. Might as well leave this unchecked.

The **Next** button is your friend. Click on it.

Step Five: Color Picking and Button Pushing for Fun and Profit

The next step lets you pick the color scheme for everything except your slides. This color scheme will affect the information page, the borders around the image, and pages that show just the text from your slides (although the people who look at these pages probably do so because they don't have a graphic monitor, so they can't see the pictures or the colors).

You can make the text the same color as the background, making it invisible to everyone!

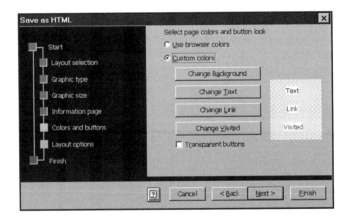

The best choice for this is **Use Browser Colors**, which lets the viewer see the page with the colors he configured as the default in his browser. He's picked colors that are best for him, no reason to mess with it.

Unless, of course, you're one of those people who likes messing with things. Click on any of the four buttons to change the background color, the color for most text, the color for linked text, and the color for links that have already been used. Clicking on any of these buttons brings up a grid of color squares. Click on the square of the color you want, then on the **OK** button. The color scheme shows up in the left edge of the dialog box, so you can see how well the colors you've chosen work together.

Clicking the **Transparent buttons** checkbox will make the slide control buttons match the color of the background. This is a Good Thing. Check this off. Then click on the **Next** button to get to choose the type of on-screen buttons the Web presentation will use.

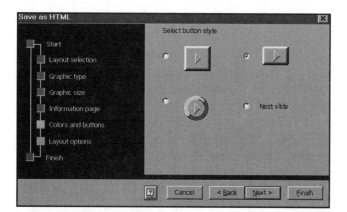

Button, button, who's got the button?

Select one of the four button types, and click the **Next** button to get to the next step. Three of the button types use symbols to describe what they do, while the fourth just uses words. I recommend using the button design that's just words (represented here by the words "Next slide") because people understand words. The Forward button symbol that they show in the example for the symbol buttons may seem pretty clear, but the other symbol buttons will have strange thing on them like a picture of a house and the letter i in a circle, neither of which is easy for the user to figure out if he doesn't already know what they mean!

Step Six: Where Do the Buttons Go? Where Do the Files Go?

The first screen of the next step lets you pick if the control buttons go above the slide, below the slide, or next to the slide. So many options! Above or below is usually the best. Click on the one you want, and that decision will be out of the way.

Perhaps presentations should be like coats, with women's presentations having buttons on the left and men's presentations having buttons on the right.

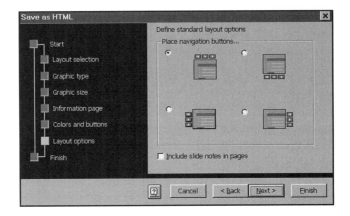

Check off the **Include slide notes in pages** checkbox if you want people to see your Speaker's Notes with each slide. Click **Next** once you've made your decision.

Finally, the system wants to know where to put all of the Web files. Click on the **Browse** button to see a file navigator. Select a folder where you want them stored, then click on the **OK** button. PowerPoint will create a new folder in that folder. This new folder will have the same name as the presentation, and in it will be all of the files that you'll have to put on the Web!

A folder to put a folder into!

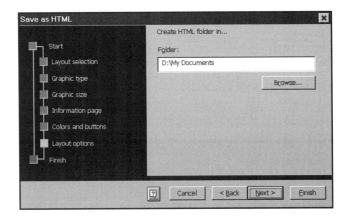

Click on the **Finish** button, and PowerPoint presents you with a Save as HTML dialog box which asks you to type a name for the settings you just entered. Type a name into the field then click on the **Save** button. Next time you want a Web presentation set up the same way, you'll be able to select this name from the Load Existing Layout list, instead of having to repick all the same settings.

Once that's out of the way, PowerPoint will start building this Web presentation! When it's done, it will tell you that the presentation has been successfully saved as HTML. Click on the **OK** button, and say "thank you" as you do. (No reason not to be polite, even to your computer.)

Publish or Perish! (Hint: Pick "Publish")

Now that you've got your presentation in Web form, it's time to *publish* it (put it up on your Web site). There are plenty of different packages out there designed to let you take the files from your hard disk and put them on the Web server. None of these tools work with all Web servers. (Some of them don't seem to work with any servers at all!)

So the best way to handle this step is to ask the person in charge of the Web site how to put the pages up there. If you fumble around a little and act only semi-competent, perhaps the Web administrator will even take care of it for you and save you all of the work!

What Hath Thou Wrought? Looking at Your Web Presentation

You can see how your Web presentation is going to look without actually getting on the Web. Start your Web browser, and tell it that you want to view a file. (If you're using Netscape, hit **Ctrl+O** to get a file browser. If you're using Internet Explorer, hit **Ctrl+O**, then hit the **Browse** button.) Find the folder where your presentation is stored, and select the file **index.htm**. This is the first page that most Web visitors will see, and first impressions are very important (although not as important as eating your vegetables).

The information page.

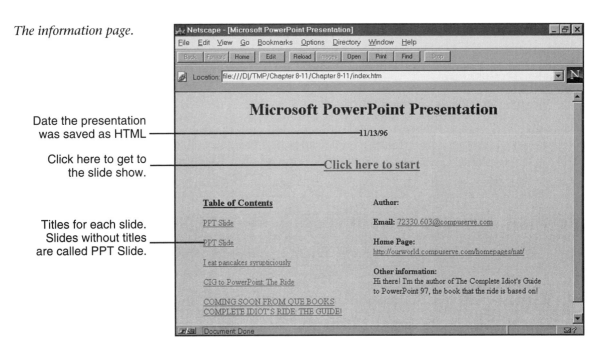

Date the presentation was saved as HTML

Click here to get to the slide show.

Titles for each slide. Slides without titles are called PPT Slide.

To start viewing the presentation, click on where it says **Click here to start** (a not-so-subtle clue). The first slide will show up, with a set of control buttons that let you move to the previous slide, the next slide, the first slide, the last slide, the information page, your home page (if you entered a homepage address), or a page that shows just the text from the slide. That seems to cover all the bases!

In addition, any hyperlinks that you built into your slide still work, so people can skip to wherever they want.

Not Perfect?

Once you've saved your presentation as HTML, you can use any standard Web page design product to change how it looks.

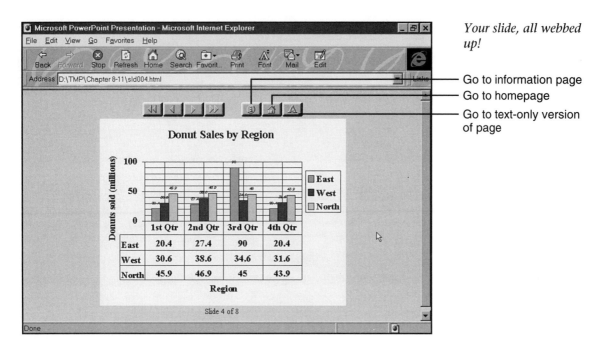

Your slide, all webbed up!

Go to information page
Go to homepage
Go to text-only version of page

The Least You Need to Know

➤ When you put your presentation on the World Wide Web, you should expect to lose all of the audio, video, animation, and transitions.

➤ To save your presentation in Web-ready form, use the **File**, **Save as HTML** command.

➤ Step through the Save as HTML Wizard by picking from the set of options presented, then clicking on **Next** to go to the next set of options.

➤ Don't check off the PowerPoint Animation option, as that will make things difficult on people viewing your presentation.

➤ When you pick the size, pick the smallest size and then select 3/4 or 1/2 of screen width, so people with the smaller resolutions can see your presentation easily.

➤ Your presentation will start with an information page, and then will show the slides one at a time, with the user pushing a button to move to the next slide.

Chapter 22

Printing Printouts and Handling Handouts

In This Chapter

➤ Print your slides and information about them onto genuine paper

➤ Specify what to print, how many copies, and how they should look

➤ Print up handouts with several slides per page

➤ Run the paper through a shredder to destroy the evidence (actually, you can figure that out for yourself!)

The advent of computers was supposed to bring us the paperless office, with everything being taken care of electronically. Alas, this has not happened. About the only part of the office that is likely to be paperless is the bathroom, and then only if the janitor has been lax about refilling the dispensers.

Instead, computers have given us the ability to create more items and many copies of those items with great efficiency. The office is now being buried under a mountain of paper—and there's no reason that PowerPoint shouldn't be in on the act!

Quick Print

If you want to quickly print out your presentation, just click on the **Print** button. This will print it all out. However, the printed version may not look just like you want it to. PowerPoint has a lot of different options to set about how the printed version should look, and when you use the Print button, it uses whatever settings you set the last time you printed using the File menu Print command described below.

Printing PowerPoint Presentations Perfectly

For greater control over the printout, yank down the ol' **File** menu and select the **Print** commands. You'll see that PowerPoint gives you a lot of control over how your printouts turn out. There's probably more options than you're ever going to use, but that's what a powerful program is all about. If it didn't have all that power, they'd probably have to call it just Point, which is a really dumb name for a program.

The Print dialog box has lots of things to click on!

What printer?

Which slides?

How should it look?

How many copies?

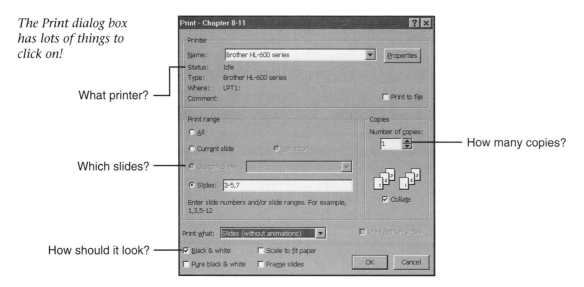

Which Printer?

Click on the arrow button on the end of the **Name** field to see a drop-down list of all of the printer devices on your system. Even if you only have one printer, you may have a number of devices set up. This is because Windows counts printers on the network and fax-modem systems as printers. You can even have actual printers configured that aren't attached to your computer. (This can be handy if you want to create a file that you can carry to someone else's computer and print on their printer.)

Select the printer that you want to print to. If you need to change something about how that printer is set up (such as which paper tray it should use or how dark the printout should be), click on the **Properties** button. If you don't actually want to print now, but rather create a file that you can print from another computer, select the right sort of printer and put a check in the **Print to File** checkbox.

Paperless Fax

If you have a properly configured fax modem, you can fax your presentation from PowerPoint without printing it out. Just select the fax driver from the printer list. When you click on **OK**, a fax program will appear asking you for details like what number to call and what the cover sheet should be.

Which Slides?

The Print Range area of the dialog box has a number of choices that let you control which parts of your presentation get printed. Click on **All**, and all the slides are printed. Choose **Current Slide**, and just the slide you're working on gets printed. Choose **Selection**, and all the slides that are currently selected get printed. (This is usually the same as Current Slide, unless you've selected multiple slides.)

Pick **Slides**, and the text box next to it lights up. Type the numbers of the slides that you want printed, separated by commas. You can include *ranges* of slides, all of the slides from one slide to another, by listing the first slide, then a dash, then the last slide. For example, if you put 3–5,7,9 into this field, PowerPoint will print slides 3,4,5,7, and 9.

How Should It Look?

When it comes to figuring how your printout should look, it would be nice if there was an option marked Just Right. There isn't such a thing, so you have to pick for yourself.

First, click on the drop-down arrow on the **Print What** field. One option is **Slides**, which prints out one slide per page. (If you have animation on some slides, you'll get to choose either **Slides (With Animations)** or **Slides (Without Animations).** With Animations will print a copy of how the slide looks before any animations, plus for every animated object on the slide, one copy of how the slide looks after that animation. (Without Animations only prints how the slide looks after all the animations are over.) There are three Handouts options, which are explained later in the chapter. Choosing **Notes Pages** will print one slide at the top of each page, with the Speaker Notes for that page under it. Choosing **Outline View** will print the text outline for the pages, much as you see when looking at your presentation in Outline view.

Underneath that are a series of checkboxes. The first one, **Print Hidden Slides**, tells the computer to include the hidden slides in your presentation. This check box will already be selected if you have chosen a hidden slide to print (except with the All choice). Since the other range selections besides All let you pick individual slides, PowerPoint assumes that if you selected a hidden slide, you must want it!

Photocopying?
If your print-outs are going to be photocopied, choose **Black & White**. That will copy better than a color printout.

Selecting **Black & White** will cause the printout not to include any colors. Colors will be turned into shades of gray, instead. If you have a black and white printer, PowerPoint will automatically use this feature for you. (It would be a neat trick for PowerPoint to find a way to print in color on your black and white printer, wouldn't it?) Selecting **Pure Black & White** means that there are no shades of gray. Your colors will turn black or white. In cases where you have color text on a color background, this may be easier to read than Black & White, or it may be impossible to read (if both colors turn black or both turn white).

Picking **Scale to Fit Paper** will stretch the slide to fill up the page. Picking **Frame Slides** will draw a square around each slide, to show where the edges of the slide are (much like the way that they appear in the Slide Sorter view).

How Many Copies?

If you want to print out more than one copy, enter the number of copies that you want to print into the **Number of Copies** field. If you want to print out *less* than one copy, then you're really wasting your time here, aren't you?

When you're printing out more than one copy of more than one page, then collation becomes important. If you put a check into the **Collate** checkbox, it will print out the entire first copy, then the entire second copy, and so on. If there isn't a check there, it will print all the copies of the first page, then all the copies of the second page, and on to the last page. Not using collation may get it to print faster in many cases, but then you have to waste time putting all the pages in order.

What Are You Waiting for?

Once you've got everything selected, click **OK** to start printing. Okay, the printing doesn't start immediately. That doesn't mean that the computer's ignoring you. What's happening is that the computer is sending the information on what to print to the disk. Then the information will be sent from the disk to your printer. This way, you don't have to wait for your printing to be finished before you go back to working with your presentation.

Handouts That No Panhandler Would Want

A *handout* is a set of pages that reprint all of the slides in your presentation, several slides to a page. They're called handouts because you're supposed to hand them out to your audience, so they can take your presentation with them when they go. It also helps the viewer follow the presentation.

There are three different Handout selections on the Print What list. If you select **Handouts (2 Slides per Page)** you will get two slides on each page (surprise), one printed on top and one on the bottom. If you choose **Handouts (6 Slides per Page)**, the slides are arranged in three rows of two.

If you choose **Handouts (3 Slides per Page)**, you get something a little different. Instead of just printed slides, you get three slides on the left side of the page each accompanied by a row of lines on the right. These lines can be used for making notes about the slide, which makes this form of handout great for handing out *before* your presentation.

The Least You Need to Know

➤ To print out all or part of your presentation, use the **File**, **Print** command.

➤ On the Print dialog box, first select the printer that you want to use from the list on the Name field.

➤ You can select **All** to print out all of the slides, **Selection** to print just the selected slides, or **Slides** to type in a list of the slides that you want to print.

➤ In the Print What field, selecting **Slides** will print one slide per page, **Handouts** will print 2, 3, or 6 slides per page depending on the option you pick, **Notes** will print one slide per page with your Speaker Notes, and **Outline** will print the text outline of your presentation.

➤ Put the number of copies you want printed in the **Number of Copies** field. If it's more than one, make sure **Collation** is checked, or you will have to arrange the sets yourself.

➤ Selecting the **Black & White** option will print it in black, white, and shades of gray, while **Pure Black & White** won't use gray.

➤ If you want to print the hidden slides as well as the non-hidden ones, select **Hidden Slides**.

➤ When you're ready to print, click the **OK** button.

A three-slides-per-page handout.

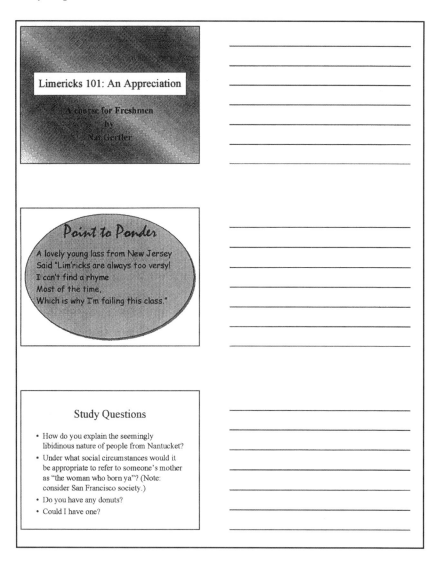

Part 5
Getting the Most Out of PowerPoint

If you like giving presentations, then you'll want to get the most out of PowerPoint. If you don't like giving presentations, then you'll want to get out of PowerPoint altogether. But by this point in the book, it's too late! You're now the expert!

In this part lies the secrets to making a good presentation, one that communicates clearly and straightforwardly, one that people want to pay attention to and can understand. And you'll learn to take things from other programs (and pass them back to), in order to save yourself effort.

Chapter 23

Office Gossip: Swapping Info with Other Office Products

In This Chapter

➤ Copy words and pictures from any word processor or painting program into your presentation

➤ Turn a Word document into a presentation (Kazam!)

➤ Turn a presentation into a Word document (Unkazam!)

➤ Build a Word table or Excel spreadsheet onto your page

➤ Copy numbers and charts from Microsoft Excel into your presentation

You're probably using your computer for more than just PowerPoint. There's Tetris, there's Doom, there's Solitaire… and oh yes, there are all those word processors and spreadsheets and other silly things you have to use in order to get your work done.

Since you have a copy of PowerPoint, odds are that you have all of Microsoft Office installed on your machine, including the Microsoft Word word processor and Microsoft Excel spreadsheet. Sometimes, you'll have information you created in one of those programs that you want to use in PowerPoint.

Stealing Bits from Anywhere

Windows has a built-in set of copying and pasting tools that make it easy to yank words out of a document, no matter what program you created them in, and slam them into your presentation. To do this, select the text in the document. Hit **Ctrl+C**, which is the standard copy command. The text will be stored in an area of memory called the clipboard. Then, go to your presentation, open up a text box for it (or select a spot in existing text), and hit **Ctrl+V**, the Paste command. This will take the text from the clipboard and slam it into the text box.

Working with pictures is much the same. In whatever picture program you're using, select the area of the picture that you want to copy. Hit **Ctrl+C**. Go to your presentation, in slide show mode, and hit **Ctrl+V**. The copied material will appear on the page.

Documents That Are Out of this Word!

Microsoft Word is a very good outline editor. It's so full of rich features and tools that I really can't describe how to use it here (although if you hunker on down to your bookstore and grab a copy of *The Complete Idiot's Guide to Word 97*, you should find it in there). So it's certainly reasonable that you'd want to make the outline for your presentation in Word, or take an outline that you already made there and make a presentation out of it.

How a Word outline becomes a presentation.

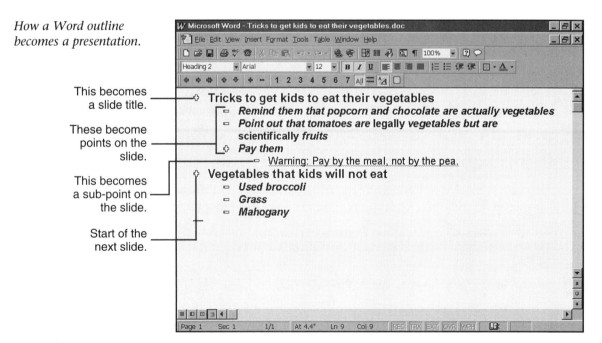

This becomes a slide title.

These become points on the slide.

This becomes a sub-point on the slide.

Start of the next slide.

Doing this is as easy as pie (one of those easy sorts of pie, not one of those tricky lattice pies). Load the document up in Word, pull down Word's **File** menu and, from the **Send To** submenu, select **Microsoft PowerPoint**. Word will start up PowerPoint (unless it's already running, in which case it doesn't have to), and the outline will appear as a new presentation. Each main point will be the title at the top of a new slide, and the items under that will appear as the text on the slide.

Even if you're not comfortable with outline mode, you can still turn your Word document into a presentation. For each slide, you'll want one paragraph to be the title, and one or more paragraphs of text for the slide. Once you have that all set up, hit **Ctrl+A** to select all the text in your document. Then click on the **Style** drop-down menu and select **Heading 2** as the style. Then, for each of the title paragraphs, click on the paragraph, pull down the **Style** list, and select **Heading 1**. Finally, use the **File**, **Send To**, **Microsoft PowerPoint** command to turn it into a presentation.

Word-ward Ho!

You can turn your presentation into one of several sorts of Word documents. You can create a Word document with pictures of the slides accompanied by your notes. You can make one with pictures of your slides accompanied by underlines. Or, you can just make one with all the text from your slide. It's up to you. I really don't care which you choose. I have a problem with apathy.

Doing any of these is as easy as a very-slightly-more-difficult pie. With your presentation loaded in PowerPoint, pull down the **File** menu, find the **Send To** submenu, and select the **Microsoft Word** command that you find there. A Write Up dialog box will appear, wanting to know what sort of document you want to make out of it.

Pick from a range of formats for the Word document.

Select the style of Word document you want by clicking on the radio button next to that style, then click on the **OK** button. The new document will appear in Word.

Bouncing Back and Forth

You can take an outline that you've been working on in PowerPoint, send it to Word, make some changes there, and then send it back to PowerPoint. When you do this, you'll lose all your graphics, and your bullet formatting may change, so only do this if you haven't put much work into those things yet, or had so much fun doing the graphics the first time that you want to do it all over again!

Table Setting

You can put a Word table on your slide without even seeming to leave PowerPoint. Just click on the **Insert MS Word Table** button, and a little 4×5 grid will appear under the button. No, it's not time to play super-tic-tac-toe, it's time to pick how many rows and columns are going to be in your table. Click on any square in the grid, and you will get a table with a grid that's the same number of squares down and from the left.

Just point to where you want the lower right edge of the table.

2 x 4 Table

When you select the size, PowerPoint will display a small Word window on the page, and the PowerPoint menus and toolbars will be replaced by the Word menus and toolbars. Fill in the information that you want in the table, then click outside of the Word window. The window will go away, leaving just the table (without the borders), and the toolbars will return to normal. You can double-click on the table at any time to go back to editing it.

Picnic Time: Spreading a Sheet Instead of a Table

Adding an Excel spreadsheet works the same as adding the Word table. Click on the Insert Microsoft Excel Worksheet button, then select the grid size, and a spreadsheet window will appear on the slide, with the Excel toolbars appearing. Fill in the information you want, then click outside the window, and the spreadsheet will be part of the slide. (Unlike the Word table, the spreadsheet will include the grid lines.)

Excel-erating Your Presentation

If you want to do pie, well, that's about as easy as copying a spreadsheet from Excel into PowerPoint. However, I won't teach you to do pie here. (Write in and insist that they have me write *The Complete Idiot's Guide to Pie*!) In Excel, select the cells that you want to copy over, then hit the **Copy** button or press **Ctrl+C** to copy it. Then head over to PowerPoint, pull down the **Edit** menu, and select **Paste Special**. Why Paste Special instead of paste normally? Because this will allow us some special tricks.

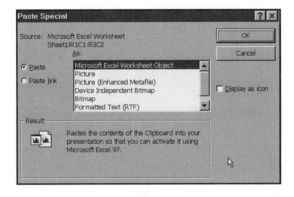

This is a special paste, even better than library paste!

When you select Paste Special, a dialog box comes up. At the center of this dialog box is a list of styles that it can paste. Pick **Microsoft Excel Worksheet Object**.

Over at the right is a pair of radio buttons. If you select the one marked **Paste**, then this will be pasted as its own little worksheet in PowerPoint. If you choose **Paste Link**, you get a nifty side benefit: whenever someone changes the original spreadsheet, the change is automatically made in your presentation! This is because PowerPoint doesn't actually store the spreadsheet. Instead, it stores it as "Here we'll display cells A3 through J27 from the Profits 97 spreadsheet." Whenever PowerPoint loads up the presentation, it checks the spreadsheet again for what is currently there.

You may not want to use Paste Link, however. For one thing, you might want your presentation to reflect the spreadsheet as it currently is, rather than change with the time. For another thing, if someone moves or deletes that spreadsheet, it can mess up your presentation.

The Web Ain't Up to Date

The copy of your presentation you saved as HTML will not automatically update when the graph changes. You have to load the presentation again and save it as HTML again.

Once you've got that selection settled, click **OK**. The spreadsheet section appears on your slide (although you may have to resize it using its sizing handles to get a clear look at it).

Moving a Chart

Copying a chart from Excel is as easy as pie chart! In fact, it's almost the same as copying a spreadsheet. In Excel, select the chart by clicking on it near the edge. (Make sure you're not clicking on part of the chart or its markings.) Hit the **Copy** button to copy it to the clipboard. In PowerPoint, pull down the **Edit** menu and select **Paste Special**. This time, the type you select is **Microsoft Excel Chart Object**. Once again, you can choose between Paste and Paste Link, for the same reasons. Click on **OK**, and the chart appears on the slide!

It's a Complete Copy

When you use Paste Special to paste a spreadsheet or chart in, PowerPoint actually gets the whole spreadsheet, not just the part you copied. It only shows the part you copied, but if you double-click on it, you'll get the Excel menus and toolbars and will be able to work with all the data of the spreadsheet.

The Least You Need to Know

 ➤ To copy text or pictures from any editing program, select them, hit **Ctrl+C** to copy, then go to PowerPoint and click on the **Paste** button to paste them in.

➤ To use a Word outline as the basis for a new presentation, load up the outline in Word and use the **File**, **Send To**, **Microsoft PowerPoint** command.

➤ To copy all the text from your presentation to a new Word document, use PowerPoint's **File**, **Send To**, **Microsoft Word** command.

 ➤ To add a new Word table to your slide, click on **Insert Microsoft Word Table** button.

 ➤ To add a new Excel spreadsheet to your slide, click on the **Insert Microsoft Excel Worksheet** button.

 ➤ To copy an Excel chart or section of a spreadsheet to your slide, first select it in Excel, then click on the **Copy** button. Then, in PowerPoint, use the **Edit**, **Paste Special** command, select the appropriate type of **Microsoft Excel** object from the Paste Special dialog box, and click on **OK**.

➤ The Paste Link option in the Paste Special dialog box tells PowerPoint to recheck the source document every time the presentation is loaded, and update the copied part to match any changes.

Chapter 24

Making Your Presentation a Doozy! (Not a Don'tzy!)

In This Chapter

➤ Make a slide show that people can see

➤ Make a slide show that people want to see

➤ Put control links on your slide that people can use

➤ Keep your slide show on topic and interesting

➤ Avoid getting carried away

So far, the book has told you how to put together a presentation. That's like a book on painting teaching you how to dip the brush into the paint and then to drag the brush across the canvas. You now have all the tools to make a really good presentation, or a really tremendously awful one. This chapter has a few hints that should let you know just which you are doing.

Can You See the Forest Through the Polychromatic Hyperlinked Trees?

PowerPoint is a powerful tool, full of features and tricks that let you make an amazing slam-bam presentation. With all the things you can do with your presentation, it's easy to forget that you don't really want a presentation. Having a presentation is not your ultimate goal.

Unless you're just sitting around using PowerPoint for the fun of it (and if that's how you have fun, there's nothing wrong with that), your ultimate goal is to give information to people (and even that may well be a step toward something else, such as getting people to buy your new all-plastic reusable donuts). Your presentation is just a tool to inform people. PowerPoint is a tool-making tool.

Keeping the Point in PowerPoint

The first step to making a good presentation is to have something worth telling people about. Before you put in the big effort, think about what you're doing. Do you have information that people will want to know? Do you have all the information they want, or are you going to leave them with more questions than answers? You should know the information that you're going to tell them before you put the very first word on a slide.

It isn't hard to find out if what you have will interest people. All you have to do is find people, tell them what you know, and see if it interests them. (This may sound tricky because there is no entry for *people* in the yellow pages, but if you check the white pages, you'll find some there. Odds are, someone you know may already be a people!) Get someone who would be a member of your audience, and then just talk to them about the topic at hand. Don't tell them you're planning a presentation, just talk a bit and see if they're interested. If so, you've got something. If not, it may be time to rethink. And if they ask questions about it, pay attention to those questions, and consider putting the answers in your presentation.

Cool-looking Augmented Obfuscation

The tools in PowerPoint have a lot of options. You can spend hours trying different metallic background fills on your logo, using different gradients, different directions, and so on. You probably *will* spend hours doing this, in fact, because it's so easy to get caught up in doing that, and rotating it to just the right angle, and adjusting the shadow, and tweaking the spacing between letters, all the while so caught up in it that you don't notice that the words in the logo say *How To Talk Goodly*.

Having a clear and understandable presentation is a lot more important than having a keen-looking one. Sure, you should take care that it looks good, but adding in all the flashes and gimmicks, the multimedia bells and hyperlink whistles, should be the last thing on the list, not the first.

It's more important that the information be in a reasonable order, so that you don't need something that comes later in order to understand something that comes earlier, than it is to have your logo in 3-D on each slide. If you spend some time planning the presentation before you even start PowerPoint, you'll save a lot of time that you would have wasted rearranging things later.

If you find yourself spending more time in PowerPoint than you did putting together the information for the presentation in the first place, you've probably turned into a PowerPoint addict, and should try to do a little less.

Watch Your Language

A picture is said to be worth a thousand words, although I have no idea where you'd go to make that trade. However, a few words, well chosen, can communicate an awful lot. A few words, badly chosen, can quickly confuse your entire audience.

Check your spelling. The built in spell-checker is really handy, underlining words that it doesn't recognize. However, it's not smart enough to recognize a typo that turns one word into another. If you're trying to type Shakespeare's phrase Now is the winter of our discontent, and accidentally hit the space bar instead of the n, PowerPoint will have absolutely no complaint about Now is the winter of our disco tent.

One good tool to catch your typing mistakes is the AutoCorrect feature. This keeps an eye on your typing, finding the most common mistakes and correcting them automatically, without even bothering to ask. To take advantage of this helper, pull down the **Tools** menu and select **AutoCorrect**. An AutoCorrect dialog box listing all of the kinds of things that AutoCorrect can catch appears, with checkboxes for each type. Make sure all of your favorite mistakes are checked, particularly that the **Replace Text as you Type** box is checked.

Exceptional Exceptions

If you use an abbreviation that ends in a period (such as abbr. for abbreviations), click on the **Exceptions** button and add the abbreviation to the list on the **First Letter** tab, so that AutoCorrect won't assume it's the end of a sentence and capitalize the next letter.

I keep trying to type a list of mistakes that AutoCorrect corrects, but the same feature in my word processor keeps correcting them!

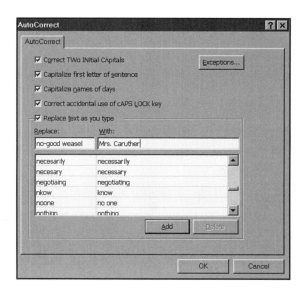

AutoIncorrect
AutoCorrect automatically replaces with the copyright symbol, which can be a problem if you're trying to display lettered points. You may want to delete this one.

You can even add the typos that you make most often, so that AutoCorrect will always fix them for you. Just type the typo into the **Replace** field, and the correct version into the **With** field, then click on the **Add** button. It will be added to the list of common mistakes at the bottom of the dialog box. To remove one from the list, just click on it then on the **Delete** button.

Some of the corrections on the list aren't even errors. For example, if you type (tm), AutoCorrect will turn that into a little trademark symbol at the end of the word.

Grammar is something that you'll have to catch yourself, unless you're wily enough to rope someone else into checking it for you (which isn't a bad idea, since your own mistakes are the hardest to catch. I have a whole team of editors working on this book, so my grammar be perfect). Pay attention to this, since a blatant grammar mistake can make you look less intelligent and more careless.

The grammar mistake that seems to get people's bad attention most quickly is the mis-used apostrophe. Apostrophes are easy to mess up, because while there are only a few exceptions to each apostrophe rule, those exceptions appear often. Don't use an apostrophe to make a word plural (*The monkey's got their report cards* is wrong) unless what you're pluralizing is a single letter (*The monkey got all A's on his report card* is right.) Do use the apostrophe when adding an s to make something possessive (*The monkey's report card was delicious* is right, because it's the report card belonging to the monkey), except when you're adding it to a pronoun, as with its, ours, hers, and yours. (*The monkey ate its report card*, not *it's report card*.) Always use an apostrophe when contracting two words into one. (*It's a bad idea to make edible report cards* is right, because *it's* is short for *it is*.) Don't confuse the contractions *you're* and *we're* with the similar-looking *your* and *were*.

Watch Someone Else's Language

When it comes to technical terms, be aware of who your audience is. Are they going to know the terms you're using? If you're not sure, you've got two choices. You can either avoid using the term altogether, or you can define it for them. A definition doesn't have to be a big, meticulous thing that interrupts the flow of what you're saying. You can use quick *sidebar definitions* (short definitions in parentheses after you use the word) without jarring much. There, I just used one! That was pretty painless, wasn't it.

In some applications, you have to worry about the entire language. This is particularly true of consumer applications like kiosks. There are large parts of the U.S. and Canada where a significant number of people have something besides English as their first language. You'll usually run into French (Canada) or Spanish (U.S.), but in specific areas there are other languages as well. Bringing your message to someone in a tongue they are comfortable with is not only good business, it may be legally required in certain situations.

There are several ways of dealing with the multilingual problem. One is to avoid language altogether, which you may be able to pull of in a store window display with nothing but pictures and prices, but cases where you can pull this off easily are more the exception than the rule. You can also put multiple languages on the screen at once. If you're doing this, you should be consistent from slide to slide about exactly where each version is placed. You also have to be sure that you're not using audio in that case. Finally, you can have a hyperlink on your first slide that is marked with the name of the language, taking the viewer to a version of the slide show in that language.

Make sure you get a good translation. Translations which have upon them much badnesses are hard read and you be to avoiding them like the turtle that snaps!

That Isn't Wrong, It's Foreign

When you include foreign language text, select it and use the **Tools, Language** command. This way, the automatic spell checker knows not to check it, and the spell checking part of the Style Checker knows to check a foreign dictionary (sold separately) for it.

Make the area's dominant language easier to notice, so that most people gravitate to the correct text. Smaller type is useful for languages with long or many words.

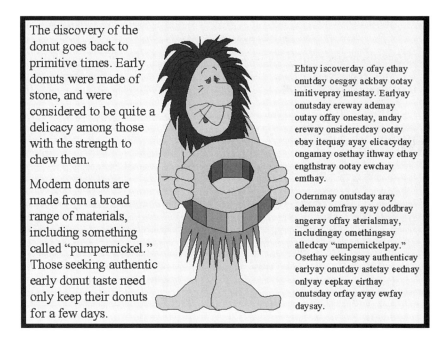

The discovery of the donut goes back to primitive times. Early donuts were made of stone, and were considered to be quite a delicacy among those with the strength to chew them.

Modern donuts are made from a broad range of materials, including something called "pumpernickel." Those seeking authentic early donut taste need only keep their donuts for a few days.

Ehtay iscoverday ofay ethay onutday oesgay ackbay ootay imitivepray imestay. Earlyay onutsday ereway ademay outay offay onestay, anday ereway onsideredcay ootay ebay itequay ayay elicacyday ongamay osethay ithway ethay engthstray ootay ewchay emthay.

Odernmay onutsday aray ademay omfray ayay oddbray angeray offay aterialsmay, includingay omethingsay alledcay "umpernickelpay." Osethay eekingsay authenticay earlyay onutday astetay eednay onlyay eepkay eirthay onutsday orfay ayay ewfay daysay.

The Awful Eyeful: Slides That Are Hard to Look at

Making a truly ugly slide is like making a truly ugly house—it usually happens not from trying to do too little, but from trying to do too much, all at once, throwing in so many different styles and clashing colors. Trying to do less will often let your slide have more effect.

Look Here! No, There! No, Wait, Over Here!

A slide show shouldn't be like three-ring circus, with a bunch of things calling for the viewer's attention all at the same time. This isn't to say that you can't have a reasonable amount of things on a slide, but there should only be one thing that says "look at me first," and should lead to looking at all the other important things.

There are several ways of deciding what gets seen first. Bigger items tend to get seen before smaller items. (That's why people read headlines first, then the articles: the text is bigger.) Colors that stand out against the background are more visible than colors that are similar to the background. The eye picks up on simpler designs (like a cartoon drawing) quicker than on more detailed things (like a photograph). Things at the top of the slide are read before things lower on the slide. Things that are animated call attention to themselves before things that are standing still.

All of this isn't to say that you can't put a number of things on a slide, but if you do, many of them should seem more a part of a background design rather than individual eye-grabbers. If you want to put your logo on every slide, just make it a key element on the first slide, and put it in a subtle color on all the rest. If you want control buttons that appear on every slide, put them at the bottom of the slide. People will be able to find them if they look for them.

When Colors Collide!

Color is tricky.

When you want something to be easily visible, the natural reaction is to just use a different color than the background. Put red words on a green background, and it should be easy to look at, right? Not necessarily.

What really makes things easy or hard to look at doesn't have much to do with what color they are. Instead, it has to do with how bright or dark they are. If you put light blue text on a dark blue background, it will be easy to read. If you put bright red text on a bright green background, it will be hard to read. Black will stand out on any light background, and white will stand out on any dark one.

There's a neat trick for checking the readability of the colors you've chosen, and that's to forget the colors altogether! Click the **Black and White** button on the Standard toolbar. The black and white display doesn't show the colors (obviously), but merely the darkness level, turning bright colors into light grays and dark ones into dark grays. If it's hard to read in this mode, it will be a strain on people's eyes in color modes.

Color Concern
Checking the black and white view also assures you that color-blind people will be able to read your slide. Color-blindness hits about 1 person in 25.

Similarly, things that are supposed to be part of the background design of the page shouldn't stand out. This doesn't mean that they have to be the same color, just the same brightness. Using the contrast and brightness controls on the picture toolbar will let you make washed-out versions of pictures, which will be just fine for use in the background.

Be aware of the moods color creates. Red is often associated with danger, warning, and financial losses, so it shouldn't be used to convey good news or positive financial results. Green is often associated with moving ahead, and is good for messages of encouragement. Blue has a calming effect, while purple suggests strangeness. Don't overladen your presentation with colors; if you're using more than 3 or 4 basic colors for text, chart colors, and backgrounds in your presentation, you're probably overdoing it.

Too Textravagant

There are already far too many ugly words in this world, like *famine*, *hatred*, and *disease*. The text on your slides shouldn't add their own form of ugliness. There are a lot of ways you can go wrong with the look of your text.

Having text that's too small to read easily is an obvious problem. How small is too small is a tough decision, but keep in mind that just because it looks fine on a computer display doesn't mean it will be fine on a projected display. In projection environments, not only are people trying to read it from clear across the room, but you also have the problem of focusing. Unless you focus exactly right, the text will be blurry.

Having too many bulleted points on a slide is also a problem. A bullet should call attention to a point. Too many bullets and they stop calling attention to anything.

By now, we've all seen forms of font abuse. One common form of this is taking a font with complex capital letters and using them for all-capitals, so that every letter is calling out for attention. This is usually pretty blatant. A subtler problem, easier to fall into, is using too many different fonts on a page. Every time you use a new font family, the reader has to adjust somewhat. This isn't too bad if there are two or even three fonts on a page, used for different things. When you get above three, you're looking for trouble. You're usually better off going for variations in the same font (using bold or italic or a different size) than going with a completely different font.

Fonts often get divided into two categories, called serif and sans-serif. *Serif* fonts have little detail lines (called *serifs*) on the end of many letters. These little lines help the eye recognize the letters, so serif fonts are good if you have a lot of text (for example, this paragraph is in a serif font). *Sans-serif* fonts don't have these little lines, which make them simpler and thus more eye-catching for headlines and short amounts of text. That's why all the section names in this book are in san-serif fonts.

To save the eyes of the world, PowerPoint includes a feature called Style Checker. Pull down the **Tools** menu and select **Style Checker**, and a Style Checker dialog box will appear, with a checklist of the three sorts of checking it can do.

You can check off the checkboxes on the check-list of things to check!

If you leave the check in the **Spelling** checkbox, it will check the spelling of your document. Sure, the automatic spell-checker that underlines wrong words will catch the same misspellings, but this will call your attention to them, in case you thought that the wavy red underline was just the international sign for "snake." If you have sections of text marked as being in a foreign language, this will use the appropriate dictionary to check them, *if* you have it installed on your system.

The **Visual Clarity** checkbox lets you check all of the different forms of text atrocities listed above, except for ugly usage of all-capitals. For that, you'll just have to develop some taste… or steer clear of all-capitals altogether.

The **Case and End Punctuation** checkbox sounds like it will make a case for bringing an end to punctuation as we know it. Actually, it will make sure that you've put a capital letter at the start of each sentence, and end the sentences with a period, exclamation point, or a question mark.

I Think 53 Fonts Is Fine

Clicking the **Options** button in the Style Checker dialog box will bring up the Options dialog box, letting you set how small type can be, how many fonts are too many, and other limits for the Style Checker to check against.

Controls: Don't Reinvent the Steering Wheel

If you're building an interactive presentation, you have to let the user know how to use it. Otherwise, they'll just stare at it for a while, then they'll go away.

The first trick is to make it clear that it is interactive. Don't just put a couple of pictures up and expect that someone will know to click on one of them. You should also avoid trying to come up with some new way of communicating what to click on. There are several good existing ways of doing this.

One way is simply to tell it straight out. If you put the words "Click here to learn more about ironing soup," then people will know that they can click there to learn more about ironing soup (unless they don't know enough to understand that sentence, in which case they're probably not smart enough to iron soup).

Another way is to take advantage of the 3-D buttons in AutoShape. Put a word on a button, and suddenly the idea of clicking there becomes very clear.

You should be careful, however, about using the buttons with the pictures on them. You may know what a triangle pointing toward a straight line is, perhaps because you have something similar on your VCR. However, there's a lot of people out there who don't have a VCR, and many others who have one and can't use it. The international symbol for information may be the best way to address an international audience, but if your presentation is in English, you should count on your audience using English.

Use words! Put the word Information on a button, and people will have a clue of what it's for. Put the phrase Click here for information on it, and it may take up more space but it will be hard not to understand. Putting the word on an arrow shape (pointing left to go back a slide or right to move to the next slide) may help folks find the right thing to click on, but the word makes it clear what it's for.

Are Your Controls Out of Control?

If you have too many controls, your presentation will be difficult to use. Imagine trying to use a mouse with 37 buttons on it, each of which does a different thing, and you'll get the sense of what I mean.

If you want your user to be able to do a lot of things, don't do it with a lot of controls on the same page with your information. Keep it down to four or five controls on each page, and have one of them be hyperlinked to a slide with the full set of controls on it. That way, only the person who is looking to do something tricky needs to face the controls, and they aren't cluttering up the rest of your presentation.

People shouldn't have to go hunting for the controls on each slide. Keep your controls in a standard spot on each slide, rather than moving them from slide to slide. Don't change what the controls look like, either.

Yelp for Help!

There was a home computer put out in the 1980's that had a lot of innovative features, but perhaps the best and the simplest was that it had a big button on the keypad marked Help. You were supposed to press that button if you needed information on how to do what you wanted to do.

Unfortunately, most of the programs didn't take advantage of the button. You'd be calling for help, but none would be coming.

If you have a complex interactive presentation, you may want to consider having an on-screen button marked Help. It's very comforting for the user to have it there, even if he doesn't use it. But if he does use it, he better be taken to a slide full of useful information!

Keep Your Content Interesting

Sometimes, people have to pay attention. If you're the boss, and it's your meeting, then they have to pay attention. Even if they're forced to pay attention, they'll get much more out of it if they're interested.

If they're not interested and they don't have to pay attention, they'll just walk away.

The first step is to make sure you're giving them the right amount of information. There are three levels of information that you have to keep your eye on.

➤ The *least* you should tell them is what they need to know.

➤ The *best* you should tell them is what they want to know. This doesn't mean that you want to tell them everything that any of them might want to know; if your presentation is trying to sell a car to everyone, you can't put in all the information that a big car-aholic will want, because you'll bore everyone else. Which brings up the third amount.

➤ The *most* you should tell them is the most they want to know. What you're talking about may have a big history, and you may have spent the past decade of your life investigating it, but unless that history is either extremely fascinating or very important to them, skip it.

The Topic: The Topic

You should always be clear on what the topic of the presentation is, and what the ultimate goal is. Every single slide in your presentation should be about that topic and head toward that goal in some way. This doesn't mean that you can't put side comments in, but you should know when you're doing so and not give them a whole slide, much less a bunch of slides.

Part of the trick is to define your topic very precisely. A title can be a good place for this description of your topic, so long as it's not too long. If your presentation's title is *How to Iron Soup*, then you know that you don't need those three slides on the history of ironing soup, because this isn't a history lesson, it's a how to lesson.

Pictures Tell a Story

School teaches us to be word people. We're always told to write essays, never to draw them. That's a shame, because pictures are both incredibly interesting and incredibly informative.

You can write fifteen paragraphs about how the new NG-57 automobile has a transwhoopdidoo suspension system which gives it a turning radius of 3.79 inches, and people will sit there and try to parse what all the technology is about. But if you show them a film clip of the car taking a tight corner, not only will they understand it all better, they will also believe it.

A drawing may not carry the sense of reality of a photograph, but it can highlight what you want to show very effectively. Of course, to get a drawing of something original, you either have to learn to draw, or find someone else who can. Even a simple diagram, however, can go far.

Graphs turn numbers (which are hard to understand) into pictures (which are easy to understand). This is a good thing.

If You Can't Please One Person, How Can You Please Them All?

I know this suggestion has popped up in various specific forms, but here is the general version: The best way to make sure you have a good presentation is to have someone try it out for you. Pick a person who doesn't already know the information that the presentation has to offer. Let them tell you what's wrong with it. They'll find the missing things, the unneeded things, and the confusing things. Listen to them, and don't put down what they say. Then fix those things, and find someone new to test it next time.

The Least You Need to Know

➤ Have something to say. Spend your time on content that communicates rather than on making your presentation as pretty as possible.

➤ Grammar and spelling count. The **Tools**, **AutoCorrect** command can keep an eye on your work as you type, and protect you from hundreds of common errors.

➤ There should be one main thing on each slide, calling your attention to look at it first.

➤ If the text is not easy to read in the **View**, **Black and White** mode, it won't be easy to read in full color.

➤ Make it clear what the user can click on, either by making it into a 3-D button or by having something that says "Click here to" whatever. Don't use too many control buttons on a page. A button marked Help can be extremely useful on a complex slide, if it goes to a useful slide of helpful information.

➤ Don't tell people more than they want to know, unless they need to know it.

➤ Pictures communicate more effectively than text, often.

Chapter 25

Express to Impress: Delivering Good Oral Presentations

In This Chapter

➤ Speak with confidence

➤ Speak with pride

➤ Speak with people

➤ Get people to listen and understand you

When someone knows something that we want to know, when they get good at something we understand, we want them to tell us about it. The problem is that most of the time, what they're good at isn't talking to people and explaining things. Do one thing well, and you're expected to do something else well as well. Luckily, it isn't a hard thing to learn.

Actually, you've already learned most of it. You've already learned the mechanics of it. You can open your mouth and make noises come out, and not just belches, either. You can make sounds that mean something to other people (such as "Excuse me for belching!"). That's the hardest part, and it took a lot of work way back when. Now all you've got to do is learn the art of delivering the presentation, and luckily, there are a handful of things that, if you keep them in mind, can move you quickly in that direction. Delivery is important. Great delivery won't make a lousy presentation great (although it will improve it), but lousy delivery can slaughter a great presentation.

Rule 1: Don't Picture Your Audience Naked

Picturing your entire audience naked is an old piece of advice, and it's a really bad one. Unless you're working in the nudist colony business, standing in front of a roomful of naked people is apt to make you nervous or revolted or excited or just plain giggly. At the very least, you're going to feel overdressed for the occasion (and delivering your presentation naked to avoid that problem is not a good idea either).

Rule 2: Rehearse

Some people in this world can "wing it." They can go out, unprepared, and just talk about whatever needs to be talked about. If you're one of those people, you probably already know that you are. Otherwise, it pays to practice. This doesn't mean memorizing exactly what you're going to say, because you shouldn't lock yourself in that tightly. But if you try to wing it to yourself, you can find out what you're comfortable talking about, what you need to make notes on, and probably anticipate where you are likely to get questions. (Close your office door when you do this, if possible, or people will think you've gone crazy, and are sitting there talking to your computer.) This is also a good way to catch mistakes on your slides, as well as places where you can arrange things better.

You can also rehearse in front of another person, who may have suggestions. If you don't trust other people (it's not the "people" that worries me so much as the "other"), video tape yourself rehearsing, then watch the tape. You'll notice things about your body language you might otherwise miss.

Rule 3: Use Notes, but Don't Use a Script

Make up some notes for your presentation. These can include a list of points you want to cover, specific phrases that you want to use (particularly if they explain something clearly, pithily, and memorably), quotes, and other details. If you're using a two-screen presentation, use the Speaker Notes feature to bring them up on-screen. Otherwise, you can use the printed version of Speaker Notes, or even just write it on a sheet of paper or on some index cards. There is no "right" or "official" way to organize your notes; you're the one who has to understand them. If anyone else tries to look at your notes, roll them up and bop that person on the nose. (This is particularly difficult but effective if you're using on-screen Speaker Notes.)

However, you shouldn't write out everything you're going to say. First of all, you don't need that. If you are smart enough to write it out, you're smart enough to say it. Secondly, a script can't adapt to the situation; if you discover your audience knows different things than you thought they knew, a script can't adapt. Finally, if you have a script, or even very long notes, you end up staring at the paper, talking to the paper, and focusing on reading rather than what you're saying. This is a good way to become both boring and unintelligible.

Rule 4: Talk to Someone

If your response to that is, "Of course I'm talking to someone! I'm talking to a *whole room* of someones!" then that's exactly the problem. You're trying to talk with a room, but it's not the room that's listening to you. You have to feel like you're dealing with people. If you aren't dealing with people, it will show in the way that you speak. You're going to sound distanced and boring.

Instead, as you say each thing, look at someone specific in the audience and talk to them. When you're looking at them, you're subconsciously shaping what you're saying to make sure it's understood, and you're picking up their reaction (including body language) to see that it's understood. This will make your presentation better and keep it sounding human.

Rule 5: Don't Always Talk to the Same Someone

If you constantly direct what you're saying to the same person, it will look like a one-on-one conversation to people, and they will start mentally tuning you out. Their thoughts will drift, and they will start thinking about donuts. Donuts are a good thing to think about. Did you know that donuts can provide all four major food groups: chewy stuff, squishy stuff, powder, and chocolate? Mmm, yes, donuts.

Oh, wait, now *I've* drifted off. If you address one point to one person and then address the next to someone on the other side of the room, suddenly everyone feels included, even if you never get to speak directly to them. This doesn't mean that you can't go back to the same person fairly regularly. If you have a friendly face in the audience, take advantage of them and return to them frequently. However, by going to different people, you also see how others are reacting to what you're saying, and that will help shape your talk. You may also wake up a few people who have drifted off.

Check This Out...

Stand Up Comedians are Good Examples

Good stand-up comedians will look at different members of the audience as they deliver each line. Many of them find a friendly face in the audience, someone who laughs well and easily, and will deliver some quick laugh-getters to that person… but then talk to other people.

Rule 6: Look at Each New Slide

Whenever you put a new slide up, pause and look at it for a few seconds, reading it over. This isn't just to remind you of what's on the slide (although that never hurts). It also gives your audience a few seconds to read the slide, to assimilate the information that's there. By turning away from your audience and looking at the slide, you take the attention off of yourself and put it on the slide, making sure people read it.

Rule 7: Don't Talk to the Slide

If you're facing the screen, people will have trouble hearing you. When they can't see your face, they're less likely to pay attention to you.

Rule 8: Stop for Questions

A lot of speakers will take questions during a short presentation, but for long presentations will ask you to save your questions for the end, so that they can get through everything. However, the aim of a presentation is not to *get through* everything, but to have people *understand* as much as possible. If you confuse people on your first slide by using the word *squidfiddlology*, and wait until after slide 3327 to answer questions about what it means, then there are 3326 other slides that your audience probably didn't understand, since they were all on how to get work as a squidfiddlologist.

This doesn't mean that you have to stop for questions every time someone has one. If your presentation is well-organized, odds are that you'll build up questions in people's minds with one slide, and then answer it with the next one. However, you should find good stopping spots in your presentation. For example, when you've just completed a single sub-topic, you can ask if anyone has any questions so far. (You may even want to add a slide marked "Questions?" at this point, which will not only remind you that it's time for questions, but will encourage the audience to feel that asking questions is actually part of the process.) Keep your answers straightforward, and if the answer is "I'm getting to that," then say so!

Rule 9: It Can be Very Easy to Use a Lot of Words...

...when, in fact, you could have said the same thing in many fewer words, and saying it in fewer words is both easier on you and on the audience, because brevity (which is a fancy word for shortness) can augment clarity (which is to say understandability), and clarity (understandability) is a thing of value in public speaking, which is presumably what you are doing.

Keep it simple.

Rule 10: Know How Sophisticated Your Audience Is

I don't mean check to see if they own their own tuxedoes. If you're giving a presentation on a technical topic, you want to know how much the audience knows about the topic. If you're discussing a new telephone with a bunch of telephony engineers, they're going to want to know what the FCC ringer equivalency of the phone is. If you use the term *ringer equivalency* with a less-technical audience, they're going to think that the phone doesn't really ring, it just does the equivalent of ringing, whatever that might be.

The truth is, though, that you're likely to face an audience with a wide range of sophistication. It's better to explain a few things that some of your audience already knows rather than make a lot of people feel that what you're talking about is over their heads. (Particularly if you're talking about anvils. No one wants anvils over their heads.)

Rule 11: Use Examples

Abstract concepts become easier to understand with a concrete example. For example, the first sentence of this paragraph is an abstract concept. If reading it made you think "Well, when does something need an example?" then it's clear that this discussion is one that needed an example. And here it is! Examples can be words (this paragraph is an example of an example being words), pictures (such as the examples of slides in this book), video, sound, or even a physical object you can pass around the room. (Warning: if the physical object is an example of a donut, don't expect it to make it all away around the room.)

Rule 12: Humor Can Be Amusing!

Throw in little humorous moments. This not only keeps your audience's attention, but also gets them on your side. People like being amused. Go figure.

You shouldn't try to turn your presentation into a stand-up routine, because that would lose the point of what you're doing, but even a few bad puns or silly names can give the presentation a positive energy.

Theoretical examples are a great time to be a little silly. Look through this book, and you should see plenty of cases of that. I could just as easily have used boring slide text from some actual presentation on the physical maturation of the fruit fly, but using the silly example didn't make the example less clear. Why use "Patient A," "John Doe," and "Smith Manufacturing, Inc." as your examples when you could use "Samantha De Hoya Von O'Goldberg," "Myron McGillicuddly," and "International Wonder-Widget And Coffee Recycling, Inc.?" Just make sure your humor doesn't obscure your point, and that it doesn't offend your audience.

Rule 13: Check Your Equipment Before the Presentation

This is particularly important if you're using someone else's slide projector or computer. If you're doing a computer presentation, you really should go through the whole thing once on their machine to make sure there's no weird happenings; just because everything is supposed to work the same doesn't mean that it does.

Slide projectors are notorious. They blow out, they disappear, or your slide carousel doesn't quite fit. Even when everything is in place and working correctly, you should still become comfortable with the remote control. Having trouble going forward and backwards is one of the most common things that keeps a presentation from getting rolling early on.

Make sure you have all the cables you need, extra bulbs for the projector, and even an extra extension cord. Turn off the slide or overhead projector when you're not using them, to reduce both noise and heat. (You don't have to turn off your LCD panel if you're using one, because it makes very little heat and no noise.)

Rule 14: Check Out the Room Ahead of Time

You want to know where everything important is. You want to make sure you'll be able to stand by the screen and still be able to control the projector. You want to know where the light switch is, and whether you can bring the lights down part way. (If possible, you don't want to bring the lights down all the way. You still want to be able to see your audience and have the audience see you. Still, you need it to be dark enough for the projected image to be clear.) Pull down the window shades to keep the glare out. Position your projector so that your image is easy for all to see. (The farther from the screen you put it, the bigger a picture you'll get, but it will look dimmer and fuzzier.)

Check out where people will be sitting. You don't want anyone blocking the projector. You want them to have comfortable seats, so their mind is on your presentation rather than their own discomfort. (Lighting and comfort have a lot of effect on people's frame of mind, and you want them in a positive mood.)

If you have a huge room (and a sizable budget), you may want to have multiple projectors projecting to multiple screens, so that everyone can see.

Rule 15: Introduce Yourself to Your Audience

This should be the first thing, to let your audience know who you are. Even if you're dealing with your own co-workers, they may not know what your exact job is or what it has to do with the matter at hand.

254

If you've got a small audience, and they aren't all people you know, get them to introduce themselves to you. Get not only their names, but what they do at the company or the club. This will help you not only aim the entire presentation properly, but also to understand why they're asking the questions that they are.

Even if you can't get them to introduce themselves to you, beware of making assumptions about who they are. In bygone days, you might have been able to count on the quiet, sharply dressed young woman in the corner being a secretary, and the dignified older gent in the front being the president. These days, however, that young woman may be Head of Programming, and the president might be the unshaven gent with a Hard Rock Cafe: Alcatraz T-shirt.

Rule 16: Don't Just Read What's On the Slide

Your talk should build on what's there. Presumably, your audience can read the slide for themselves. You can read a line of what's there, but only if you're going to expand on it.

Rule 17: Tell Them Where You're Going

Your presentation isn't a mystery story (unless, of course, it is). If you let them know in advance that the aim of the presentation is to show them the advantage of squirting the jelly into donuts after they're cooked, they'll understand why you're spending all this time explaining all the tedious work that goes into wrapping dough around the existing lump of jelly.

This doesn't mean that you have to tell everything about your conclusions. The details of the conclusion are for the end. But they should have the gist of where you're going—unless you're building up to news so bad that no one would pay attention ("As I intend to show, the company's economic situation is so bad that I will be forced to bite you all hard on the elbows.") You can even give them a brief outline of your presentation, so they know which major points you'll be covering.

Rule 18: Pronounce Clearly

You're excited. You want everyone to be as thrilled about your discovery of The East Pole as you were. Butwhenyougetsoexcitedthatyoustarttotalklikethis, then no one will understand. Slow down, and put a little bit of silence between each word. A little space is fine, and can make you look intellectually contemplative. Too much space just starts
to aggrevate people as they wait for you to get finished already!

Being too quiet is also a problem. There's no need to shout, but just bring the sound up from your throat, rather than just shaping it with your mouth. Don't be afraid to open your mouth wide!

And it doesn't have to all be at one speed or volume. If you want them to be excited about something, show your excitement by getting a bit faster and louder. If you want them to think carefully on a point, slow it down, even pause before and after it. A good pause is an attention-getter. Just don't overuse it.

Rule 19: Dress Cleanly

You don't necessarily have to dress up. If you're talking to a comfortably dressed group, you can dress just as comfortably. But even if you're in jeans and a T-shirt, they should look clean and fresh, not worn to shreds. Looking sharp shows that you pay attention to details, and people will value what you have to say.

Rule 20: Don't Talk Down

I can't explain this one to you. Just trust me on this one. For reasons you cannot understand, you shouldn't talk down to your audience.

Didn't that sound obnoxious? You bet!

Don't assume that your audience is stupid, or that they'd be unable to understand something even if you took the time to explain it fully. Sure, you know more about what you're telling them than they do (if you don't, why are you doing the talking?), but there's a reason why you want them to know what you're telling them, so they obviously are useful people. They don't already know what you're telling them, but that just means they have things to learn, as we all do.

Rule 21: Don't Take Too Long

The people you are talking to probably have other things to do. Keep an eye on the time. If you're doing a two-screen presentation, take advantage of the Slide Timer feature.

If you're falling behind and see a slide that really doesn't need explanation, then don't. Move right ahead to the next one.

Don't leave one slide up for too long. If for some reason you have a lot to say before moving to the next slide, turn the projector off, so the focus will be on you, not the same old unchanging slide. (But maybe you'd have been better off breaking the information from that slide into several separate slides?)

Rule 22: Don't Worry About It!

It's only talking, and you've been talking most of your life. You're not going to be perfect, and no one expects perfection from you. Heck, if you sound *too* perfect, people might think you're trying to put something over on them. If something goes wrong, just say "Whoops!", correct yourself, and move on. If they don't understand something, they'll ask you. There's no need to worry about everything.

And the weird thing is that if you don't worry, you'll do better. Confidence is very convincing so: Smile and Relax.

The Least You Need to Know

➤ Rehearse and prepare notes, but don't use a script.

➤ Talk to someone, but not always the same someone.

➤ Look at each new slide but don't talk to the slide and don't just read what's on the slide.

➤ Stop for questions.

➤ Keep it simple.

➤ Use examples and humor.

➤ Check your equipment and the room before the presentation.

➤ Introduce yourself to your audience, and tell them where the presentation is going.

➤ Pronounce clearly.

➤ Don't talk down.

➤ Don't take too long.

➤ Don't worry about it!

Installing PowerPoint

Microsoft PowerPoint 97 is available by itself, or as part of a Microsoft Office 97 package.

If You Bought PowerPoint Only

Before you start trying to install PowerPoint, make sure that you have enough space on your hard disk. You'll need about 50 megabytes of free space. If you don't have that much, you'll need to delete some files. Be sure to empty your Recycle Bin when you're done (by right-clicking on the **Recycle Bin** icon and selecting **Empty Recycle Bin**), or else those files may still be taking up space on your disk.

If you've bought the CD-ROM version, put it into your CD-ROM drive. The program will start automatically, bringing up a selection of things you can do. Select **Install Microsoft PowerPoint**.

If you bought PowerPoint on floppy disks, stick the disk marked Disk 1 into your floppy disk drive. Click on the **Start** button and select **Run**. In the dialog box that appears, type a:\setup then click **OK**. This will start the installation program. (You are better off getting the CD-ROM version of software when possible. They're not only easier to install than the floppy version, they often have added features.)

Once you've started the installation process, the installation program will ask you questions. Answer them. When you get to choosing between Typical Installation and Custom Installation, pick **Typical**. You'll see a list of items that you can choose whether or not to install. Items that you'll probably want are already checked off. The one thing that isn't checked off that you may really want to add is **Web Page Authoring (HTML)**. Click on the box next to that if you want to use PowerPoint to create presentations for the World Wide Web.

Once you've made your decisions, click **OK** to continue with the installation process.

If You Bought Microsoft Office

Before you start trying to install PowerPoint, make sure that you have enough space on your hard disk. If you're installing the complete Office package, you'll need about 150 megabytes of free space. If you only want to install PowerPoint, you'll only need fifty megabytes. If you're really low on disk space, you can choose to run Office from the CD-ROM, which will only take 25 megabytes of the hard disk. However, it will run slower if you choose this option, so only do it if you're not going to use Office that often.

If you don't have enough space available, you'll need to delete some files. Be sure to empty your Recycle Bin when you're done (by right-clicking on the **Recycle Bin** icon and selecting **Empty Recycle Bin**), or else those files may still be taking up space on your disk.

Put the Microsoft Office CD-ROM into your CD-ROM drive. The program will start automatically, bringing up a selection of things you can do. Select **Install Microsoft Office**.

Once you've started the installation process, the installation program will ask you questions. Answer them. For most of the questions, the program will come up with suggested answers already in place.

At one point, you'll be asked to choose between Typical Installation, Custom Installation, and Run Office from CD-ROM.

➤ If you want to run PowerPoint from CD-ROM, choose **Run from CD-ROM**. If you choose this, the Office CD-ROM must be in your computer at all times while you are using PowerPoint.

➤ If you want to install all of Office, choose **Typical Installation**. You'll see a list of items that you can choose whether you want to install. Items that you'll probably want are already checked off. The one thing that isn't checked off that you may really want to add is **Web Page Authoring (HTML)**. Click on the box next to that if you want to use PowerPoint to create presentations for the World Wide Web.

➤ If you just want to install PowerPoint, and don't want to install the rest of the Office programs, choose **Custom Installation**. You'll see a list of parts for Office. Some of them will already be checked off. Click on these entries to clear the checkboxes except for the ones marked **Microsoft PowerPoint**, **Office Tools**, and **Converters and Filters**.

Continue with the installation process. It should be smooth sailing from here.

Windows 95 and Windows NT Primer

Windows 95 and Windows NT are graphical operating systems that make your computer easy to use by providing menus and pictures. Before you can take advantage of either operating system, however, you need to learn some basics that apply to both of them.

Fortunately, Windows 95 and Windows NT operate very much alike (in fact, they're so similar I'll refer to them both just as Windows throughout the remainder of this appendix). If the figures you see in this primer don't look exactly like what's on your screen, don't sweat it. Some slight variation may occur depending on your setup, the applications you use or whether you're on a network. Rest assured, however, that the basic information presented here applies, no matter what your setup may be.

A First Look at Windows

You don't have to start Windows because it starts automatically when you turn on your PC. After the initial startup screens, you arrive at a screen like the one shown below.

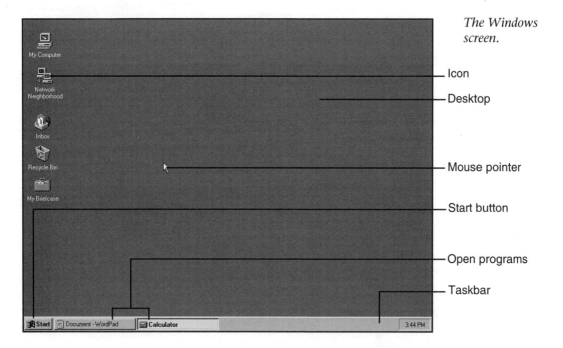

The Windows screen.

Icon

Desktop

Mouse pointer

Start button

Open programs

Taskbar

Parts of the Screen

As you can see, the Windows screen contains lots of special elements and controls. Here's a brief summary:

➤ The Desktop consists of the background and icons that represent programs, tools, and other elements.

➤ The Taskbar shows a button for each open window and program. You can switch between open windows and programs by clicking on the taskbar button representing the program you want. (The program you are currently working on is highlighted in the taskbar.)

➤ The Start button opens a menu from which you can start programs, get Help, and find files. To use it, you click on the **Start** button, then click on a selection from the list that appears. When you move your pointer over a command that has a right-facing arrow beside it, a secondary—or cascading—menu appears.

Getting started.

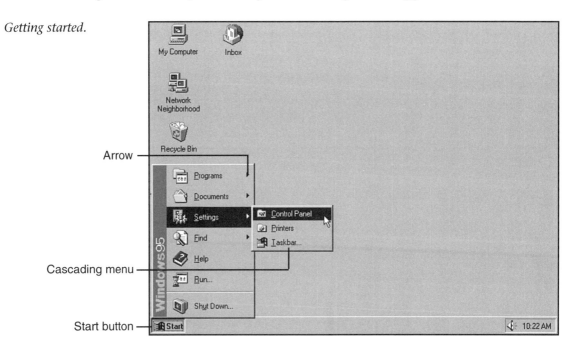

➤ The icons that appear on your desktop give you access to certain programs and computer components. You open an icon by double-clicking on it. (An open icon displays a window containing programs, files, or other items.)

➤ The mouse pointer moves around the screen in relation to your movement of the mouse. You use the mouse pointer to select what you want to work with.

You'll learn more about these elements as you work through the rest of this Windows primer.

Also Appearing: Microsoft Office

If your computer has Microsoft Office installed on it, the Office Short-cuts toolbar also appears on-screen. It's a series of little pictures (strung together horizontally) that represent Office programs. Hold the mouse over a picture (icon) to see what it does; click on it to launch the program. See your Microsoft Office documentation to learn more.

You may have some other icons on your desktop (representing networks, folders, printers, files, and so on), depending upon what options you chose during initial setup. Double-click an icon to view the items it contains.

Using a Mouse

To work most efficiently in Windows, you need a mouse. You will perform the following mouse actions as you work:

➤ **Point**   To move the mouse so that the on-screen pointer is touching an item.

➤ **Click**   To press and release the left mouse button once. Pointing and clicking on an item usually selects it. You click with the right button (called "right-clicking") to produce a shortcut menu. (You can reverse these mouse button actions if you want to use the mouse left-handed. To do so, click **Start**, **Settings**, **Control Panel**, **Mouse**, then choose **Left-handed** in the Button tab of the Control Panel dialog box.)

➤ **Double-click**   To press and release the left mouse button twice quickly. Pointing and double-clicking usually activates an item or opens a window, folder, or program.

Double-clicking may take some practice—the speed needs to be just right. To change the speed so it better matches your "clicking style," choose **Start**, **Settings**, **Control Panel**, **Mouse**. In the Buttons tab of the Mouse Properties dialog box, you can adjust the double-clicking speed until it's just right for you.

➤ **Drag**   To move a window, dialog box, or file from one location to another, place the mouse pointer over the element you want to move, press and hold down the left mouse button, and move the mouse to a new location. Unless you're told to do otherwise (for example, to right-drag), you drag with the left mouse button.

Controlling a Window with the Mouse

Ever wonder why it's called "Windows?" Well, Windows' operating system sections off rectangular areas of the desktop into work areas called "windows." These windows are used for particular purposes, such as running a program, displaying options or lists, and so on. Each window will have common features, as shown in the following figure:

Use your mouse to control and manipulate windows.

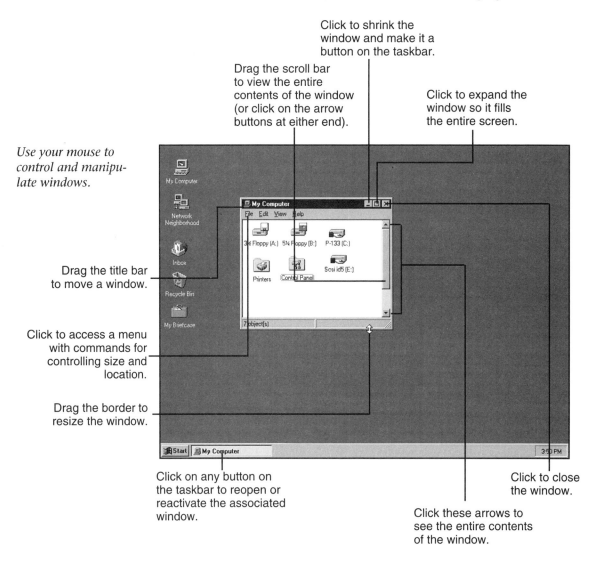

Click to shrink the window and make it a button on the taskbar.

Drag the scroll bar to view the entire contents of the window (or click on the arrow buttons at either end).

Click to expand the window so it fills the entire screen.

Drag the title bar to move a window.

Click to access a menu with commands for controlling size and location.

Drag the border to resize the window.

Click on any button on the taskbar to reopen or reactivate the associated window.

Click to close the window.

Click these arrows to see the entire contents of the window.

Scrolling for Information

If your window contains more icons than it can display at once, scroll bars appear on the bottom or right edges of the window. To move through the window's contents, click on an arrow button at either end of a scroll bar to move in that direction, or drag the scroll bar in the direction you want to move.

If you're using the professional version of Office 97, you'll also have enhanced scrolling available to you via your "Intellimouse"—a new mouse by Microsoft that includes a scrolling wheel. Using this mouse is described in all Que books that cover Microsoft Office 97 and its individual applications.

Getting Help

Windows comes with a great online Help system. To access it, click on the Start button then click on Help.

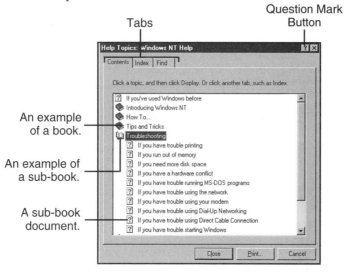

Windows offers several kinds of help—this figure illustrates the Contents tab.

The Help box contains three tabs (Contents, Index, and Find), each of which provides you with a different type of help. To move to a tab, just click on it.

Here's how to use each tab:

➤ **Contents** Double-click on any book to open it and see its sub-books and documents. Double-click on a sub-book or document to open it and read the help topic.

➤ **Index** When you click this tab, Windows will ask you for more information on what you're looking for. Type the word you want to look up, and the Index list scrolls to that part of the alphabetical listing. When you see the topic that you want to read in the list, double-click on it.

➤ **Find** The first time you click on this tab, Windows tells you it needs to create a list. Click **Next** and then **Finish** to allow this. When Windows finishes, Windows will ask you to type the word you want to find in the top text box. Click on a word in the middle box to narrow the search, review the list of Help topics at the bottom then double-click the one you want to read.

When you finish reading about a document, click on **Help Topics** to return to the main Help screen, or click **Back** to return to the previous Help topic. When you finish with the Help system itself, click the window's **Close** (X) button to exit.

Another Way to Get Help

In the upper-right corner of the Help window, you should see (next to the Close button) a question mark. This is (surprise!) the Question mark button. Whenever you see this button (it appears in other windows besides the Help window), click on it to change your mouse pointer to a combined arrow-and-question mark. You can then point at any element in the window for a quick "pop-up" description of that element.

Some applications or application suites (such as Microsoft Office 97) may also offer online help. The use of online help is discussed in the application documentation, or in any Que book that covers the application.

Starting a Program

Of the many possible ways to start a program, this is the simplest:

1. Click the **Start** button.

2. Move your mouse pointer over Programs.

3. Click on the group that contains the program you want to start (such as Accessories).

4. Click on the program you want to start (such as HyperTerminal).

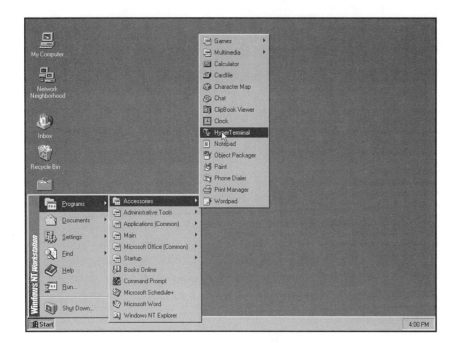

Work through the Start menu and its successive submenus until you find the program you want to start.

Here are a few more ways you can start a program in Windows:

➤ Open a document that you created in that program. The program automatically opens when the document opens. For example, double-click on the My Computer icon on the desktop, find the icon of the document you want to open, then double-click on a document file.

➤ (Optional) Open a document you created in that program by clicking the Start button, moving your pointer over Programs, and then clicking Windows Explorer. The Window Explorer window opens and looks very similar to the File Manager window you've worked with in Windows 3.1. Locate the directory (or Folder, in Windows 95/NT 4.0 terminology) and double-click on the file name. The document is opened in the program in which it was created.

➤ Click the **Start** button and select a recently used document from the Documents menu. Windows immediately starts the program in which you created the file and opens the file.

➤ If you created a shortcut to the program, You can start the program by double-clicking its shortcut icon on the desktop.

267

What's a Shortcut?

Shortcut icons are links to other files. When you use a shortcut, Windows simply follows the link back to the original file. If you find that you use any document or program frequently, you might consider creating a desktop shortcut for it. To do so, just use the right mouse button to drag an object out of Windows Explorer or My Computer and onto the desktop. In the shortcut menu that appears, select **Create Shortcut(s) Here**.

Using Menus

Almost every Windows program has a menu bar that contains menus. The menu names appear in a row across the top of the screen. To open a menu, click on its name (after you click anywhere in the menu bar, you need only point to a menu name to produce the drop-down menu). The menu drops down, displaying its commands, as shown in the next figure. To select a command, you simply click it.

A menu lists various commands you can perform.

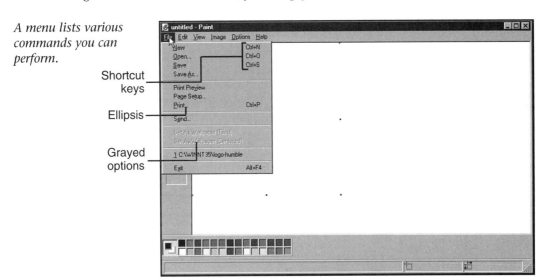

Usually, when you select a command, Windows executes the command immediately. But you need to keep the following exceptions to that rule in mind:

➤ If the command name is gray (instead of black), the command is unavailable at the moment and you cannot choose it.

➤ If the command name is followed by an arrow (as the selections on the Start menu are), selecting the command causes another menu to appear, from which you must make another selection.

➤ If the command is followed by an ellipsis (…), selecting it will cause a dialog box to appear. You'll learn about dialog boxes later in this primer.

Shortcut Keys

Key names appear after some command names (for example, Ctrl+O appears to the right of the Open command, and Ctrl+S appears next to the Save command). These are shortcut keys and you can use them to perform the command without opening the menu. You should also note that some commands have their first letter underlined. By pressing Alt+the letter underlined, you can perform the command.

Using Shortcut Menus

A new feature in Windows is the shortcut menu (or "Context-Sensitive" menu). Right-click on any object (any icon, screen element, file, or folder), and a shortcut menu like the one shown in the next figure appears. The shortcut menu contains commands that apply only to the selected object. Click on any command to select it, or click outside the menu to cancel.

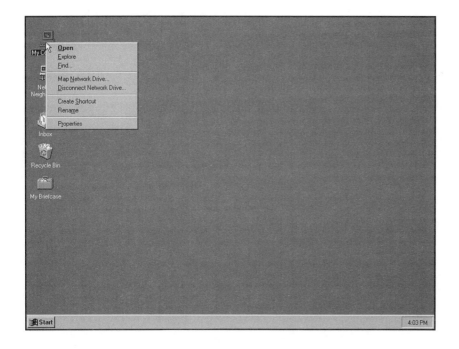

Shortcut menus are new in Windows 95 and Windows NT 4.0.

269

Navigating Dialog Boxes

A dialog box is Window's way of requesting additional information or giving you information. For example, if you choose Print from the File menu of the WordPad application, you see a dialog box something like the one shown in the figure below. (The options it displays will vary from system to system.)

A dialog box often requests additional information.

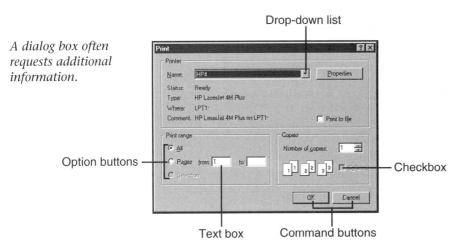

Drop-down list

Option buttons

Checkbox

Text box   Command buttons

Each dialog box contains one or more of the following elements:

➤ List boxes display available choices. Click on any item on the list to select it. If the entire list is not visible, use the scroll bar to find additional choices.

➤ Drop-down lists are similar to list boxes, but only one item in the list is shown. To see the rest of the list, click the drop-down arrow (to the right of the list box), then click on an item to select it.

➤ Text boxes allow you to type an entry—just click inside the text box and type. Text boxes that are designed to hold numbers usually have up and down arrow buttons (called increment buttons) that let you bump the number up and down.

➤ Checkboxes enable you to turn individual options on or off by clicking on them. (A checkmark or "X" appears when an option is on.) Each checkbox is an independent unit that doesn't affect other checkboxes.

➤ Option buttons are like checkboxes, except that option buttons appear in groups and you can select only one. When you select an option button, the program automatically deselects whichever one was previously selected. Click on a button to activate it and a black bullet appears inside the white option circle.

➤ Command buttons perform an action, such as executing the options you set (OK), canceling the options (Cancel), closing the dialog box, or opening another dialog box. To select a command button, click on it.

➤ Tabs bring up additional "pages" of options you can choose. Click on a tab to activate it. (See the section on Help for more information on Tabs.)

From Here

If you need more help with Windows, you may want to pick up one of these books:

The Complete Idiot's Guide to Windows 95 by Paul McFedries

Easy Windows 95 by Sue Plumley

The Big Basics Book of Windows 95 by Shelley O'Hara, Jennifer Fulton, and Ed Guilford

Using Windows 95 by Ed Bott

The Complete Idiot's Guide to Windows NT 4.0 Workstation by Paul McFedries

Using Windows NT 4.0 Workstation by Ed Bott

Speak Like a Geek: The Complete Archive

People who design or use computers like to make up new words to describe the various pieces of the computer and the things these pieces do. Even worse, they like to take already existing words like *mouse* and *window* and give them new meanings.

Here's a cheat sheet for you. With it, you should be able to understand what they're talking about, and even spit it right back out at them!

Access   A database program made by Microsoft. Database programs let you organize lists of information and help you find information on those lists.

action buttons   Special AutoShapes that look like buttons and automatically have hyperlinks attached to them.

alignment   Refers to where the text is positioned side-to-side within a text box.

animation   Moving something onto the slide during animation, or making it appear gradually instead of all at once. For example, a list may appear item by item, rather than all at once.

AutoShape   A set of pre-drawn shapes that PowerPoint lets you add to your slide easily.

box   The rectangular area containing any object on a slide.

bullet   A pointer used to highlight items on a list. Bullets are usually dots, but they can be little arrows, or any of a number of other designs.

button   The word *button* is used for two different things. There are the buttons on the mouse, which you push to tell the computer to take action on something on-screen. An on-screen button is usually a rectangular area that you click on to perform some action.

CD-ROM   Short for *Compact Disc-Read Only Memory*, this is a shiny disk that looks like an audio CD, but has computer data on it. Your computer needs a *CD-ROM* drive to be able to read the information on a CD-ROM.

chart   Refers to a numerical graph, except when used as part of the term *organizational chart*.

checkbox   A small white square that you use to select an option. Click on the square to put a checkmark in it (which means you want the option), click again to take the checkmark out.

click   *Clicking* on something is when you point the pointer at it, then press and release the left mouse button once. (If you're using a left-handed mouse, you'll use the right button.)

clip art   A piece of art meant for anyone to be able to use in their documents.

Clip Gallery   An organized collection of clip art, sounds, and videos that you can use in your documents.

clipboard   An area of memory used to store things that you've copied or cut from your document, so that you can paste them somewhere else.

Close button   The button with an X at the right end of the menu or title bar. Clicking on the menu bar's Close button closes the document while leaving the program open. Clicking on the Close button on the title bar closes the document and the program.

copying   Storing a copy of whatever is currently selected into an area of memory called the *clipboard*.

CPU   Short for *Central Processing Unit*, the CPU is the chip that does most of the computer's thinking. The 486 and the Pentium are two types of CPUs.

cropping   Trimming one or more sides of a picture.

cursor keys   Keys with arrows on them that are used to change where your typing will appear in a block of text.

cutting   Removing something from a document and storing it in an area of memory called the *clipboard*.

database   A program that helps you create and organize lists of information and makes it easy to pull specific information out of that list.

datasheet   A grid where you enter information for a numerical chart.

deleting   Removing.

desktop   The open area that is underneath any open windows in Microsoft Windows. If there aren't any programs running, then what you see is the desktop.

dialog box   A window that appears when the computer wants information from you. It can have a mixture of tabs, buttons, fields, checkboxes, and radio buttons in it.

document   Any single picture, letter, report, spreadsheet, presentation, or other item that you've created and stored on the computer.

donut   The standard source of energy used to power programmers.

double-clicking   Pointing to something with the mouse pointer and pressing and releasing the left mouse button twice, rapidly. (If you're using a left-handed mouse, use the right button.)

downloading   Copying a file from another computer to yours, using a modem connection or a network.

dragging   Moving the mouse with the left button pressed down. To drag an object, point to it, press, and move. (Left-handed mice use the right button.)

drop-down button   A button with a downward-pointing triangle on it at the end of a field. Clicking on this button makes a menu of possible values for the field appear.

e-mail   Short for *electronic mail*, this refers to letters or files sent over a computer network from one user to another.

Excel   A spreadsheet program made by Microsoft. Spreadsheet programs are used to do math and to create graphs.

field   A white rectangle where you can type information that the computer wants.

file   A group of information stored under a single name so that the computer can find it. A PowerPoint presentation can be a single file, or it can use several files, with the main file containing the information about what other files are used.

fill effects   Styles of filling a shape with a blend of colors, or a picture.

film recorder   A device that lets your computer put images onto photographic film.

floppy disk   A flat square removable item used to hold computer information. In order for the computer to read the information, you have to stick it into a *floppy disk drive*. It's called a *disk* because there's a flat magnetic circle inside that actually holds the information.

folder   The information on the hard disk is organized into *folders*. Each folder has a name, and inside each folder there can be files, and there can be more folders.

font size   How big your letters appear.

fonts   Styles of type. For instance, Courier New and Arial are fonts that come with Windows.

footer   Material that appears at the bottom of every slide, except the title slide.

function keys   A row or column of keys marked F1, F2, and so on. These are used by many programs to perform special commands. Exactly which command changes from program to program.

GIF   The *Graphics Interchange Format*, a way of organizing information about a picture so that the computer can understand it and recreate the picture.

gigabyte   Sometimes abbreviated *GB*, this is a measurement of information size. A gigabyte is about a thousand megabytes.

graph   A chart that plots numerical values.

hard disk   A device built into your computer that is used to store information permanently. Information on the hard drive doesn't go away when you turn off the machine; they have to be erased by a computer command.

header   Material that appears at the top of every slide, except the title slide.

help system   A group of many short articles and instruction guides that are organized so that you can find the one you want.

HTML   Short for *HyperText Markup Language*, this is the format used to store displays on the World Wide Web, so that your Web browser can understand it.

hyperlink   The linking of an object to a slide, a program, or a Web address, so that when you click on the object (or when you pass the mouse over it), the slide, program, or Web page is opened up.

icon   A small picture that represents a file, program, or function.

inkjet printer   A printer that prints out by squirting little dots of ink onto the paper.

Internet   A series of computers linked around the world, that lets you get information from one computer to another by passing it down the line.

Internet Assistant   A Web browser program created by Microsoft. Web browser programs let you view the displays on the World Wide Web.

intranet   A series of computers linked together within your company or organization. Intranets work like the Internet, only on a smaller scale.

JPEG   A format used for storing a picture on a computer. The name comes from the *Joint Photographic Experts Group* who developed the format.

keyboard   The part of the computer with the typewriter-like bunch of keys.

kiosk   A stand-alone computer designed to be easily accessed and easily used for getting information.

kiosk mode   A slide show display mode that doesn't allow the user any controls that aren't built into the slide itself.

laser printer   A printer that prints by pressing toner onto the paper.

LCD   Short for *Liquid Crystal Display*, a display made up of little segments that can be clear or colored, depending on whether electricity is being applied.

LCD panel   A computer monitor that you can put on an overhead projector, so that the image that would be on the computer screen is seen wherever the projector is aimed.

LCD projector   A device that is capable of projecting a computer screen image onto a movie screen.

loop   Repeat.

Meeting Minder   A PowerPoint feature that lets you take notes during the slide show and add things to your scheduling program.

megabyte   Sometimes abbreviated *MB*, this is a measurement of information size. A megabyte can store about a thousand pages of text, a dozen full-screen pictures, or 7 seconds of high quality stereo sound.

megahertz   The computer has a central rhythm, a beat that it uses to drive everything it does. The speed of this is measured in *megahertz* (abbreviated *MHz*), which stands for millions of beats per second. Today's fast computers dance to a rhythm of 200 million beats per second, or 200 megahertz.

menu   A list of commands that you can select from. You can see the menu by clicking on the right name on the menu bar.

menu bar   The second bar at the top of a window. The menu bar has a list of menus on it. Click on any menu name to see the menu.

Microsoft   The biggest PC software company. They make PowerPoint, Windows, Office, and many other products.

modem   A computer device that lets your computer share information with other computers using the phone lines.

mouse   A device that helps you control the computer. Slide the mouse across the mouse pad, and a pointer on the screen moves in the same direction. The buttons on a mouse let you tell the computer to take action on what you're pointing to.

narration   Speech that you record on the computer to play along with your slides.

Notes Page View   A PowerPoint view of your slide show where you can see one slide at a time, plus the Speaker Notes from that slide.

null-modem cable   A cable that can connect two computers so that they can act like they're connected by modems and a phone line, only without any modems or phone line being needed.

object   The word Object is used for two different things in PowerPoint. It can refer to anything that you put on a slide (a line, a picture, a sound, and so on), or specifically to anything that PowerPoint needs to run a separate program to deal with (such as a chart or graph).

Office   A set of programs sold as a group by Microsoft. Office includes the Word word processor, Excel spreadsheet, PowerPoint presentation creator, and Outlook scheduling program. The Office Professional version also includes the Access database program.

Office Assistant   An animated character that appears in a window and offers help information.

online   Refers to anything done over a network or over a modem connection.

organization chart   A diagram that shows who works for who in your company.

Outline View   A PowerPoint view of your slide show, where you can see all the text from your slides and make changes to it.

overhead   A transparent sheet with an image on it. You display overheads by putting them on an *overhead projector*, which shines light through it and magnifies it onto a screen.

overhead projector   A device that shines light through an overhead so that the image appears on a movie screen or a wall.

packing   Storing everything you need for your presentation into a single file.

pasting   Taking whatever's in the area of memory called the *clipboard* and putting it into your document.

PC   Short for *Personal Computer*, this refers to any small computer meant to be used by one person at a time, or any computer designed primarily to run MS-DOS or Windows.

pointer   A small picture on the screen that moves when you move the mouse. The picture is usually an arrow, but sometimes it can be a small bar or a finger.

PowerPoint   A program designed to let you make presentations.

presentation   An information show created with PowerPoint. Presentations can include slides, notes, and narration.

presentation conference   A presentation conducted over a network, with each person seeing the slide show on their own PC.

processor   Another term for *CPU*, the chip in the computer that does most of its thinking.

pushed in   Refers to a button that looks like it's below the level of the toolbar. A button that's pushed in means that button's feature is now in effect.

radio buttons   A set of small circles next to a list of options. Select the option you want by clicking on the radio button next to it. Only one radio button in a group can be selected at a time; when you select another button, the selected one becomes unselected.

RAM   Short for *Random Access Memory*, this is a bunch of computer chips where the computer stores information that it is currently using. Information in RAM goes away when you turn the computer off.

resizing   Changing the size of a picture or box. Resizing stretches or squishes the item to fit the new size.

right-click   Right-clicking on something is when you point the pointer at it, then press and release the right mouse button. (If you're using a left-handed mouse, you'll use the left button.)

saving   Copying the document you're working with (including all new changes) onto a disk.

scanner   A device that takes a picture of a hard copy page and sends that picture to your computer.

scroll bar   A scroll bar is used to let you select which part of a document you want to see, when that document is too big to show in the space provided. There's a box on a bar. The box shows the relative position of what you're seeing in the document. Drag the box to see another part, or use the up and down buttons at either end of the scroll bar to move up or down in the document. (Sideways scroll bars have left and right buttons.)

selecting   Indicating the item on-screen that you want your commands to affect. You select something by clicking on it or by dragging a box around it.

service bureau   An outside company that will put your computer created images onto slides, overheads, posters, and other tough-to-create forms.

shortcut menu   A menu that appears when you right-click on something. Shortcut menus usually have commands that deal specifically with the thing that you clicked on.

Slide Master   A special slide that isn't shown itself, but everything you put on the slide master appears on all your slides besides the title slide.

slide   One screen of information in PowerPoint, or a single transparent picture used with a slide projector.

slide projector   A device used to project transparent pictures onto a screen.

Slide Sorter View   A PowerPoint view of your slide show, where you see a number of slides at a time. This is good for rearranging your show, or doing things that affect a number of slides.

Slide Timer   A timer that you can display while running your show in Speaker Mode, letting you see how long your slide show is taking.

Slide View   A PowerPoint view of your slide show, where you see one slide at a time, and can change all of the contents and graphics.

sound card   A computer board inside your computer that connects your computer to speakers, giving it the ability to put out sound and music.

speaker mode   A slide show display mode that allows the most control over moving through the show or performing other functions.

Speaker Notes A PowerPoint feature that allows you to create notes for each slide and to see them on-screen as you give your presentation.

spelling checker A PowerPoint feature that checks every word on your slide, as you enter it, and underlines it with a wavy red line if it thinks it's misspelled.

spreadsheet A program that does math, using information laid out in a grid.

Start button A button on the left edge of the taskbar that you click on when you want to start a program.

tab This has two meanings. There's the tab key on the keyboard, which is used to move your typing spot to a fixed position. There's also the tabs in a dialog box, which are named buttons that let you select which set of settings you want to work with; click on a tab, and the settings having to do with the name on the tab appear.

taskbar A bar usually found at the bottom of the screen that includes the Start button as well as buttons for all the programs you are currently running.

text Typed information, such as paragraphs, numbers, and so on.

timings Stored estimated times for the showing of each slide, used to automate the slide show and used by the Slide Timer to keep you informed of whether you're running behind time.

title A special piece of text at the top of the slide that identifies the slide. PowerPoint considers the title text to be the name of the slide.

title bar The bar at the top of the window. This usually has the name of the program being used followed by the document name.

Title Master A special slide that isn't shown itself, but everything you put on the slide master appears on the title slide.

title slide Usually the first slide in your slide show, this has the title of your presentation.

toolbar A row of buttons and drop-down lists that have related functions. For example, PowerPoint uses several toolbars, including a toolbar of Web-related controls.

trackball A device used instead of a mouse. Roll the ball in any direction, and the pointer on the screen moves in that direction.

transition The visual method of replacing one slide on the computer screen with the next.

transparency Another word for *overhead*.

transparent color A color selected on a picture that will be treated as clear instead. If you put a picture with a transparent color on your slide, you'll be able to see through the parts with transparent color, on through to whatever is under the picture.

undo   A feature that takes back your last command.

uploading   Copying a file from your computer to another computer, using a modem or a network.

URL   Short for *Uniform Resource Locator*, it's another name for a Web address, the string of letters, slashes, and punctuation that tells the computer where to find a given display on the Web.

video   In computer terms, *video* refers to a changing picture that is stored as a series of still images, which are shown one after another. Video files can include the sound that goes with the picture.

Web browser   A program that lets your computer show you the displays on the World Wide Web, as well as any other displays stored in HTML format.

window   A moveable, resizable rectangular area of a computer display that has a title bar and menu bar at top.

window mode   A slide show display mode that shows the show in a window, rather than full screen.

Windows   A computer operating system made by Microsoft that's designed around using the mouse and the window displays. Windows 95 is the version of Windows released in 1995.

Wizard   A program feature that steps you through all the steps needed to do something, taking care of all the steps it can for you.

Word   A word processor made by Microsoft. Word processing programs are used for creating and changing letters, reports, and other text.

WordArt   A logo design tool built into PowerPoint and some other Microsoft products. The term can also refer to a logo designed with that tool.

word processor   A program that lets you create letters, reports, and other text documents, as well as letting you change and correct things before you print it out.

World Wide Web   A system that lets you see information displays stored on various computers that are connected to the Internet. To see these displays, you need a connection to the Internet, and you need a Web browser.

Index

Symbols

3-D button (WordArt), 3-D Settings command, 66
3-D Color button (WordArt), 67
3-D renderings, 78

A

action buttons (AutoShapes), 75
  adding, 128–129
Action Settings dialog box, 122, 128, 156
Add as Standard Scheme button, 111
Add Sound dialog box, 125
Advance button, 149
alignment button (WordArt), 61
alignment, configuring, 43–44
Animation Preview command (Slide Show menu), 133
animations, 131
  adding, 134
  charts, adding, 139–140
  colors, changing, 137
  creating, 133–141
    automatic, 134–135
    movement effects, 135–136
  deleting, 134
  dissolving, 137
  hiding, 137
  previewing, 133, 141
  sorting, 134
  sounds, adding, 136–137
  starting, 133
  styles, 132–133
  text, moving, 138–139
  troubleshooting, 133
  WWW, 209
apostrophes, 240–241
Appear animation effect, 135
Appear animation style, 132
Apply button, 111
Apply to All button, 111
Arrow button, 70
Arrow Style button, 70
arrows, block, 74
  drawing, 70
  see also lines
Assistant button, 101
Assistant style button, 102
Assistants, 8, 18–20
  changing, 20
  light bulbs, 18–20
  organization charts, adding, 102
  questions, asking, 19–20
  tips, resetting, 19
  topics, 20
audio, see sounds

AutoContent Wizard, 9–11
  completing, 11
  mistakes, correcting, 10
  presentation types, selecting, 10–11
  starting, 10
  titles, creating, 11
AutoContent Wizard option button, 10
AutoCorrect
  automatic replacements, adding, 240
  exceptions, adding, 239
  foreign languages, 241
AutoCorrect command (Tools menu), 239
AutoLayout
  boxes, grouping, 52–53
  movies, slide designs, 159
AutoShapes, 72–75
  action buttons, 75, 128–129
  basic shapes, 74
  callouts, creating, 74
  drawing
    block arrows, 74
    connector lines, 73
    happy faces, 74
    lines, 72–73
    stars and banners, 74
  flowcharts, creating, 74
  shapes, changing, 75
  text
    inserting, 75
    rotating, 75

U–V

W-X-Y-Z